The Positive Image

Women Photographers in
Turn of the Century America

C. Jane Gover

State University of New York Press

Published by
State University of New York Press, Albany

For information, address State University of New York
Press, State University Plaza, Albany, N.Y., 12246

Library of Congress Cataloging-in-Publication Data

Gover, C. Jane, 1934-
    The positive image.

    (SUNY series in the new cultural history)
    Bibliography: p.
    Includes index.
    1. Women photographers--United States--History--
19th century. 2. Women photographers--United States--
History--20th century. I. Title. II. Series.
TR23.G68 1987   770'.88042   86-30185
ISBN 0-88706-533-3
ISBN 0-88706-535-X (pbk.)

Contents

List of Photographs

Preface

Jane Gover's *The Positive Image* exemplifies the objectives in this series in New Cultural History. It is, first of all, concerned with the emergence of photography both as a profession and as a popular pastime at the turn of the century. The camera and its accompanying technology played an unrivalled role in changing cultural perceptions, in changing, that is, the meaning we attribute to experience. During the period of Gover's study, from the 1880s to the 1920s, it can be argued that the photograph provided the basis for constructing new visual "realities"—family, lifespan, news, character were all reconceived by the impact of the photograph.

More particularly, Gover succeeds in showing the ways women first became involved in photography. She explores some of the implications of this involvement, both for women and for photography. She places the appearance of women photographers in the context of more general changes in the lives of middle-class women, of their movement into the professions, of the move to forge new networks among women in order to circumvent the limits imposed by a male-dominated society. At the same time, she shows the degree to which women photographers were, for a time, assigned within photography to a subordinate "domestic" role not unlike the one they played in the larger society. It was a difficult struggle for women to achieve their own vision as photographers and some of Gover's most interesting observations have to do with the changes in women's lifestyles that appear to have resulted from the urgency of these new interests. The proportion of women photographers in this period who remained single or were divorced is far too high to be coincidental. The single life, for most of these women, appears to have been necessary for them to pursue their interests and their work as photographers. But even in the most enlightened circles, the photographic work of women was often dominated by the vision of male mentors, as those close to Alfred Stieglitz came to understand.

It is not easy to generalize about the work of this first generation of women photographers and Gover avoids easy formulations in analyzing their work. Readers will be struck by the great variety of their work, from amateurs like Alice Austen to successful and well-known photojournalists like Frances Benjamin Johnston the artistic range of women photographers seems not unlike that of men. Nonetheless, Gover finds a strain in the work of these women that is distinctly traceable to gender, what she calls their attention to the "pictorial representation of the domestic and feminine."

In inaugurating this discussion of the impact of women on photography, *The Positive Image* presents future students of the work of these and succeeding generations of women photographers with an illuminating hypothesis. Gover offers useful insight into the ways in which technology entered into and changed the lives of women in this period. The sewing machine, the typewriter and the camera all became accessible to women in this period. But the camera, it appears, offered the most creative possibilities to them.

William R. Taylor, series editor

Introduction

The golden age of photography dawned in the 1880s and lasted until the 1920s.[1] This was at once an era of technological and aesthetic development. The dry plate, rolled film, and the hand held camera were among the many mechanical advances that created modern photography. At the same time, Alfred Stieglitz, Edward Steichen, Clarence White, Gertrude Käsebier, and others demonstrated that photography was indeed an art form. Always a popular undertaking, George Eastman and his Kodak company in the 1880s made photography once and for all accessible to everyone. In that process, photography lost its status as a novelty. It emerged both as a legitimate art form, as a professional endeavor, and as an everyday technique that virtually anyone could master.

The fact that any man, woman, or child could become a photographer is important not only because so many did, but because the person taking the picture conveyed the standards and expectations of the society. Photography gave a voice to every person using a camera, creating a text that could be read. At the same time, those who turned photography into an art form developed a revitalized way of seeing that differed considerably from the conventions established by painters. The new photographic vision made use of close-ups and other angles, for example, to record everyday events and objects in unexpectedly dramatic ways.

Women played a special role in the history of photography on three levels, as artists, professionals, and amateurs, contributing to artistic innovation on the one hand, and capturing aspects of everyday life on the other. By 1900, thousands of women were actively involved as amateurs and professionals in the new medium, and the story of these women is worth telling. It is especially important to rescue the artists from oblivion. Recent exhibitions and some new literature have only begun "to repeople the artistic landscape" with the female artists—painters and sculptors as well as photographers —who rightfully belong these.[2]

Until the late 1970s little if any serious literature on photography was concerned with women's involvement in that field. Indeed, women's contributions were almost totally ignored by writers of photographic history. In Beaumont Newhall's *The History of Photography*,[3] for example, long regarded as a basic yet comprehensive history of the medium, an occasional woman is discussed. These examples represent a kind of tokenism, recognizing an idiosyncratic individual without a serious acknowledgement of the large scale and significant involvement of women in photography since 1880. William Welling also surveys the changing nature of photography as an art form.[4] In a year-by-year account he discusses the aesthetics, technology, and history of photography. Welling approaches women's activity here much in the same way as Newhall; Frances Benjamin Johnston is highlighted by Welling as an early example of a photojournalist but he fails even to suggest the presence of the thousands of other women working as amateurs and professionals during this late nineteenth century period. Coverage of the 1900 women's exhibition of photography at the Paris Exposition would have been an appropriate way of indicating the achievements of American women photographers. Numerous instances of similar treatments by writers on photography could be noted here.[5] Suffice it to say, like the work of Newhall and Welling, they deny by exclusion the fact that women were on the photographic scene. All writers have downplayed the quality and the extent of women's contributions to photography and effectively relegated these women artists and professionals to obscurity.

To be sure, there are some isolated examples of photographic history that combine biography and photographs in dealing with specific female photographers. These books, meant for a popular readership, bring the names of a handful of women photographers to general attention but in a nonscholarly and sometimes ahistorical manner.[6] The writers make sincere efforts to bring to light the contributions of special women, yet none has done so in a completely satisfying way mostly because they treat these women as idiosyncratic figures rather than women whose lives defined them as significant transitional figures in the history of women in American artistic and professional life.

Anne Tucker's book, *The Woman's Eye*,[7] widely read and frequently quoted, is a good example of this. It evaluates the photographers from a feminist perspective. In an introductory essay and in brief biographical sketches, Tucker questions the relationship between sex and art. "Can and should art be distinguished as women's art or men's art?"[8] she asks. This is an important question that should be addressed in any inquiry into women's involvement in the arts. However, Tucker's approach neither provides necessary comparisons with male photographers nor does it consider the cultural context of the periods that are examined. In addition, Tucker fails to treat photographers like Frances Benjamin Johnston and Gertrude Käsebier as nineteenth century figures. Tucker's feminist analysis is insightful but her tenuous historical framework weakens her statement.

Moreover, Tucker neglects to connect the individual women photographers to their nineteenth century contemporaries. This is a common problem of the literature. The independent and creative character of certain women are noted but none of the authors identify the commonalities shared by women photographers with other middle class women who became social workers, joined women's clubs, wrote novels, or established medical or legal practises. In each case, the photographer seems to rise from the nineteenth century landscape unconnected to social changes, unaffected by technological advances, and forever separated from the professional, artistic, and social lives of her female colleagues. In addition, the work of these women photographers is not considered as expressive of the Victorian culture and ideology that integrated the tenets of the cult of domesticity, the feminine rather than the feminist, and a moral tone that regulated behavior. A more subjective approach is required that would, as Germaine Greer has suggested, "show women artists . . . as members of a group having much in common, tormented by the same conflicts of motivation and the same practical difficulties, the obstacles both external and surmountable, internal and insurmountable of the race for achievement."[9] It is no longer enough to provide names, show pictures, or discuss individuals apart from the historical context.[10] The historian must now relate the individuals to the ideology and to the changes that shape any historical period.

These women photographers reveal themselves to have been more important, talented, and constructive than has been acknowledged. In particular, the purpose of the following analysis is to explore and reveal the multifaceted nature of women's experience in photography during the years 1880 to 1920, with particular emphasis on the turn of the century period. The discussion will draw together elements from the history of photography and the history of women, especially as it relates to women in professional and cultural life.

Many questions shaped this study of women and photography. These questions fall into two categories. First are those that relate to women as artists; does the gender of an artist affect the viewer's evaluation of the image? How do social and economic realities influence the artist's work? And how do societal notions of career, work, and family responsibilities shape the artist's self-perceptions and self-esteem? Second, in a broader social context other questions were considered; how did women respond to changes brought about by urbanization? How did the resulting shifts in gender roles affect these photographers as women, artists, professionals? Did these responses show up in the images women produced? How were women photographers connected to women in other professions?

At the inception of this research project, I held certain assumptions and expectations about women and photography that made it difficult to find answers to these questions. First, I expected to find that women's experiences in photography were entirely positive. Second, I believed the women in this unique group to be radical as compared to their middle class contemporaries. And, last, I did not see a particular female vision in the women's work. Upon investigation, however, these preconceptions had to be revised.

Although it was relatively simple for a woman to become a photographer, she had to contend with subtle forms of discrimination. Unlike women painters who had to confront outright hostility from academicians and exclusion from important art classes,[11] women could learn photography on their own or in a variety of photography schools, clubs, or classes—all open to women. Neither did women have to face the suspicion accorded women who aspired to be doctors or lawyers.[12] As photographers, women were free to combine the private and public spheres by working in home studios and reproducing domestic images. Photography journals of the period, however, revealed another perspective. These periodicals not only provide the historian with a picture of the photography scene in these years, but also express an underlying attitude that contradicted the totally positive attitudes toward women and photography. Articles appeared regularly that sought to keep women within the domestic space. On the one hand, women were encouraged to enter photography as independent workers while at the same time they were told to do so in menial roles—as receptionists for male photographers or as helpmates to photographer husbands. As the number of women photographers grew, established male photographers appeared uneasy at the possibility of the feminization of their field.

Women photographers did not emerge as the radical people I wanted them to be. In their private lives, professional women photographers appeared independent; they earned their own livings, and often remained single. Yet, certain realities of their lives belied a truly radical lifestyle. With few exceptions, women photographers kept their middle class ties intact. They rarely lived alone, for example, but rather were included in the households of close relatives and friends. The camera provided women with the means of stepping beyond the private, domestic space. At the same time, the women's lifestyles and imagery sustained middle class ideology as it celebrated the domestic ideal and woman's place as nurturer.

The question of whether or not women's work in photography reflected a distinct female vision had to be answered. At first few differences were apparent between the work of male and female photographers in this period. Gertrude Käsebier's photographs and the early pictorialism of Alfred Stieglitz displayed similar soft focus, painterly effects. The interiors of Joseph Byron and Alice Austen both suggested the Victorian reverence for home and concern with elaborate detail. The nudes of Anne Brigman and the figure studies of Edward Steichen shared artistic similarities. In these early years of photography, there seemed little relationship between one's sex, class, and art.[13] Male and female photographers of the late nineteenth century subscribed to contemporary artistic conventions usually established by males who dominated the field. Photographers appeared more affected by the dictates of pictorialism than by factors of gender or class.

These initial assessments shifted with a closer decoding of the iconography of the women photographers and through an intense scrutiny of the details of the women's lives; gender as well as class did indeed affect women's pictorial interpretations of their world.

The middle class orientation of these women shaped their perceptions; leisure time, education, family ties, and marital status inspired a special perspective. Frances Benjamin Johnston, for example, might not have expressed a clear cut "feminine" view, but implicit in her work is a distinct, middle class, progressive mentality. And the seemingly genteel tone of Alice Austen's photographs disguises a satirical and sensual strain in her imagery that derived from her hermetic lifestye. The photographs of the many female amateurs connected them to the home. In portraits and in genre pictures these women reaffirmed Victorian values of home and motherhood. And although the women photographers of this era exclude much of the outside world in their photography, it nevertheless allows the historian a close-up of their comfortable, genteel environment.

The value of women's photography from this period has not been properly assessed nor viewed in its proper context. Critics have complained about the absence in the women's imagery of the modernist tendencies that finally intrigued photographers Alfred Stieglitz, Edward Steichen and Paul Strand.[14] Instead, the women generally remained within the pictorial tradition and their photographs have been judged by contemporary standards to be stilted and sentimental. In this sense nineteenth century women photographers did not emerge as innovators, yet their self-contained visions looked to the interior, the domestic, and often sought to capture the reality of women's special place in Victorian society. These photographs cannot be dismissed. Women used the stylistic conventions of the time but this does not imply their women's view to be of less importance than their male counterparts. Photography surfaces as a perfect medium of expression for these nineteenth century women.

Women's photography during these golden years retains a special relationship to history. The record left by them from the years 1880 to 1920 stands as a product of the culture of the time. For these photographs exist as much as a pictorial journal of everyday life as evidence of historic events and public personalities. The contributions of these women photographers have heretofore rarely been acknowledged. But when these women are viewed as formulators of culture their significance cannot be underestimated.

This pictorial portfolio reveals many of the social trends and ideology of turn of the century American life. The rise of the professional woman, the impulse toward organization, (as seen for example in the camera club and women's networks), the gentility and complexity of Victorian home life, the connections of women photographers to the aesthetics of nineteenth and early twentieth century photography (especially in the person of Alfred Stieglitz), and indeed, the very perceptions of women themselves, all further an understanding of women in the social and cultural contexts of the time.

1

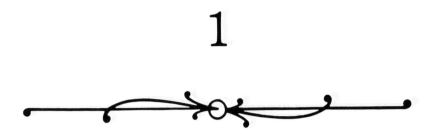

There Will Be a New Era

The popularity of the camera in the last two decades of the nineteenth century coincided with the vast technological, industrial, and urbanizing processes of the period. The United States emerged from the nineteenth century as a full fledged modern nation with enormous corporations, mass production, and ever-growing metropolitan centers. It was an environment dominated by men; men invented the new machinery, controlled the monopolies, engineered the building of cities. Yet, women were involved in the changing world as well. Not only did certain new innovations free women, to a large extent, from the burdens of domestic drudgery but other products of modern technology came to be associated with women. By the late nineteenth century, for example, women and the typewriter became synonomous, while women ran the sewing machines in the garment center of New York City and filled the work rooms and factories of other industries.

In turn of the century America, the camera similarly became one of the few mechanical devices to be linked to women. Indeed, a "fit"[1] occurred between the technological events of the late nineteenth century and society's perception of women and their proper sphere. The modern technology embodied by the camera coincided with the desires of many middle class women who yearned both to fulfill artistic ambitions and participate in the public arena. The woman with her camera, in effect, found one way to bridge the gap between two eras.

In 1904, an editorial in *The Photographer* described a Kodak advertisement, an illustration by Jessie Willcox Smith,[2] an artist famous for her representations of women and children. The work depicted a small girl in bed surrounded by her Christmas toys. Her mother, Kodak in hand, is photographing the child. The editorial lauds Kodak for the tasteful, charming advertisement that utilized a popular artist's talents. Both the editorial and the advertisement highlight the connections between women, the camera, art, and contemporary advertising. From the 1880s on, these links became more and more evident, culminating by the end of the decade in George Eastman's history-making advertising campaign that brought the camera into thousands of homes and made the device especially appealing to women as amateur or professional photographers.

Dramatic improvements in camera technology coincided with social changes that affected gender roles and the place of women in American life. An excerpt from a letter written by photographer Eva Watson-Schütze to her colleague Frances Benjamin Johnston in 1897 expressed the writer's passion for photography and her belief in women's future in the medium. "There will be a new era," wrote Watson-Schütze, "and women will fly to photography."[3] And indeed, in the late nineteenth century, many believed that a new era for women had arrived—not only for photographers but also for women in American professional and cultural life.

Women who turned to photography at the end of the nineteenth century, whether as professionals or as amateurs, did so at a time when the public arena appeared more accessible to women. Feminists, in 1900, demanded not only voting rights for women but their right to higher education and the right to earn an income. In other words, these activists perceived a role for women beyond the prescribed women's sphere. And while feminists' voices were the loudest, other women, mostly from the middle class, began to integrate the message into their personal lives.

The Victorian heritage, however, proved difficult to shed. The cult of true womanhood had become so entrenched throughout the century that the ideal of "a lady" still meant piety, purity, submissiveness, and domesticity. For middle class women, however, the base of the pedestal on which they had stood for so long was beginning to erode. By 1900, technological innovations eased the burdens of housework, the birthrate declined dramatically, and higher education became more available for women.[4] The resulting new leisure meant fresh opportunities and incentives for women to push against the restrictions that had circumscribed their lives. Through women's clubs, for example, women not only read poetry and Shakespeare's plays, they also developed the talent for organization and the confidence to enter (even if tentatively) the public sphere.[5] Clubs were only a first step, however. Most middle class club women continued to believe in their essential domestic roles; club members were reluctant, for instance, to endorse women's suffrage until late in that campaign.

Other middle class women were stepping out in different ways. Between 1890 and 1920 women's attendance at colleges almost tripled and the numbers of women in the work force more than doubled between 1880 and 1900.[6] Of this number, many became increasingly active in professions. Nursing, teaching, and social work were, of course, traditional female fields but in 1900, 7,387 women had overcome intense male opposition to become doctors.[7] Unfortunately, the high numbers did not always reflect the reality accurately. In some states women were barred from law practise and were excluded from admission to many top law schools. Elizabeth Blackwell may have paved the way for women doctors but comparatively few chose the difficult route she pioneered.[8] And in all fields women opted to remain unmarried. Almost 50 percent of female college graduates in this generation remained single. Career, marriage, and motherhood did not typically mix in turn of the century America. College graduates expressed concern over their futures. Hilda Smith (Bryn Mawr, 1908) was asked, "What came after college?" Her answer, "I don't know,"[9] echoed the dilemma of many well educated women who, like Smith and Jane Addams, agonized over their correct response to career and the demands of the "family claim."[10]

Similar difficulties and choices confronted women artists. There had, of course, always been women artists in America. Despite their accomplishments they were not, however, perceived as well suited to the so-called fine arts; painters and sculptors were usually men and this male presence defined these arts as part of the public and professional world. Instead, women were thought to be naturally disposed toward the "lesser" arts—needlework, embroidery, china, and miniature painting[11]—arts and crafts easily linked to women in domestic settings. These artistic pursuits synonomous with women were evaluated by nineteenth century contemporaries as subordinate to the "fine" arts. Women's craft work was perceived as requiring less intellectual and artistic ability.

By the nineteenth century, such traditional female activities as embroidery and needlework even helped to sustain an ideology that imposed societal restrictions on women because they were performed at home with time-consuming attention to detail. In addition, the middle class nature of late nineteenth century America assumed that women's art would express their feminine and domestic proclivities. Restricted to the home, denied access to the academy, the marketplace and, for the most part, to educational opportunities, women cultivated their arts and crafts. Until quite recently[12] this category of artistic endeavor remained separate from and subordinate to the prevailing masculine standards of what art should be.

Despite its low status in the artistic hierarchy, decorative art produced by women formed an aspect of women's culture that expressed their special perspectives within a society dominated by men. By the nineteenth century, middle class women had expanded the meaning of domestic arts and crafts to connote status and accomplishment—a badge of leisure and middle class respectability far different from the crafts created out of necessity by working class women.

In the late nineteenth century the camera was similarly perceived as an example of minor technology and the photograph was evaluated as subordinate to painting. In addition, like the decorative arts, photography was described as "painstaking" and as requiring "abnegation and devotion," singularly feminine traits. Writers on photography discussed the "delicate touch" required by the demands of photography. These kinds of perceptions tended stereotypically to justify women's use of the camera while placing them in suitable subordinate roles within the art world.[13]

Thus, middle class women added photography to their home-based arts. Here was an instance of the encroachment of a specifically nondomestic piece of modern technology into the nineteenth century middle class household, a heretofore private sector not penetrated by such symbols of the public sphere or the modern age. The camera presented a new way for women to represent and record their lives. The photo album replaced the sampler, the quilt, and the miniature portrait.

Before the 1880s photography, like many areas of professional endeavor, was inaccessible to women. In the early years of the history of the medium, the appearance of a woman with a camera was quite unusual. The cumbersome, heavy equipment required by the photographer discouraged many people of both sexes but especially limted the interest of women as amateurs or professionals. The photographic outfit could weigh from 50 to 70 pounds and often required a large steamer trunk to hold the necessary paraphernalia: glass plates and lenses, a heavy wooden tripod, at least two cameras with their plate holders, a dozen or so plates, solution bottles, a heavy glass tank for sensitizing—and the list goes on. The photographer was further encumbered by the necessity of a portable darkroom for the developing process when away from the home darkroom.

The bulky, weighty outfit was only part of the story. To be a photographer also meant diligence, dedication, and study. An article in *Anthony's Photographic Bulletin* warned of the challenging task; one had to be familiar with the entire process of producing a print in the pre-dry plate days. This meant knowing how to "make collodion, coat, sensitize, and develop a plate, construct the silver bath . . . print, tone, and fix the prints."[14] Glass plates not only had to be kept moist but also required development immediately after exposure. The wet plate process was a complex one involving seven steps, and a mistake at any point meant a ruined photograph.

Despite the problems, however, isolated examples of women photographers do surface as early as 1846. Their experiences were diverse. Sarah Holcomb was known to have worked in New Hampshire, combatting the cold, harsh winters that froze chemicals. She also faced the equally hostile competition of male photographers working in the area.[15] In these early days some women turned to photography as a supplementary source of income. Jane Cook, an amateur artist, was listed in the New York City Directory of 1846 as a daguerreotypist.[16] Caroline Hopes of St. Louis, Missouri and Mary Hoyt of Syracuse, New York also did daguerreotype work. The San Francisco City Directory of 1850 noted a Mrs. J. Shannon as both a midwife and daguerreotypist.[17] Still another photographer, Madame Weinert Beckman, impressed her male colleagues with her 1852 exhibition of calotypes.[18]

Women were encouraged as early as the late 1850s and early 1860s to become photographers. Photography journals and other publications urged women to try the new field pointing out that photography did not require nearly as much effort as did regular needlework.

Probably the most common way in which women participated in photography during these pioneer days was as assistants to photographer husbands. These husband and wife associations occurred from the earliest days of photography. In England in the 1840s, Constance Talbot, wife of William Henry Fox Talbot (an early figure in the development of photography) established herself as the first woman photographer and photographic technician. Mrs. Talbot learned photography from her husband and then went on to produce her own photographs. This was in addition to assisting Talbot with his photographic experiments.[19]

Indeed it was not unusual to find instances in towns and cities throughout America of women who became photographers through marriage, and of women who, having learned the craft, took over the studio after a divorce or the death of a spouse.[20]

But it was the technological advances from 1880 to 1909 that had definitive and far-reaching implications for women's expanded involvement in the medium. The introduction of dry plates[21] during the 1880s, the invention of celluloid roll film, and the development of the hand held camera at the end of the century, made the camera a practical, simple, and easily handled device for both amateurs and professionals.[22] These innovations changed and expanded the already burgeoning mass amateur market that was making photography accessible to all.

Further, the introduction in 1883 of the detective camera emerged as another highly popular advance.[23] Regardless of the make, it attracted little attention even when used on busy streets or while traveling. By the early 1880s thousands of men, women, and children had adopted the new, compact device which was so convenient that a "lady might without attracting any attention go upon Broadway, and take a series of photographs, feeling perfectly sure that she would attract no more attention that she would if she carried a work box or work basket."[24] Most women, admonished by their mothers "to behave like a lady under all circumstances" and to "do nothing that will attract the least notice"[25] found the changes in the camera to be compatible with the behavioral expectations of their middle class world. Women in photography were no longer a curiosity or particularly exceptional.

This burgeoning interest in photography was enhanced by the introduction of the Kodak camera and nitro-cellulose film in 1889. At this time Kodak became a household word; thousands were urged to "press the button" and let "Kodak . . . do the rest."[26] And indeed photographers by the thousands sent their exposed rolls of film to Kodak for processing. George Eastman's introduction of the Kodak system (a series of operations which cocked the shutter, exposed the film, and advanced the film to the next frame) totally revolutionized the entire medium, eliminating still other technical and chemical problems. Now anyone with the purchase price of 25 dollars for the easily operated camera could become a photographer. Instead of the novice being involved in the technical functions of the photographic process, trained specialists at the Eastman factory developed, printed, and reloaded the camera before sending it back to the eager amateur. George Eastman had produced a camera which created a new mass market.

By the 1880s and 1890s photography had passed through its formative phases. The earliest developments of the 1840s and 1850s, the daguerreotype and the calotype, had evolved into the photographic compositions of the 1860s and 1870s that included the snapshot and the motion experiments of Eadweard Muybridge.[27] By the last decades of nineteenth century the perceptions of photography as strictly a science or merely a novelty changed even further. The end of the century marked photography's modern era in which the medium became an artistic form of expression and accessible to all.

Women entering photography in the mid 1880s were able to take advantage of the technological advances and the shifts in perceptions toward the new medium. They approached the field when the aesthetic nature of photography was being fervently debated. Was photography an art form or was it just another minor technological device of the modern age? In England, the ideas of British photographer H.P. Emerson sparked the debate. Photography, admitted Emerson in 1886, was "superior to etching, woodcutting, and chemical drawing"[28] in the correctness of its reproduced image, but he found it lacking when compared to painting. Photography was devoid of color and without accurate tonal characteristics. By 1891, Emerson's declarations on photography became more extreme and discussion over them intensified. He declared that photography was not an art at all. Photographers, he wrote, lacked control over their images and the art was a limited one. Emerson, despite his denunciations, did not give up photography; his work and his words stimulated controversy as others responded and attempted to define the aesthetics of the medium. Prestigious European camera clubs, like the Vienna Camera Club and London's Linked Ring, took opposing positions to Emerson's. They asserted photography's artistic identity.[29]

In America, Alfred Stieglitz was intensely convinced of the artistic nature of photography and made consistent efforts to elevate photography to a fine art. Unlike Emerson, Stieglitz recognized no limits within photography but rather understood the ability of the camera to uncover new meanings in the ordinary and raise the commonplace subject to evoke universal truths and express the highest emotions. As photographer, writer, editor, and art patron, Stieglitz from 1890 on developed the artistic potential in photography.

It was mainly through Stieglitz's endeavors that photography finally became recognized as a fine art and not merely the favorite hobby of the leisured middle class nor the province of the greedy commercial portrait photographer. Through his editorship of Camera Notes (1897–1902) and, even more importantly, Camera Work (1903–1917), Stieglitz proclaimed his faith in photography's artistic qualities. Even as photography, through the early decades of the twentieth century, continued to be degraded as a fashionable hobby, a fad, and the "lowest of all the arts," Stieglitz and his followers (known as Photo-Secessionists for their rejection of the banal and routine in photography) promoted photography's right to be equated with painting. Other magazines like The Craftsman and The Outlook followed the lead of Camera Work and celebrated the work of the Photo-Secessionists and the talents of the photographer as a skilled artist.[30] These periodicals addressed themselves to those artists and critics in the fine arts who were reticent about admitting photographers and photography to their hallowed precincts. Gertrude Käsebier, for example, often featured in these pages, exemplified in her career the passage from photographic hobbyist to a full time professional committed to artistic photography. Exhibitions and publications of Käsebier's work proved inspiring to scores of photographers and provided examples of the creativity involved in photography. Photography gained adherents and they radiated confidence about its potential.

Between 1890 and 1898 the movement toward fine art photography flourished. Several small salons were held that emulated the European practice of a highly selective showing of pictorial work. It was, however, the photographic salon at the Philadelphia Academy of Fine Arts (1898) that enhanced the position of American photography. "For the first time it was realized that a Stieglitz, a Hinton, or a Day was as distinctive in style as a Breton, a Corot or a Verestchagin; that photography is open to broad as well as sharp treatment; that it had its impressionists and its realists."[31] In other words, photography was finally being recognized as an art form comparable to painting.

Salon exhibitions, the claims of Stieglitz, the publication of serious photography journals, and the establishment of respected camera clubs were developments that elevated photography's status. Significantly, by 1898, collectors for the first time were buying photographs shown at salon and camera club exhibitions. Even more importantly, in 1896 the National Museum bought fifty photographs at the Washington, D.C. salon held that year.

The intellectual arguments among Stieglitz and his followers and the salon movement contrasted, however, with the growing commercialism to be found in photography. The presence and proliferation of opulent and elaborate portrait studios, for example, indicated the fashionable and exploitive sides of the profession. In the 1890s thousands of stage celebrities, society figures, as well as those who aspired to elite positions flocked to have their pictures taken by Bachrach or Falk or Pach or by hundreds of less well-known commercial portraitists.

The differences between the work done by commercial studios and that produced by pictorialists or by Stieglitz's followers among the Photo-Secessionists epitomized a developing artistic split among the photographic ranks. Those who utilized the "old" approach were unconcerned with the pictorial qualities of their prints. Theirs was a plain, straight-forward style. On the other hand, the "new school" adherents sought a "painter-like" result in their photography. The softly focused photographs of Steichen, Clarence White, and Alvin Langdon Coburn, for example, were influenced by Whistler, Japanese prints, impressionism, and symbolism. In fact, the work of these and other photographers was so close to painting that viewers frequently mistook the photographs for paintings.

Many women professionals and amateurs adopted the pictorial mode. In doing so they were affected by the work of Stieglitz, and the Photo-Secessionists. Eva Watson-Schütze, Gertrude Käsebier, Anne Brigman, Alice Boughton, and many others were welcomed as Photo-Secessionists. The term "secession" seemed to link this group of photographers to the art world where artists in the forefront of a new movement might "secede" from what they judged to be the more traditional mainstream. Most women of this group appeared content to follow pictorial principles throughout most of their careers. Käsebier, for example, founded the Pictorial Association of America in 1916 when it was clear that Stieglitz was turning to modernism and away from his earlier pictorial stance; Anne Brigman clung to pictorialism long after it had lapsed into disfavor among both photographers and critics. Yet although women photographers of the Photo-Secession adhered to artistic trends formulated by males in the field, they did not necessarily project a similar vision in their work. Women like Brigman and Käsebier often contributed an identifiable female perspective.[32]

As the nineteenth century evolved, photography became an acceptable profession and respectable hobby for women; they faced neither hostility nor disapproval for using the camera. This was due, in part, to changing notions regarding women and the new technologies. In the expanding urban and industrial American society machinery continued to be assigned to men. Cars, trucks, boats, and later, planes and computers, at least initially were associated with males and designated for male use. But due largely to the sales efforts of manufacturers like George Eastman and Isaac Singer, American women became validated for the handling of certain other machines. Indeed, both the sewing machine and the camera emerged as mechanical devices that, because of their domestic associations, fit in with accepted perceptions of women.

During the late nineteenth and into the twentieth century advertisers recognized such connections and became increasingly concerned with persuading women to buy their products, often by creating a demand for the goods among that group of potential customers. An advertisement for *McCall's* magazine in 1904 recognized that "90% of the family income is expended by the women of a household." It went on to explain that "every wife and mother at the head of a home holds the clasp of the family pocketbook."[33] The ad referred to the three million readers and the 600,000 paid subscribers to *McCall's*, a "new kind" of woman who oversees and controls household finances and purchases. Not surprisingly, advertisers directed their sales pitches to this class of buyers. Women's magazines proved useful to these late nineteenth and early twentieth century advertisers. Not only *McCall's* but *The Ladies Home Journal*, *Women's Home Companion*, *Good Housekeeping*, and *Cosmopolitan* dated from the last three decades of the nineteenth century and all directed their articles and advertising to the city-bred, economically comfortable woman who comprised the bulk of their readership.[34] The large circulation of these periodicals testified to the double assumptions that women not only comprised most of magazine readers, but also that women bought the majority of consumer goods.

The story of the marketing of the early sewing machines in the 1870s usefully illustrates both the emerging recognition of women as consumers and demonstrates an advertising campaign that capitalized on women's changing roles in that period. First patented by Elias Howe in 1846 and later improved and developed by Isaac Singer, the sewing machine had a world-wide impact as "the first consumer appliance."[35] The domestic implications of this innovation were obvious. But even though it was greeted enthusiastically in farm or factory environments, the sewing machine was at first more often viewed suspiciously as a home tool. Men, usually husbands, held the buying power that could introduce the new labor saving device into the world of their wives. They rarely saw the need to replace the satisfactions derived from their wives' hand sewing with machine stitched work. Women, on the other hand, did not yet possess the finanical independence necessary for the purchase of a machine of their own. Buying a machine, in fact, might indicate a wife's inclination to assume a degree of personal autonomy over her activities, an already growing and troubling phenomenon of the period. Cognizant of this situation, the Singer Company geared its original campaigns to male rather than female needs; a women with a machine would become a more refined companion for she could devote additional time to cultivating herself.

Still another factor that deterred purchases of sewing machines for home use was the nineteenth century perception of woman as unable to operate complex machinery. Women themselves admitted to feeling inept and often moved to tears when faced with such a mechanical device.

Singer, in an effort to encourage sewing machine sales, finally directed the company's message to women instead of men, urging them to act independently. In doing so Singer created, in fact, a new market. By no means a feminist, but rather prompted by business priorities, Singer concentrated on the female buyer. Not only did the company aim its advertising at women, but Singer also hired women to instruct prospective purchasers on operating techniques. This would prove to any doubters that women were capable of handling such machinery. Advertising also pointed to the new leisure within the reach of housewives—time that might now be directed toward child-rearing, caring for a husband's needs, or even earning her own money as a sewing machine operator. A Singer advertisement, around 1870, pronounced the machines advantages: "During the nineteenth century the Singer Sewing Machine has added countless hours to women's leisure for rest and refinement, it has opened new avenues for her employment, and it has brought comforts which were formerly attainable to a few within the reach of all."[35]

Of course, the sewing machine as a domestic labor saving device coincided with traditional perceptions of women's role as homemaker whose job included mastery of the needle and its related sewing and embroidery skills. The camera, classifiable as a cultural mechanism, existed as a different type of domestic vehicle to be utilized at an artistic level by those very women freed by Singer's product to enjoy or professionally use the now accessible leisure.

However, women's possession of both machines meant not only the ability to run up a faster seam or snap a picture of a smiling baby. Unexpectedly, these innovations also provided women with a means of stepping beyond the limitations of the domestic world. As things turned out, both examples of modern technology established creative outlets and finanical opportunities for women of the late nineteenth century.

The years from 1879 to 1889 produced a veritable revolution in photography and George Eastman, through his inventions, was in the forefront of those changes. The camera and photography became a new technique that created vitalized worlds in industry, commerce, and creativity. Through large quantity machine production, low prices, national and international distribution, and widespread advertising Eastman sought to develop the commercial potential of photography while still promoting his belief in photography's artistic possibilities. In 1885 he envisioned the expansion of photography—"We should be able to popularize photography to an extent as yet scarcely dreamed of."[37] In keeping with this conception, Eastman, in the 1880s, set up an advertising department that acquired space in popular periodicals with country-wide circulations. Ads in Scribner's, Century, Harper's, Scientific American, Frank Leslie, and others created new markets while expanded product distribution from only stock dealers to drug and department stores helped to make Eastman's cameras and equipment familiar to consumers.[38] Eastman understood the need to develop new consumers to absorb the large scale production that was part of Eastman industries. Like many large producers (Burpee's, Ivory, Remington) of the 1880-1890 period, Kodak relied upon a systematic advertising campaign in national magazines. Even a brief examination of Eastman's promotion of the Kodak points to the prevailing turn of the century belief in the creation of product demand. Indeed, Walter Dill Scott wrote in 1903 that businessmen should make their ads as appealing as possible in order to enhance the product and encourage and prod the consumer to buy.[39] In other words, advertisers were not merely to describe their goods but rather to make people want to spend money on their products.

Prior to 1885, Eastman's advertising had been limited and sporadic. In that year, however, he used full page ads in widely read photography periodicals in both the United States and England. Kodak's advertising campaign continued to expand; the company became as prominent an advertiser as Sears Roebuck, H.L. Heinz, and Quaker Oats, among others.[40] The adoption of the famous slogan, "You press the button; we do the rest" achieved in 1889 an unprecedented reknown for the Kodak name and product. The catchy phrase was applied by the general public to all cameras.

Recognizing the nineteenth century woman's reluctance to handle mechanical equipment, Eastman stressed, as Singer had done, the ease of operation and the simplicity of the Kodak's mechanism. Prior to the late 1880s the camera was considered a device for professional photographers. Between 1840 and 1870, for example, camera purchases were made mostly by commercial studio photographers and only occasionally by a dedicated amateur.[41] Even in the early 1880s potential buyers displayed a reluctance to purchase a camera that required the complex developing and printing processes necessary in that period. George Eastman in the late 1880s devised his simple, fairly inexpensive camera for the general amateur market. In 1888 he expressed his belief in the enormous possibilities of photography for "everybody" through the three step Kodak system.[42] This was a camera for those who probably had never taken a picture before nor had even considered the purchase of a camera.

Camera companies related their products to women as early as 1886. Advertisements for a variety of cameras and camera products appeared in women's magazines and appealed to the curiosity of female buyers. Women were asked to buy the magic lantern and the stereopticon; they were even urged to start their own photography businesses. Women were cajoled into entering contests that offered cash rewards for images of infants and gardens.[43] The typical magazine advertisements for camera equipment that appeared before 1888 presented the product, stated its usefulness, listed its price. By this year, however, Eastman recognized the need to create a market for his photographic products and placed women in a crucial spot in his advertising scheme.

Concomitant with its advertising in professional journals, the Eastman company promoted its wares in the pages of women's magazines. Emphasizing the simplicity of operation, Eastman not only contacted a large general public but within these ranks reached a whole new clientele.[44] By 1900 amateur photographers owned 100,000 Kodak cameras and Eastman Kodak was on the verge of releasing the Brownie, a dollar box camera that would continue to revolutionize photography and expand camera sales.[45] Almost every man, woman, and child was a potential customer. And from the late 1880s onward, Eastman paid particular attention to the consumer capacity of the leisured middle class woman with money to spend on such things as cameras, and time to devote to the technique. Throughout the advertising buildups, women appeared crucial not only as potential consumers but also as an advertising image to sell cameras. Eastman's goal was to create new markets. Toward this purpose, Eastman, like Singer, concentrated on women and created the illusion of their independence.

Thus, women amateurs of the period were personified by the image of "the Kodak girl":

> Dressed in a shirtwaist
> And her sailor hat and shirt
> Of natty gray, she sallies forth
> And snaps and snaps away . . .[46]

Determined, dedicated, good-looking, the Kodak girl was everywhere—at Chatauqua, the World's Fair, or next door, directing her camera at everything and anyone within range. "It matters little whether the subject be religious or romantic or the spot sacred or very ordinary, the Kodak girl will be found around, adjusting her lens to a proper focus and 'taking in' the sights."[47] Lady amateurs and Kodak girls were particularly evident during the summer months. Off to the seashore, the countryside, or to Europe, women were inevitably seen with cameras and cases as their companions. These real life examples of the Kodak girl came from all over the United States—many from small cities like Potsdam, New York, Phillipsburg, Pennsylvania, or Cambridge, Massachusetts.

The image promoted by Kodak of its Kodak girl enjoyed widespread popularity and competed with other advertising symbols like Sunny Jim and Johnny Walker. The public perceived this symbol as representing a "nice girl," and many even adopted her striped shirt as a fashion fad.[48] The Kodak girl possessed a sweet smile and a sympathetic air. Pretty, wholesome, and sweet, the woman in camera ads fit the expected image of turn of the century women. But, in part, she portrayed as well a new kind of freedom. Women, for example, on the covers of *Kodakery*[49] are not passive buttonpressers but are participants in their surroundings. With camera in hand, this woman photographer is active and curious yet accepted and welcomed everywhere. What began as an advertising gimmick emerged as a symbol of a new middle class woman who, though not yet fully emancipated, could still enjoy an expanded notion of acceptable behavior. The nineteenth century woman with her camera projected the image of a "modern" look; the reality, it turned out, was harder to achieve.

Innovations in the camera industry as evidenced in George Eastman's improvements in the camera and other photographic equipment, a modern trend in advertising, and the advances in publishing and printing, expanded the photographic experience generally and women's involvement in the medium in particular. Middle class women freed by technology from the worst aspects of household drudgery now found their lives shaped, in part, by a search for activity to fill leisured hours. By the late 1880s thousands of women, uncomfortable with this leisure, found an active, creative, and sometimes even a lucrative outlet in photography.

2

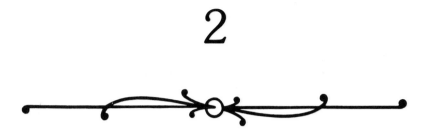

A New Profession
for Women

In the years 1880 to 1920, photography, a male bastion before
1880, emerged as a career option and avocation for women. By 1900,
more than 3500 women worked as professional photographers[1] where
25 years before only an occasional woman could be seen toting the
burdensome equipment necessary for camera work. Now many
women chose to support themselves with their cameras, even while
others considered it merely a fascinating diversion. Whatever the
degree of commitment, women and their cameras became linked
and society approved of the merger. This represents, in fact, a con-
vergence of technical advances, attitudinal shifts toward women's
roles, changing perceptions about the very nature of photography
itself, and, for many women, a burgeoning consciousness of the
restrictions present in late Victorian America. What began for
thousands of women as a fad in the 1880s evolved as a profession
for a significant number of them by the early decades of the twentieth century.

Coincidental with the popularity of the camera in American cultural life were other late nineteenth century social changes which also affected women's involvement with photography. Advances in household technology, for instance, transformed accepted patterns of women's lives. Their experiences, heretofore restricted to the domestic sector, now reflected the encroachments of the new industrial order, particularly among the young urban and suburban middle class. By the turn of the century these advantaged daughters were being sent to high school and college where, exposed to a life beyond the bounds of household duties and routines, they learned of other possibilities. Education provided women with the training and, even more importantly, with the desire to take advantage of the many opportunities offered by the expanding urban economy. Alongside the educational advantages now available for women were the more liberal attitudes toward women and their work. Both society's outlook and women's perceptions regarding their lives were being redefined. No longer trapped by the expectations of the cult of true womanhood, women found themselves in transit from nineteenth century traditions to modern twentieth century trends.

Indeed, an acute dilemma arose over the position of the middle class woman who worked in late nineteenth century America. This was revealed in books and articles which attempted to deal with the issue but often sent out mixed messages. On the one hand, women were seen as capable, trainable and, in fact, as people who "should be trained to do some sort of work by which [they] can earn a livelihood, if need be."[2] But underlying these expressed beliefs in women's competency and ability to earn their own incomes was the persistence of earlier notions of women's nurturing and domestic roles. The media, for example, often acknowledged women's shortcomings and warned them of the inevitable obstacles that would surely subvert them. An 1882 article in *The Century*, clearly warned that "no womanly woman ever takes the helm and sails out into the strong waters with all the responsibilities of life resting on her without great suffering."[3] Denunciations of working women surfaced frequently. Indeed, passionate reassertions, often by women themselves, of home as woman's proper place and motherhood and homemaking as woman's special mission vied with urgings to prepare women for roles in the workplace.[4]

In their search for a suitable occupation or an intriguing hobby, women were advised in a variety of prescriptive literature to consider taking their places in the working world. A demand for career information led to the publication of numerous books and articles on the subject. This literature was directed, in particular, to middle class women. Catherine Filene's *Careers for Women*,[5] a collection of essays on work opportunities, was compiled to answer an apparent need for data on vocational choices. The author sought to transmit information for job-seekers in order to save them time, money, and effort. Mrs. M.L. Rayne in *What Can A Woman Do?* hoped that her book would aid women in finding useful employment and that her suggestions would even be valuable for "those fortunate ones who do not need to step beyond the horizon of home, it will give a deeper interest in 'women's work,' and cause them to feel a personal role in her labor and achievement."[6]

Rayne recognized the changing position of middle class women in nineteenth century America; it was imperative that women develop an income-producing skill. She perceived the happy woman as one who worked at something she enjoyed. Society must therefore provide the education which would allow a woman, like a man, the freedom to pursue her life's profession. Rayne's concern with the working woman is reflected in other literature of the time and coincided with such activities as the vocational movement of the early twentieth century. Pursued in colleges and in large American cities, this activity, sponsored by educational organizations, helped the educated, bright ambitious woman to find an appropriate position.[7]

Increasing numbers of women perceived their roles to be outside the domestic sphere. The special capacities of women proclaimed by nineteenth century prescriptive literature were interpreted by feminist Julia Ward Howe as empowering women to enter the public sphere to "do nothing less than to redeem the world."[8] Indeed, the membership of the Association for the Advancement of Women agreed that women could enter any profession for which they were suited. Speeches on all aspects of women's work ("Women's Work in the Pulpit," "What Practical Measures Will Promote the Financial Independence of Women," and so on)[9] resonated with the notion that women's activities need no longer be restricted to traditional domestic tasks. The mutual support of AAW members helped to dissipate long held, preconceived images of working women and the invectives heaped upon those women bold enough to infiltrate the male work place. Yet it was still a rare occurrence to encounter a woman doctor, lawyer, or painter. Intrusions by

women would not only mean unwanted competition into traditionally male fields but worst of all, such changes might "feminize"
the profession, a step that, it was feared, would lower the prestige of
those males already in the field. In medicine, for example, these
reasons created a male backlash in the last third of the nineteenth
century, thwarting women's applications to medical schools.

In spite of such barriers, by the turn of the century, people
realized that professional women were on the American scene. Articles and speeches devoted considerable attention not only to the
idealization of "the clever woman"[10] but to the many vocations
opened to them. *The Outlook* featured a series dealing with women
and their work: "The School-Teacher," "The Woman on the
Farm," and "Woman in the Professions" described these and other
careers   and   offered   encouragement   for   those   seeking
employment.[11] *The Ladies Home Journal* and *The Outlook* contributed additional encouragement to the working woman by
publishing ideas on meal planning and appropriate dress for the
woman with a job.[12] At the same time, however, these periodicals
reassured their women readers that successful professionals attained
their status because they remained womanly throughout the pursuit
of a career. Thus, the tacit approval given to women in the
workplace was tempered by an attempt to sustain traditional concepts. Amidst these debates, photography afforded a unique solution for women, one that combined domesticity with a profession.

For many women, initial forays with cameras were largely
determined by the popular and fashionable nature of photography
in the 1880s and 1890s. In the spring of 1884, *Anthony's Photographic Bulletin* declared that the use of the camera was so widespread that it had "no parallel in the history of any other art."[13] The
phenomenon of photography was, in fact, described as a disease,
The New York Times equating the camera epidemic with the
cholera epidemic.[14] In women's magazines the new recreation was
consistently promoted as a charming, practical, and fulfilling amusement. "Photography for the Girls"[15] appeared the perfect pastime
for young women in the interval between boarding school and marriage. In America and in Europe the "new pursuit" was discussed.
Dances, rides, walks, the theater, drawing, the piano—accepted
Victorian pastimes for young ladies—all seemed to pale when compared to the possibilities of the camera.

As a hobby, photography was taken up by European royalty; Princess Victoria of Wales, the Duchess of York, and the Duchess of Fife were ardent amateurs who won prizes for their work.[16] In London, in 1886, Princess Fredericka opened the second annual amateur photographic exhibition. At this showing two hundred prints were the work of women.[17] *The Photo-American* reported the extensive photographic interest of the Empress of Germany who "takes her own pictures, develops her own plates, makes her own copies, tones them and mounts them. . . . She goes nowhere without her beloved camera . . ."[18] In 1898, still another journal, *The Professional Photographer* described other princesses, baronesses, and countesses committed to photography and commented that: "If these representatives of royalty who can adorn a court and grace society, and who possess every means of enjoyment that birth and culture and position afford, can find pleasure in photography, there must be much in it for people in general not yet disclosed."[19] Closer to home, Mrs. Cleveland, the wife of the President, enthusiastically took up photography.

This focus on foreign princesses and other elites involved in photography popularized the medium and legitimized photography for the American middle class woman. This fashionable aspect also reflected a tradition of sorts in photography. The camera had long been associated with celebrities and much that was trend-setting and diverting in American life. The *carte de visite* (visiting card) craze of the 1850s and 1860s and later, in the 1880s, the popularity of cabinet photographs, not only established connections between the portrait photographer and the fashionable world but also contributed to the categorization of photography as a fad and not a fine art.[20] These card photographs, particularly popular in urban areas, reproduced images of actresses and politicians, businessmen, and students. The visiting card vogue included not only the reproduction of one's own image, but also collecting photographs of family, friends, and the period's celebrities. These cards were accumulated in albums in which portraits of family members mingled with the faces of queens and presidents. The Victorian attraction to the cult of the celebrity and the age's celebration of the family further accounted for the perception of the faddish nature of the photograph.

The very popularity of the camera among middle class people conversely brought to photography the taint of "ordinariness," which diminished the new art in many eyes but helped to make photography accessible to women. The careless and aimless use of the camera by both snap-shooting amateurs and nondiscerning professionals was criticized. Photography critic, Joseph T. Keiley caustically degraded the activities of "art-babbling, plate-spoiling" amateurs.[21] The well known photographer, Arnold Genthe, commented on the commercial and unartistic state of the medium in these early years when "everyone claimed to be a photographer and yet few displayed any imagination or picture sense."[22] And, the president of the Photographer's Association commented in the spring of 1899 that, "Photography as other professions has suffered from the acts of unworthy men. Law has its shysters, medicine its quacks, theology its hypocrites, and it is not wonderful that photography has had men . . . whose conduct degraded it."[23]

Detractors disputed the claims of those who elevated photography and photographers to a higher sphere. One contemporary commentator noted that:

> "In the minds of most persons he [the photographer] ranks a good deal below an artist, and a little above a book-agent. He is shabby genteel, the man who serves mammon and misses the true artistic inspiration. He is regarded by painters much as the family doctor regards the quack who advertises."[24]

Such assessments caused photographers to defend themselves and their art. They consistently sought to justify an improved position for photography in American cultural life. Too few, it seemed to photographer J. Pitcher Spooner, were concerned with raising the quality of their photographic work. Without higher standards, he asserted, critics would continue to say "only a photographer," demeaning the profession as a whole.[25] Anne Brigman remembers braving jeers that mocked photography as "merely a mechanical process."[26]

Others denigrated the new medium because of its popularity among women and children. Well known pictorialist photographer, F. Holland Day, stated his concern that the use of the camera by these groups would prevent the medium from being taken seriously as a fine art.[27] Day was aware of the contempt that artists and sculptors often expressed toward photography. These impressions of photography were widely published and shaped perceptions of it as a second class art form. It seemed quite natural then that its was so easily taken up by women, similarly treated as second class members of nineteenth century society.

With no formal academic requirements, the aspiring photographer entered a profession which appeared to be an untried frontier promising easy achievement with a minimum of preparation and financial outlay. Women of the middle class, still tied to husbands and hearths, yet chafing under the restrictions implied by such commitments were attracted to photography by advertising that stressed the simplicity of merely pressing the button on their Kodaks,[28] unaware at first of the realities of becoming a serious camera operator. Alice Hughes, a leading portrait photographer in turn of the century England, expressed dismay over the naiveté of aspiring women amateurs who thought photography to be merely an amusing and glamorous pursuit. They failed to recognize the hard work and ability required to succeed.[29]

Stories abounded which encouraged the pretty, patient, willing woman. Typical of these tales was a story published in *The Amateur Photographer* in 1884. This scenario depicted a beautiful, young woman working behind the counter in her husband's unsuccessful photography studio. An unconventional switch occurs when the wife emerges from the counter to take over the photography duties while the husband retreats behind the counter. The article explains the woman's success in a tone and style often used in photography journal anecdotes that relate to women:

> . . . she was pretty . . . prettiness has a bewitching effect on mankind . . . the business has been brisk ever since the change . . . Her garments are not frayed and blotched, but neat and becoming; and the scent of her is not acid but geranium . . . The gentle touch of her hand electrifies him [male sitter].[30]

A more realistic picture of the woman in photography emerged throughout the 1880s and 1890s, as photography continued to be encouraged for women by successful female photographers. These women, exuding confidence based on their personal accomplishments as photographers, recommended all aspects of the field. Their comments attempted to present an honest picture of life in and out of the studio; details were freely given about fees, training, and the hard work involved. Direct appraisals of the craft stressed both its rigorous nature and the financial and artistic satisfactions. Two articles in 1894 by Elizabeth Flint Wade lauded photography in grandiose terms as "the handmaiden of science, the artist's assistant, the tourist's notetaker, the mainstay of the lecturer and historian, the chronicler of current events . . . the discoverer of unknown worlds."[31] She pointed to the opportunities in scientific and industrial photography as well as genre and interior work. Directing her advice to "the perservering amateur" rather than to the professional, Wade depicted the medium in glowing terms.

Photography was promoted for the artistic woman, whether amateur or professional. It was easier to enter than painting which required a greater expenditure in both time and training. Emilie V. Clarkson, a "woman expert in photography," started as a painter. Discovering certain deficiencies in her artistic skills, Clarkson switched her mode of expression. She frankly discussed her change of interest.

> I was always very fond of drawing and painting . . . but to accomplish anything in that direction a thorough course in drawing is necessary, also a certain degree of talent and genius which I soon discovered I did not possess, and rather than be a mere dauber, I turned to photography, for by its aid I found I could compose figure compositions . . . without the talent necessary for drawing them.[32]

In photography, *The New York Times* asserted, a girl "can become an artist photographer, in half the time and at far less expense than painting . . . at hand are scenes, gardens, homes, and historic buildings."[33] To prove the validity of such statements, women described their early experiences in photography in order to inspire hesitant beginners. For Lillian Baynes Griffin, photography began after an illness forced her to give up magazine writing. Indeed, photography helped her recovery. Mattie Edwards Hewitt entered photography to make a living and kept with it because "it is the most fascinating of arts . . . "[34] For Lily Selby, an Englishwoman with a science degree, photography was "all an accident." Looking for an artist's studio with her sister, Selby was offered a photographer's studio with all its equipment. This serendipitous incident coincided with her own knowledge of chemicals and her sister's business expertise to propel the women into a photographic career. Edith Tracy and her sister began photography as a diversion which grew into a paying business while Mme. Aimé Dupont took over her husband's studio after his death.[35]

The experience of other women photographers considered successful in late nineteenth century America provided positive incentives for women's entry into photography. Mary Patten, a portrait photographer for 20 years, only worked nine months of the year but proudly asserted that after the first year she made a good income from photography. Patten advised aspiring photographers to experiment and train in both school and studio. Then, according to Patten, woman's natural characteristics would enhance her chances for achievement. Her emphasis on these assets reiterated the prevailing belief in women's unique character, especially as applied to the arts.[36]

J.H. Parson's woeful tale of widowhood was transformed into one with a happy ending, thanks to photography. Parsons learned the photography business as her husband's assistant, mastering printing and other techniques in this capacity. On her husband's death, she took over the studio and became successful enough at the business to support her family. She hoped that her story would inspire other women "compelled . . . to support themselves, for all cannot be teachers, clerks, or seamstresses."[37] Photography here is equated with traditionally female jobs; the new field appeared both respectable and acceptable for women because it merged home and business.

These success stories offered many routes for women to follow. With "pluck, sincerity, and the will to succeed" it appeared that any ambitious woman could become a professional photographer or enjoy the fulfillment of amateur status. In addition, women could learn photography in a home setting where sitters, subjects, and a ready made studio were easily available. Women could arrange a work space within the domestic environs. In fact, a regular darkroom was not required to develop plates. Rather, the kitchen or bathroom could and did serve the purpose for either the successful professional or the beginner. For a time, Frances Benjamin Johnston used her bedroom window for printing and developed her plates in the bathroom.[38] At the beginning of her career, Alice Hughes turned the small upstairs rooms of her family's house into a darkroom. Hughes, like Johnson, printed her negatives in a window.[39] Catherine Weed Ward told of similar early experiences.[40]

However, the emphatic statements by and about successful women photographers alternated in contemporary newspapers, magazines, and photography journals with articles and anecdotes that continued to emphasize the homely virtues and subtley portrayed ways to divert women's photographic ambitions. This duality prevailed in much of the late nineteenth and early twentieth century periodical literature and reflected the conflicts aroused by the period's changing ideology. On the one hand society encouraged women to enter the public arena while at the same time it disparaged and discouraged those women who actually emerged from the domestic sphere. The field of photography proved no exception to this ambivalence.

Certain observers, for example, denounced women who earned income from photography. The well known art and photography critic, Sadachiki Hartmann, resented women's role in the profession. He persisted in identifying women with the traditional domestic sphere.[45] Viewed from this perspective, any compensatory work for "ladies" was abhorrent and demeaned the proper male role as provider. Likewise, most husbands and fathers sought to protect their wives and daughters from the coarse, cruel marketplace, a world in which contacts with unknown men could only bring humiliation and affronts to a woman's natural delicacy and grace.[46]

The pervasiveness of these values was apparent in literature of the late Victorian period. *The Outlook* described the emerging woman of the early twentieth century as possessing qualities similar to her sisters of a past age. Adept at "homely tasks" and suffused with the knowledge of "the spiritual world," these "mothers of the race . . . will become in still deeper measure the mothers of society."[47] In the early days of the new century, articles continued to advise young women to marry and become mothers, "real partners in the life bond with men who must honor them."[48]

Writers in serious photography journals also tried to keep women photographers in their proper place. Aware of the growing numbers of women in the field and perhaps, like Sadachiki Hartmann threatened by their presence, certain articles consigned women to domestic roles within photography. Recurrent writings about women (and sometimes even by women) described a subordinate role for their sex in photography. Women appeared as martyred wives, receptionists for male photographers, or else eager to appropriate the print or the negative for domestic use. These notions denied women's potential as independent, creative photographers and expressed in subtle ways both male and female confusion over gender expectations.

Women sometimes participated in sustaining such negative images. The martyred wife (or sometimes martyred daughter) emerged as a popular stereotype that appeared often in photography journals in the early years of the twentieth century. It was well suited to the period's perception of the Victorian lady, a woman who often remained at home patiently acceding to her husband's whims and needs. The wife of a fanatical amateur photographer often played out this role. She endured the pain and suffering of her husband's neglect, her own passivity, and the disruption of her household by odorous chemicals and cumbersome equipment. These women appeared suspicious of photography and resentful of their male relative's involvement. Photography journals published these letters as amusing anecdotes that caricatured the husband/ wife relationship. Mrs. J.T.'s letter to the *Detroit Free Press* described herself as oppressed by her husband's involvement with the "villainous practise" of photography. Spending all his money on camera equipment rather than on new clothes for his distracted wife, this husband compounded the tension-filled home situation by staining every part of the house with "horrible solution."[49] Louise Yellott enumerated her unhappy experiences with a photographer husband in similar language. "I am," she wrote, "a martyr to photography—in other words, I am the wife of an amateur photographer . . . and I write to the martyred wives of amateur photographers."[50] Julia M. Crane, a martyred daughter, complained of similar distractions. Both she and her mother sacrificed new hats and were frequently provoked and embarrassed by her father's pursuit of this photographic hobby.[51]

Of course, at times a husband's devotion to his hobby had an opposite effect on family members. Department store head Frederick Constable's wife once despaired over her husband's involvement. Distracted by the silver nitrite stains on his clothing, she, like other wives, resented the intrusions of the camera. However, with the onset of technological advances which simplified the printing and developing processes, Mrs. Constable committed herself to photography as her husband's assistant.[52] This case does not describe the oppressed wife. It does, however, reiterate the nineteenth century notion that woman's place was in service to her husband.

A particularly favored position recommended to women in the pages of photography journals was as receptionist to a male photographer. The receptionist role implied a number of womanly virtues —hospitality, charm, cleanliness. Women were frequently advised to serve as receptionists in order to aid the photographer in his contacts with customers. A neat, lady-like woman would properly maintain the reception area and would necessarily please women clients and attract males.[53] The female receptionist was celebrated as integral to a successful studio. She "could with a few subtle touches so metamorphose the gallery that it wouldn't be recognized . . . She will coo to the baby while enlarging truthfully to the proud mother on its perfections."[54] In this capacity, a woman would enhance the studio so that this workplace might simulate the home as nearly as possible.

Addressing themselves to women's place in the domestic sphere, photography journals continued, into the 1890s, to appeal to their women readers' more feminine and frivolous sides. "A Page for Women" in *The Amateur Journal of Photography* in 1896 offered tips on bridal etiquette and pointers on style.[55] Similarly, in *Photo-American* Mrs. A.D. Waterbury offered "A Menu Hint to Housewives." Women amateurs were advised to utilize negatives to decorate menu cards, "a souvenir highly appreciated by guests who do not do photographic work."[56]

Women, with photographic interests and aspirations were frequently encouraged to apply their talents to "thimble and pencil" rather than "developers and plates." Women's work clearly meant creation of the embroidered focusing cloth, sewing an apron for the serious male photographer, or a velveteen cover for plateholders, albums, and portfolios.[57] Photography was promoted for women here but in a context which clearly sustained her image as a homemaker. A woman could easily divert her needlework ability from a new blouse to a utilitarian camera cover. Dress photography was still another option promoted as appropriate for women. This activity involved, in part, the photographic reproduction of bridal trousseaus. For this task brides clearly expressed a preference for female photographers.[58]

These admonitions represented subtle pressures toward domesticity as promulgated by photography journals published by males for a largely male readership. In a sense, these prescriptions were one means of reconciling women's active participation in the field with prevailing Victorian ideology. The sporadic efforts to bolster women's faltering domestic image coincided with material in other magazines that generally encouraged women's entry into the public arena yet occasionally seemed obliged to present a picture of the educated accomplished woman who would still combine "gracious manners" with a "trained mind" and still be "capable of all homely tasks."[59]

The prescriptive advice in contemporary magazines, and the often ambivalent position toward women evinced in photography journals suggest the dual, and often negative, perspectives from which middle class working women were viewed. In a society which throughout the nineteenth century had insisted on women's obedience to the tenets of piety, purity, domesticity, and submission, the new professional working woman in and out of photography appeared a threatening figure. Yet, women who did enter photography in lesser capacities used these positions to learn the craft and shape a role for themselves within the medium. This, despite those mysoginists in the field who would create subordinate and noncreative tasks for women.

The nineteenth century concerns with the special feminine traits of women paralleled similar cultural attitudes toward photography itself. From its very early days, women and photography were often linked together in the public mind, a connection that helped to make photography accessible for women. Mid-nineteenth century photography was regarded by many as a respite in a chaotic world, an art that "cherishes domestic and social sentiments" as well as spiritual ideals. In 1852, for example, the daguerreotype was described as bringing one closer to heaven: "who can be without a Daguerreotype of him or her they love? That embodiment of the form's spirit . . . it does raise the mind from earth and heaven, and bring to the imagination the fairy, spiritual forms of the departed . . ."[60]

From birth until death and throughout the uncertainties of nineteenth century life, the camera evoked spiritual thoughts and imagery. Whether recording the death of a first born or capturing the "sacred momento" of a decrepit old man, the photographer performed a hallowed service. M.A. Root, photographer and artist, observed in 1862 that through photography "our loved ones, dead and distant; our friends and acquaintances, however far removed, are retained within daily and hourly vision."[61] Recognizing the materialism and competitive nature of contemporary society he conceived of photography as helping to restore some kind of order. It was a "benediction", a presence that "tends to vivify and strengthen the social feelings."[62]

Root went on to say that the use of the photographic art "inspires to virtuous and noble deeds" for ". . . the great and the good, the heroes, saints, and sages of all lands are, by these life-like presentiments, brought within the constant purview of the young, the middle-aged, and the old."[63] Renowned English photographer, Julia Margaret Cameron (1815-1879), also described photography with religious undertones, likening her portraits to prayers.[64] Understandably, when the camera-wielding person turned out to be a woman, her character and influence were greatly enhanced.

Women were viewed from similar perspectives in the nineteenth century; they symbolized stability for family and friends, were viewed as a refuge in a world of change, holy enough to redeem erring men, a source of spiritual inspiration.[65] As portrait photographers, a genre which became the particular province of women, female photographers were esteemed for perpetuating the memories of deceased family members. The photographer bolstered traditional ties through this work; the studio, like the home, could inspire such a spirit. Root, in fact, described the studio as a "temple of beauty and grandeur,"[66] language coincidental with other nineteenth century literature that identified woman, her sphere, and her function.

Indeed, the public studios of female photographers frequently reflected the haven described by Root. Nineteenth century women bore the responsibility for creating a home environment that would serve as a spiritual and peaceful retreat and testify as well to the family's social status. Woman photographers similarly created studios evocative of elegant, inviting middle class homes. The studio of the Selby sisters, for example, reflected a woman's world. Originally from England, the Selbys set up a "lovely old blue and ivory studio" on Fifth Avenue in New York City. Here they served afternoon tea and became known for their feminine style, ". . . a sort of delicate distinction in the effect of a thoroughly 'nice' and sympathetic understanding of the social world . . . "[67]

Other women photographers worked in feminine settings. In 1890 Mrs. L. Condon of Atlanta, Georgia, an experienced professional photographer, opened a studio. In this workplace, lavishly decorated with Turkish rugs, silk drapes, upholstered chairs, pottery, and works of art, Mrs. Condon specialized in photographing children, brides, and society women.[68] The "dainty rooms" that made up the studio of Helen McCaul and Elizabeth Dickson on West 33rd Street in New York City provided still another appropriate background for their specialties—"soft and delicate" portraits of mothers and children of the New York City and Newport social world.[69]

Dickson, McCaul, Condon, and the Selbys were professional photographers with public studios who supported themselves with their cameras. All were perceived as having special women's traits that included an innate sense of fine taste as well as an intuitive understanding of children and women. These sensibilities, presumed natural among women of the middle and upper classes, were expressed in studios that reflected such traits.

Other enobling qualities attributed to photography easily merged with the image of ideal womanhood. Patience, a much exalted nineteenth century virtue, especially for women, was frequently mentioned in relation to photography. Photographer, H.P. Robinson, for one, generalized the trait to apply to photographers. "The patience of Job," he said, was necessary for any aspiring photographer.[70] Frances Benjamin Johnston spoke of the need for women photographers to possess "unlimited patience to carry through her endless failures." Johnston noted not only patience but also tact as vital qualities for women photographers. Using tact properly, Johnston advised, "a woman can, without difficulty, manage to please and conciliate the great majority of her customers—even the most exacting ones."[71] Mrs. M.L. Rayne, in a chapter on work for women in photography, also asserted that patience was basic to one's progess in that field.[72] Root too specified patience as a characteristic important to a successful photographer.[73]

In an 1890 article for Outing magazine, Margaret Bisland noted the reasons why photography held a special appeal for women. Bisland recognized the connections between women, home, and photography: "Photography makes a strong appeal to women for the reason that she may study and practise it in her own home . . . yet it does not interfere with daily duties . . . it is an art within the reach of women of modest means . . . but a corner of a family drawing-room or one's own private apartment . . ."

If indeed women at the turn of the century continued to perceive themselves and were perceived in terms of the private rather than the public sphere and chose work related to their prescribed domestic function, then the association of photography with women and of their roles is crucial for an understanding of women's easy access to that profession. Here was an opportunity to adjust the career/mothering dilemma, for within photography women could keep one foot at home while taking first steps to expand their vistas. The three interrelated directions for educated women, as defined by historian Joyce Antler, as "whether to live at home or away from home, whether to pursue a leisurely avocation or a specific vocation . . . and finally whether to marry or remain single,"[74] were neatly resolved within the scope of commercial and artistic photography. One could work in a home studio, record family and friends, and photograph domestic scenes that might include gardens, pets, and intimate interiors. Photography as vocation or avocation gave a woman room to find her own identity while remaining close to the hearth.

Mary Lyon Taylor's life in photography stands as a good illustration of a woman who integrated the camera with the domestic sphere.[75] Trained as an artist, Taylor followed the expected path for aspiring women painters—she specialized in miniature painting on porcelain and ivory and also did portrait paintings. These genres even by the twentieth century, were traditionally associated with women artists. Long denied access to life classes, to many apprenticeships, and to acceptance by the academies, women like Taylor tended to focus on so-called "feminine" subjects (mothers, children, pets, domestic scenes). When Taylor married, family responsibilities took precedence and painting was relegated to a pastime status. In 1906 she became ill and was forced to give up painting totally; she then turned to photography as a diversion. The diversion, however, became a career, one that apparently could accommodate home and work. Friends and family served as subjects and a home studio was set up to facilitate the photographic endeavor. Taylor's romantic, impressionistic images of women and children, children and their fathers, reflected, according to one commentator, the "quiet peacefulness of happy, domestic life." "The Goldfish," for example, a portrait of Mrs. Alexander Paton of London, was described by a contemporary as "not so much a portrait as an embodiment of happy motherhood, a woman absolutely content in her home."[76]

The domestic and family orientation and values of women like Mary Taylor, placed them within a larger segment of middle class

women who, unprepared for work in an environment often dominated by male values of aggression and acquisitiveness and
separated from a world of domesticity, perceived the only option to
be marriage and motherhood. Usually not the "experimentor" of
Antler, "a free spirit, one who has fabricated a life-style that was ec-
centric and unconventional yet devoid of the conflicts with which
many of her peers had struggled,"[77] but rather an adherent of conventional nineteenth century ideology, the middle class woman at
this time found in photography a place where she could express her
femininity and still participate in the exciting changes of the time
which projected the spirit of the new science and technology.

3

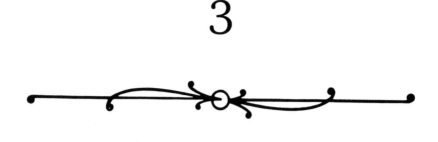

Group Portrait

The personal lives of women who entered photography in the last decades of the nineteenth century reveal many similarities. These middle class women shared attitudes toward family, marriage, and career; they shared educational experiences and an intense dedication to photography. Women photographers were characterized by these sociological factors and in these respects were connected to their sisters in other professions, as well as to late nineteenth century cultural and social expectations that circumscribed the options available to women.[1]

Women photographers were attached in a distinctive way to the conventional middle class ideology of the late Victorian period which celebrated women, home, and family. This middle class background not only shaped their personal values but proved particularly useful to the creative and goal-oriented woman in pursuing lives outside the domestic sphere. Their class status implied financial well-being and leisure time. In addition, their families neither inhibited nor objected to the photographic pursuits of wives or daughters. Instead, women photographers found their families to be encouraging; parents, brothers, sisters, and other relatives provided psychological and economic supports.

At the same time, however, women photographers made certain choices which set them apart, not only from their families, but from prescribed behavior for women in this period. These women often displayed unconventional characteristics that appeared idiosyncratic but really displayed their independent frames of mind. They shared a willingness to flaunt social standards and expectations. In life style and/or behavior they managed to reject some basic tenet of nineteenth century ideology. They were often single women in a period when marriage and motherhood were glorified; they were business women at a time when the market place was deemed ill-suited for ladies; and they were creative women when the kind of independence that implied was suspect. Alice Austen chose not to marry; Jessie Tarbox Beals became a lone news photojournalist in an otherwise exclusively male field; Frances Benjamin Johnston daringly descended into the Kohinoor mines for a photostory; Eva Watson-Schütze never dropped her maiden name; Alice Boughton was both a feminist and a socialist. In all cases, these women, in one respect or another, went beyond both late nineteenth century prescriptions for lady-like behavior and contemporary definitions of women as mere "passive spectators and consumers."[2]

The dichotomous lives of these women set them apart from the mainstream but not, significantly, from other creative women of the time. Like other professionals in education, nursing, and the arts, women photographers had to face up to society's standards and expectations. That included marriage, childbearing, the stigma of spinsterhood, the nurturant rather than the productive role in families. They still had to confront, in other words, the pervasive and stifling cult of domesticity.

However, their choices were facilitated by the unexpected erosion of traditional standards. Women were experimenting with outside choices; they joined the work force and attended college. Feminists and social scientists called for the reform of marriage and urged a reexamination of alternatives to marriage.[3] The implications here for the nineteenth century professional woman are obvious, and by the 1880s it had become increasingly difficult for the urban, middle class, career-oriented woman to remain aloof from the debate over long cherished and still only occasionally challenged ideals. As historians reassess the lives of professional women of this generation, the personal tensions which reflected the public argument become strikingly apparent. The dilemma of Alice Freeman Palmer who gave up the presidency of Wellesley College for marriage clearly and painfully illustrates the difficulties for many women who attempted to reconcile career and marriage.[4] Other well known women made similar decisions. Charlotte Perkins Gilman divorced her husband and separated from her child. Marriage for Gilman had meant nervous depression and a loss of independence.[5] Crystal Eastman's solution to the marital state was untraditional in a different way, involving communal living arrangements and frequent separations.[6]

In photography, Sallie E. Garrity's story presents a similar situation. Garrity's decision to marry stifled her expanding career and confirmed the idea that marriage could destroy a woman's career and creativity. Sallie Garrity opened her first public studio in 1886, in Louisville, Kentucky, and went on to establish a large and successful photography business in Chicago. While working at the 1893 World's Fair she met a Mr. Rothery "who wooed her away from Chicago and photography to Los Angeles and matrimony."[7] By 1900, photography circles lost touch with Sallie E. Garrity. In that year, Frances Benjamin Johnston received news of Garrity while assembling her Paris exhibition of women photographers. An editor of a photography journal reported to Johnston that Garrity had "made a new deal by marrying an old man with money."[8] Once the subject of newspaper articles that extolled her accomplishments in photography, Garrity's professional life appeared finished by the turn of the century.

Some professionals, of course, married without such fatal consequences. Catherine Weed (Ward) and Eva Watson (Schütze) established seemingly solid relationships with their husbands. Still other women managed to save or recover a professional life through divorce or, as in the case of Gertrude Käsebier, by finding career fulfillment at middle age. Many women photographers, however, chose to remain single.

In fact, the majority of achieving women in the 1880s and 1890s chose not to marry. Born between 1850 and 1880, these educators, artists, social reformers, and nurses were part of a generation of American women that became significantly and distinctively active outside the domestic sphere. The fact that so many of these women never married provides evidence of the deep concern they felt when confronted with the career/marriage dilemma.[9] This conscious decision to stay single expressed their fears of being dominated by husbands or thwarted by marriage. Women aspiring towards a vocation or committed to independent work easily perceived the inequality that could undercut achievement; family and career for the most part appeared irreconcilable. Apparently the experiences of late nineteenth century feminists who, like Charlotte Perkins Gilman, urged women to maximize their potential unrestrained by social conventions did not go unheeded. Women were prepared to accept the necessity of going it alone.

Yet the traditional view remained: single women in late nineteenth century America were perceived as outside the mainstream of approved social life. Often criticized as deviants, single women offset such social judgments by remaining within the family sphere, by living with other relatives or with close friends. They rarely lived alone. This was particularly true of single professional women who were twice condemned because of their pursuit of careers. Sharing their lives with others provided respectability and security for these women. In this sense, the nurturant, familial, or friendly connection proved to be a buffer between the unmarried career woman and society.

In 1897, Frances Benjamin Johnston had the finishing touches put on her photography studio. A skylight, low raftered ceilings, simple angular lines, and innovative decorative touches made this workplace the model of a well planned studio. Thoughtfully designed by Johnston and executed by a Washington D.C. architectural firm, Frances Benjamin Johnston's long awaited studio was built onto the rear of her parents' home. The symbolic merging here of Johnston's professional life with her family residence significantly reflects the experiences of others among Johnston's female colleagues. These women consistently adhered to that middle class ideology which professed strong familial ties coupled with a daughter's demonstrated artistic independence and professional goals. Johnston's life as an unmarried woman, however, hardly coincided with stereotypical images of the "old maid." Far from falling into barren spinsterhood, Johnston built a world of intimate family connections, long-lasting friendships and a successful career. Unlike the negative effects of the family claim described by Jane Addams, the encouragement offered by Johnston's parents helped her to forge ahead in photography. And, like other achieving women, Johnston's life was characterized by involvement in female bonding patterns with friends and colleagues. This, of course, is reflected in Johnston's dynamic presence in the female network in photography which fostered accomplishment among women.

Remaining single, Johnston avoided the career/marriage conflict by drawing instead on the psychological and financial resources provided by her family. The socially prominent and well-to-do Johnstons sent their daughter to a woman's seminary in Washington and then to art school in Paris. In later years, family connections were useful in promoting Johnston's burgeoning portrait business. Kinship continued to be important throughout the photographer's career. During the intervals when Johnston was on assignment abroad, Anderson Johnston handled his daughter's business correspondence; his wife assumed other studio related responsibilities. While in Paris in 1900, Johnston's instructions to her parents detailed a schedule for decorating the house, paying bills, and disposing of her complete work. During that summer, Anderson Johnston took care of bills from photographic supply firms.[10] In 1905 he performed similar duties. Her "loving mother" oversaw the redecorating of Johnston's studio, paying bills when necessary. In addition, Mrs. Johnston forwarded her daughter's mail and supervised the duties of Mr. Coover, Johnston's studio helper. Mrs. Johnston reported on Coover's activities in the dark room and studio where he did enlarging, filled orders, mounted prints, and took messages. She noted his occasional absences in her frequent letters to her daughter which also detailed the gossip and events of the hot Washington summers.[11]

Like Frances Benjamin Johnston, Alice Austen remained single throughout her life. Born and brought up in the genteel environment of nineteenth century Staten Island, Austen spent her life at the family residence, Clear Comfort.[12] Alice Austen grew up within a close circle of family and friends. In fact, her uncles Peter and Oswald introduced the young Alice to photography, teaching her camera techniques and building a home dark room for her. As she grew up on Staten Island, Austen toted her camera and tripod everywhere—to picnics and parties, tennis matches, and musicales. Friends posed for her and family members consistently supported her hobby. This loving, accepting atmosphere enabled Austen to produce the myriad images of nineteenth century social life in and around the Austen home. In addition, the family's financial backing provided Austen with the equipment she needed to pursue photography.[13]

Austen spent her later years at Clear Comfort with her long time friend, Gertrude Tate. The fifty year relationship with Tate seemed a fulfilling alternative to marriage. Indeed, the marital state for Austen never appeared to be a serious consideration despite a lively social life as a young woman. Early memories of her father's desertion might have, in the end, shaped her attitudes toward and influenced her choice of the unmarried life.[14]

Austen's life style was not unique in late nineteenth century America. Close female friendships and long lasting relationships between two women were still accepted as part of women's socialization. The literature of the period discussed these arrangements. In 1883, for example, Louisa May Alcott wrote a fictional account of such a relationship in her novel, *An Old Fashioned Girl*. Henry James in *The Bostonians* described a now classic study of an intense friendship between two women. Real life attachments were notable as well, especially in intellectual and artistic circles. Jane Addams, Vida Scudder, Frances Willard, and M. Carey Thomas are only a few renowned women born between 1850 and 1880 who lived intimately with other women. This generation of women represented the greatest number of unmarried, childless women in American history.[15]

The single life as lived by Austen and Tate embodied a world apart from the experience of a nineteenth century bachelor. Unlike the single male who lived alone, belonged to a club (usually a male bastion), and enjoyed the public's acceptance, single women instead committed themselves to a women-identified household. The world of the unmarried woman in the nineteenth century was distinct from that of her male counterpart. For a woman, remaining single often meant exile to the domestic sphere. These women might have given up husbands, but their lives still remained connected to traditional female activities and expectations. Their personal experiences provided another perspective on conventional middle class family life. For without children or husbands, these women continued to recapitulate the values inherent in the cult of domesticity and the belief in the ideology of true womanhood.

Indeed, Austen and Tate's arrangements were akin to a marriage.[16] They shared household responsibilities, travelled together

and though very different in personality, the two women comple-
mented one another. In addition, by pooling their financial and
emotional resources Austen was able to dedicate herself to photography. Tate, apparently less intent on artistic pursuits, fulfilled
household duties. Theirs was a union in the traditional sense of the
word. Unfettered by conventional domestic demands, Austen
devoted her time to producing work that must be "just so." Her total
commitment to photography might not have been possible in a
more typically prescribed household situation.

Other women photographers manifested similar traits of independence and ambition while finding sustenance in close family
associations. Beatrice Tonneson became a professional photographer when, at the age of twenty-two, she bought the business of a
successful male photographer.[17] Tonneson never married but her
well-to-do father provided both financial and moral support for her
early photographic endeavors. Later, Tonneson established a studio
in her widowed sister's home. Tonneson drew up the plans for the
sky-light, dark room, operating, and finishing room. The arrangement proved useful for both women; by 1900 Beatrice became
known as the acknowledged artist of the association and her sister,
the business manager. Beatrice, in fact, along with Frances Benjamin Johnston represented American women photographers as
delegates to the Paris Exposition in 1900, an indication of her artistic
achievement. The involvement of father and sister in Beatrice Tonneson's career supplied a domestic support system that freed the ambitious photographer from the period's traditional family restraints.[18]

Among women photographers, Gertrude Käsebier's solution to
the career/marriage/family dilemma appeared unique. In 1897,
Gertrude Käsebier opened her first public studio in New York City.
An impressive feat in itself, this act implied even greater significance,
for the 45 year old Käsebier was the wife of Eduard Käsebier and the
mother of three teenaged children. In effect, Käsebier had declared
her independence with her recently completed art studies at Pratt
Institute and in Europe. Now the decisiveness of setting up her own
studio emphatically proclaimed her choice of career over hearth.

Born in 1852, Käsebier came of age after the mid-century point
when suffrage activity was publicized and women's unequal position
was increasingly acknowledged. Issues regarding not only the vote,
but also women's education, work and career, dress and health

were addressed by church and government representatives and by a proliferation of articles in the popular press.[19] Women's entrance to colleges and universities similarly aroused a new consciousness of possibilities for women. During this period of societal transformations Gertrude Stanton married Eduard Käsebier, a shellac importer from Germany. He was industrious and his business prospered providing well for his growing family. But Gertrude Käsebier always appeared restless within the conventions of married life. The small town character of life in Brooklyn stifled Käsebier, "her artistic abilities . . . fermenting under the hausfrau surface."[20]

In 1889 Käsebier entered Pratt Institute in Brooklyn where she studied portrait painting. Käsebier always displayed independence of thought and action; this decision to study art was consistent with her "head-strong" character. In her late thirties, she was probably one of the oldest students, a fact that did not deter her from entertaining her fellow students at Sunday evening open houses. She also helped the poorer students by commissioning them to paint or sketch her children. By the late 1890s she became committed to photography and opened her New York portrait studio.[21]

Other women of the 1890s expressed similar dissatisfactions with domesticity and directed their energies to such activities as literary clubs, a social and cultural phenomenon of the late nineteenth century. Käsebier, therefore, was not alone in her recognition of woman's need to reassess her life in middle age. By the late decades of the nineteenth century, still a period in which women were esteemed for their mothering roles, women in their forties who had completed child care responsibilities often felt an emptiness in their lives. For the married woman who had subordinated personal aspirations for maternal duties, the middle years appeared a time to pursue earlier dreams. For the majority of this group, club life emerged as an acceptable and satisfying route allowing participation in areas beyond the home.[22] For a minority, of which Käsebier was one, an independent career provided still another option.

Gertrude Käsebier's decision to strike out on her own after her children were grown indicates both her fidelity to the concept of motherhood and her belief in her own abilities and potential. Her life clearly integrated the public and private spheres by achieving a balance between both worlds. By remaining home until middle age she satisfied the demands of domesticity; as a photographer she established herself within the world of developing technologies, new social roles, and changing artistic values.

Divorce among women photographers existed as yet another alternative to marriage. Anne Brigman and Jessie Tarbox Beals, perhaps the most idiosyncratic individuals of the group, divorced their husbands after several years of marriage. Brigman and Beals were not unique in this time to have chosen divorce. In the Progressive Era, the movement for divorce reached enormous proportions. From 1880 to 1916 the implications of the rising divorce rate reflected in various ways the social transformations of the period.[23]

Poet, actress, feminist, photographer, Anne Brigman displayed few qualities in common with the traditional nineteenth century woman. Brigman, born in Hawaii in 1869, was in many ways the "new woman" of the period, and unlike many of her sisters in photography or other professions, appeared to retain few Victorian values in her personal and professional life.

One has only to look at Brigman's photographs to detect the idiosyncratic qualities of her personality. Brigman's favorite subject was the female nude set in the natural surroundings of the northern California mountains. Her models were often close friends and sometimes herself. The photographing of nudes by a woman was rare in this period but Brigman's images had, in any event, a very avant-garde quality. The sensuous forms reproduced in the symbolist tradition appeared romantic and dreamlike, close to surreal in their fascinating juxtaposition of woods, waterfalls, and an unclothed figure. Brigman's work contrasts sharply with the mother/child portrayals of Käsebier, the Washington elites of Frances Benjamin Johnston, and the domestic scenes of Alice Austen. Though Brigman retains the expressiveness of the pictorialists, her subject matter remains distinct from the genre studies of most of her female colleagues.[24]

In 1910, Anne Brigman separated from her husband, Martin, a retired master mariner. Said Brigman of that decision, "he had his way of looking at things and I had mine. We developed along different lines. So here I am working out my own destiny!"[25] Over forty at the time, Brigman recognized the need for a woman artist's personal and creative freedom, apparently unobtainable for her in marriage.

After altering her marital status, Brigman temporarily shared her mother's house in Oakland. Then in 1913 she lived alone "'in a tiny cabin studio . . . with [a] red dog . . . [and] 12 tame birds . . ."[26] Separation brought Brigman the freedom she desired. Unfortunately, however, the war and the gradual dissolution of the Photo-Secession affected her artistic output. She continued to participate in pictorialist shows when available, but these exhibits evinced little critical response or approval. The currents of modernism seemed to pass by Brigman unnoticed.

Throughout her life, Brigman sought outlets for her intense creative energies. She acted in local stage productions and wrote poetry. The poetry described the "wild trees" that stand "aloof . . . supreme . . . flames against the wind."[27] This personal vision of the poetry complements her romantic, symbolist photographs. Both speak of the artist's self-perception as free, wild, and independent amidst a convention bound society.

Jessie Tarbox Beals divorced her husband Alfred after several years of marriage. Prior to their separation the Beals' worked together at photography. Alfred's special role was setting up the dark room as well as processing the negatives and prints; Jessie acted as photographer and business manager. The Beals' arrangement is reminiscent of husband and wife partnerships throughout the history of photography—with one major distinction: Jessie Tarbox Beals hardly fit the nineteenth century image of helpmate. She consistently dominated the relationship. By 1917, however, both the professional and personal relationship had deteriorated, causing Jessie Tarbox Beals to leave her husband. The end of the marriage was marked by a revealing poem written by Jessie:

> I close my eyes, less
> he should see the hate
> That burns beneath their lids
> And then I wait and wait, until
> he leaves my side[28]

Although very unhappy within the marriage, Beals' marital status never appeared to impose constraints on her personal style. During the course of the Beals' life together, Jessie's career flourished and marriage did not prohibit her from taking a lover. Diary entries and emotion laden poetry, however, expressed her deep unhappiness and lack of filfillment.

> Intense you say: yes I am intense
> A pessimist deep brooding over life-
> A woman with strong feeling, proud
>   instincts and heart sorrows
> With hope of little joy save that of work,
> With longings for sweet tenderness . . .
> A home, a comrade and deep sympathy . . . [29]

Divorce, an extramarital affair, and involvement with Greenwich Village intellectual life distinguish Beals from most of her female contemporaries. Still, in an historical sense, Beals remained connected to this group. Her independent (if not idiosyncratic) behavior places her in a special relationship to her times and to the women of the period. That is, in her personal and professional life she took advantage of the expanding options for women at a time of particular kinds of social change. Her work as a photojournalist set her apart from turn of the century women photographers who chose subjects closer to their intimate domestic worlds. But this imagery and her independent life style bridged the gap between the two centuries.

There were, of course, marriages among professional women photographers that not only worked, but appeared to provide fulfillment for both partners in the relationship. Eva Watson-Schütze and Catherine Weed Ward were two outstanding photographers who prior to their marriages had established clear cut places in the world of photography. Marriage did not inhibit either woman from continuing to pursue their photographic goals. And both marriages coincided to some degree with prevailing nineteenth and early-twentieth century patterns. Both women married professional men of the same class and with similar intellectual interests.[30]

In 1891, Catherine Weed Barnes (Ward) was described as "the best known woman amateur in photography on this side of the Atlantic."[31] Working in Albany as a photographer, she also found time to write and lecture on the subject, especially about women's future in the field. In addition, Ward held the joint editorship of *American Amateur Photographer*. In 1892 Ward left that journal (to be replaced by Alfred Stieglitz) to travel to London where she married photography editor, H. Snowden Ward. In this case, marriage did not signify an end to her activities. Ward continued to lecture and write; she published *Shakespeare's Town and Times* illustrated with her own photographs. She lectured on the book as well. As editor of the woman's department of the English journal, *Photogram*, Ward unflaggingly encouraged women's activities in photography.[32] Few details are known about the personal life of Snowden and Catherine Weed Ward. Yet they seem to have achieved a working relationship; two people in the same field, both with established reputations, neither seeming to diminish the other.[33]

Eva Lawrence Watson married Martin Schütze in 1901. Born in Germany, Dr. Schütze was trained as a lawyer. Unable to use this legal background in the United States, Schütze became a professor of German Literature and Philosophy at the University of Chicago.[34] Watson, a well known and respected photographer at the time of her marriage, had exhibited widely and had achieved an international reputation. Due to this reknown she was invited to serve on the juries of the Philadelphia Salons (1899, 1900) and of the Art Institute of Chicago. Eva Watson was one of the women included in Alfred Steiglitz's elite circle of artists and photographers. She was acclaimed by critics as a "master in photography"[35] and in 1905, in a *Camera Work* article devoted to Watson-Schütze, critic Joseph Keiley described her as "one of the staunchest and sincerest upholders of the pictorialist movement in America."[36]

After her marriage Watson-Schütze maintained her married name, asserting her self-perception as an individual unwilling to be subsumed in the marital role. Watson-Schütze, in fact, continued to work and consistently affirm her belief in her own ability and her place in photography. A tough-minded woman, Eva Watson-Schütze in 1893 rejected the notion of a separate display of women's work in a women's pavillion at the World's Fair. She was emphatic in wanting her photography "judged by one standard, irrespective of sex."[35]

Women photographers mostly remained single and maintained close family ties. They also found common ground in their educational experiences and art training backgrounds. Most women's middle class parents saw to it that their daughters received an education suitable for young Victorian women. This usually meant boarding school rather than college, preferably at a school close to home.[38] Gertrude Käsebier, Alice Austen, and Frances Benjamin Johnston, the three most well known photographers of the group, all attended seminaries for young women near their homes; Käsebier went to the Moravian Seminary in Pennsylvania; Austen was a student at Miss

Enington's School for Young Ladies on Staten Island; Johnston, from Washington, D.C. attended the Notre Dame Convent in nearby Maryland. These seminary educations are found in the lives of other women photographers as well.

Most women photographers, active at the turn of the century, aspired first to be painters and only turned to photography after their contacts with the more traditional art form. Sarah Sears studied at the Boston Museum of Fine Arts; Emma Fitz was an art student at Wellesley College; Edith Lounsberry and Emma Farnsworth were also art students. Alice Boughton boasted of art training in Paris; Beatrice Tonneson began by "dabbling a little in art."[39] Rose Clark and Eva Watson-Schütze were very serious art students. Clark was known as a leading portraitist. Watson-Schütze studied with Thomas Eakins, but she found that her art training was "artificial" with "no outlet for creative impulses."[40] It was then that she turned to the camera, finding that this instrument allowed her the artistic fulfillment she craved.[41] The two foremost women photographers in America at this time, Frances Benjamin Johnston and Gertrude Käsebier, acquired art backgrounds at prestigious institutions in the United States and in Europe and consistently stressed the significance of that experience to their photography.[42]

For nineteenth century women interested in developing drawing and painting skills, art training in Europe was accepted and expected. And, although many nineteenth century women "took up" painting, few perceived this involvement as leading toward a career. Families, in fact, actually supported young women's artistic pursuits as an acceptable activity in the period prior to the arrangement of a proper marriage. In 1885, women's search for leisure activities led many to learn drawing, sketching, and painting—accomplishments viewed as character enhancing for young ladies. The acceptance of art as a natural extension of women's domestic role allowed genteel but impoverished women to occasionally find employment and provided middle and upper class women with an outlet for artistic ambitions. Women, long perceived as the mainstays of American culture, found that art training actually improved their place in the domestic sphere. "Nice girls" with artistic pretensions from large cities throughout the country made the obligatory trip to Europe to study at those academies, which by the 1860s provided art education for women.[43] Middle class familial ideology could accept the diversionary nature of their daughters' artistic whims and only balked at painting when taken seriously as a career. Mary Cassatt's father's now famous retort to his daughter's announcement of her intended painting career, "I would rather see you dead," was not an untypical reaction to such a proposal.[44]

After the mid-century point, women from the United States (and, indeed, from all over the world) streamed into classes taught by Robert Fleury at the *Académie Julian* in Paris.[45] The *Académie* became the best known of the French art schools for women, although it was not unique. By the second half of the century, women seeking both careers and personal fulfillment could be found in numbers of similar institutions.

Frances Benjamin Johnston studied at the *Académie Julian*, the same school at which painter Cecilia Beaux was enrolled during her Parisian art student days.[46] Johnston's early ambitions centered on becoming an illustrator and to that purpose she studied in the Paris *ateliers*. Here she established her belief in "art in photography." Her European training taught Johnston the artist's concern for detail and arrangement.[47] Returning from Paris, Johnston organized and taught classes at the Art Students League in Washington. Soon after this, on a friend's suggestion, Johnston invested in a camera, a step which led to her life-long commitment to that art form. Johnston's art training instilled in her an understanding of the beneficial connection between art and photography. Obviously drawing from her own experiences, she advised aspiring women photographers to "study art first and photography afterward."[48] Considering both an art background and a tasteful, creative imagination as essential to portrait photography, Johnston always encouraged artistic effects.

Other women photographers also trained first as painters and suggested that course for other aspiring photographers. Catherine Weed Ward credited her work with "brushes and palette"[49] as an experience which aided her progress in photography. It was a part of the liberal education necessary in the evolution of a successful photographer.[50]

Painting, of course, was considered a serious art form, very different from photography which was frequently denigrated as a fad or a quasi-science. Gertrude Käsebier, for one, initially chose to study painting. In 1888, she enrolled at Pratt to pursue her long deferred artistic aspirations. For five years Käsebier studied painting, relegating photography to the subordinate position accorded it by many of her art teachers.[51] Käsebier continued her art education in Europe. In the 1890s she spent two summers in France taking art classes with Frank Vincent Dumard.[52] While in France, Käsebier discovered photography to be her vocation and from that time on recognized the camera as a means to artistic expression. "Why," she asked, "should it not be required of the photographer, desiring to be known as an artist, that he serve an apprenticeship in an art school?"[53]

Virginia Sharp never attained the renown of Frances Benjamin Johnston or Gertrude Käsebier. Nevertheless, Sharp, like so many of her female colleagues became a photographer after earlier study and experience as a painter. As a young woman with artistic ambitions, Sharp trained as a painter both in Europe and the United States. She studied for three years at the Boston Museum of Fine Arts and continued her art education abroad spending two winters in Paris.[54] After feeling the stifling effects of marriage upon her creativity, Sharp finally turned to photography as a means of satisfying her thwarted artistic aspirations. Photography for Sharp represented a substitute for her first love, painting. Her early evaluation of painting as the more serious pursuit reflected the prevailing late-nineteenth century judgement and accounted in part for so many artistic women's initial attraction to painting.

The life of Catherine Weed Ward is useful to examine because it typifies in many ways the shared backgrounds of women photographers in the late nineteenth century. Her professional and personal experiences link her to women photographers and to women in other professions as well. Active as a devoted amateur photographer as early as 1886 and well known by 1891, Ward's life and career reflects much of nineteenth century middle class social and cultural ideology as it applied to women's work, class, and gender. As an upper middle class woman, Ward entered photography without it necessarily becoming a paying proposition. Her education at a women's college, European travel, devoted family ties before marriage, and independent work and interests within marriage all define Ward as one who bridged the gap between the traditional woman of the nineteenth century and the "new woman" of the twentieth. In her public life, her personal experiences, and in her writings Ward revealed the duality of her place within society. In addition, the position of almost total obscurity to which Ward has been relegated in the 1980s calls attention to the fate of so many women in American artistic life who, despite productive lives, have been lost from the historical record.

Catherine Weed Barnes Ward was born circa 1860s in Albany, New York, the daughter of Emily Weed and the Honorable William Barnes and the granddaughter of New York publisher, Thurlow Weed. Her life reflected these associations and advantages.

Like so many young women of her class, Ward traveled extensively with her family. In 1872, for example, she accompanied her parents to Russia where William Barnes served as a United States delegate to the International Statistical Congress held in St. Petersburg.[55] Trips to Europe were usually part of the upbringing of young middle class women. Francis Benjamin Johnston traveled to Europe and Alice Austen spent many summers abroad. Sojourns in Europe meant cultural enrichment or, as in the case of social reformer Jane Addams, it provided, at different times, career inspiration and an opportunity to recuperate from mental and physical problems.[56]

Ward's experience at Vassar College, an elite school for women, again corresponds to other aspects of middle class women's lives. Ward attended Vassar in the 1880s but her stay there was short-lived. While at school, overwork caused "an illness which threatened congestion of the brain."[57] Such a diagnosis reflected nineteenth century medical opinion that described women's smaller brains and their intellectual inferiority. Indeed education and particularly advanced learning was believed to produce adverse effects on large numbers of women "whose mental powers are overtaxed before their brains are sufficiently developed."[58] As a sensitive young woman aware of such medical prescriptions, Ward might well have internalized such ideology. If she did, Ward was not alone in her response. One only has to glance at the lives of other achieving women to confirm the commonplace nature of this experience: Jane Addams, Charlotte Perkins Gilman, and others expressed in their own lives the calamity of illness in connection with dilemmas over education, vocation, or marriage.

In 1889, her mother's death changed the routine of Catherine Ward's life. At that time she assumed the responsibility for the running of the family's Albany home. Like other women of her class, Ward did not question the assumption of such a role. Indeed she was able to integrate household duties with her photography. It was at this time that Ward's interest in photography burgeoned. As in the case of other women photographers, the art that began as a pastime emerged by 1890 as her "life work."[59] She combined respect for the family claim and her devotion to photography by setting up her first studio on the top floor of the family home, very much in the manner of Johnston and Tonneson. Shortly after this Catherine Weed Ward established a new studio in a separate building. This marked her developing autonomy and increased dedication to her art. No longer a tentative beginner, Ward did all her own work including posing, lighting, developing, and printing.[60]

In addition to a personal background that related to patterns present in the lives of other female photographers, Ward's writings on women and photography reveal her consistent support and encouragement of women in the field. Early in her career, Ward expressed her awareness of woman's place in a changing world. In 1891 in an article for *Wilson's Photographic Magazine*, Ward noted the human struggle and the competitive nature of the hectic late nineteenth century society but was optimistic about women's role in chaotic times.[61] She commented on the very practical need for women to prepare themselves to earn a living by taking advantage of the newly created market place opportunities. Not surprisingly, Ward enthusiastically endorsed women's entry into photography, stressing the hard work and commitment required. In this connection she expressed concern over prevailing male/female stereotypes:

> Men have so long held the most advantageous place in the
> various professions simply because they are expected to make a
> business and not a pastime of what they undertake. This is not
> caused by the size of the masculine brain . . . but is largely the
> result of their training, and if women will go through the same
> hard work . . . they will deserve and win the same rewards.[62]

Ward predicted a special role for women in photography arguing that their unique "feminine" qualities of patience, attention to detail, their delicacy and neatness particularly prepared them for photography. These views reaffirmed similar urgings by contemporaries who acknowledged a natural affinity between women and photography and perceived a special role for women in American cultural life.

However, Ward stated emphatically that women were not entitled to special treatment and in 1890 she appealed to the Joint Exhibition Committee to abolish the special "ladies diploma."[63] In subsequent articles she continued to stress the same point. "Do not think . . . my sisters, that because you are women your work should be praised where man's would be blamed, but expect only such credit as you fairly earn."[64]

Throughout her life Ward proved to be strong-minded and independent. Successful as a photographer, lecturer, writer, and editor Ward displayed many traits of the "new woman" of the era. She publicly espoused women's rights, traveled freely, and exhibited a commitment to her work. Having taken advantage of the leisure, education, and vocational opportunities provided by her middle class origins, Ward apparently determined to bring the virtues of middle class womanhood to a new and untried endeavor.

In her roles as editor and lecturer, Ward consistently asserted views favoring women's participation in the workforce in general and photography in particular. As joint editor of *American Amateur Photography* (with F.C. Beach and W.H. Burbank), Catherine Weed Ward headed the ladies' department. Later, while editor of *The Photogram*, Catherine Weed Ward and her husband, H. Snowden Ward, were always interested in the work of women.[65] In fact, Catherine Weed Ward edited a special department in *The Photogram* recording women's contributions to photography. Her frequent talks to women's groups such as the Women's Industrial Union of Syracuse and the Association for the Advancement of Women similarly testify to her focus on women's changing place in society. Ward's membership in Sorosis, the well known women's club, allowed her to associate with other women in the arts and other professional fields who, like Ward, were cognizant of the problems faced by women in the public arena.

However, despite her seemingly "modern" attitudes toward women and work, Ward continued to express nineteenth century ideals and expectations. In urging photography for women she frequently connected the field to images of domesticity. She likened the studio to the home, seeing both as sheltered environments with "little noise or confusion."[66] In fact, she believed that household training enhanced women's traits of orderliness and thoroughness, advantages easily transferable to the darkroom. Unlike men, women with such backgrounds would be conscientious enough "to cork the bottles, turn off the gas and water . . . and generally leave things in good order."[67]

Ward specifically directed her advice to well-educated, middle class women "with refinement, art tastes, literary culture . . . and considerable business ability."[68] The class nature of Ward's argument for women's entry into photography implied that uneducated, working class women were not equipped for photography. To Ward, this segment of the population lacked the "superior fitness" that she perceived as a prerequisite for becoming a photographer.

Catherine Ward regarded photography as an art with an "enobling sense of creation"[69] that placed it well beyond the realm of mere recreation. Ward's eloquent descriptions of photography make it almost spiritual. Here was a profession that would naturally appeal to women, perceived as they were at the end of the century as custodians of culture, purity, and morality.[70]

4

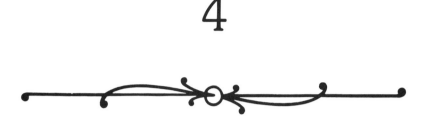

Association: The Watchword of the Age

In the clearly gender-oriented world that still existed in late Victorian America, women photographers took advantage of two forms of organization that bore relationships to nineteenth century social trends toward association. Amateur and professional women photographers participated in an informal female network, the center of which was famed photographer Frances Benjamin Johnston. Women encountered positive experiences through this support system that had ties to a long tradition of female bonding practices in America.

Women also joined camera clubs, associations that included both male and female photographers and provided encouragement and artistic reinforcement for members. Women benefitted from belonging to these clubs, a nineteenth century phenomenon that reflected the era's impulse toward association among men and women in many professions and in artistic and leisure activities.

The following chapter discusses, in two parts, these different forms of organization and the affirmative effects the network and camera clubs had for women photographers.

Frances Benjamin Johnston and
Female Networks in Photography

Women artists in the nineteenth century had long felt a need for the support of other women. A shared consciousness emerged among these creative women of themselves as a group with special needs and objectives. Women in the Arts and Crafts movement of the late nineteenth century, for example, were known to have received support and encouragement from women with common goals and interests.[1] Support among female painters was demonstrated in various ways: club membership, classes organized by women, and occasionally, an institution, like the Philadelphia School of Design, was established just for women. However, such activity was sporadic and often resulted from the difficulties encountered by women painters; men dominated the art academies and women were excluded from the prestigious art schools and from life drawing classes.[2] And in a professon that was concerned, like all the others, with advancing male careers and not at all with the aspirations and interests of women, the presence of women's prizes, women's exhibitions, special scholarships for women, and even an association of women artists, attested more to a token recognition than to any widespread awareness of women's unequal status or special needs.

Significantly, the presence of an identifiable network of women photographers from the 1880s until the beginning of the twentieth century provided encouragement for aspiring women in that field. Throughout the nineteenth century, women's connections to other women were evident; intense female friendships and other forms of bonding widened women's domestic boundaries and, in so doing, effected a positive impact on society. These female relationships have been described by historians.[3] Fostered both in response to the exclusionary male world of the marketplace and in part by discomfort with the limitations of home and family life, women sought "kindred spirits" among their own sex. Female bonding in church, reform, and social groups similarly reflected women's need to identify with one another and to find acceptable tasks away from the domestic sphere. Two familiar examples of these practices were the quilting bee and the women's club. The quilting bee was a social activity in which women as a group performed the clearly domestic art of putting together quilt tops sewn by individual women. Strictly a women's activity, the bee meant not only work but also some form of socialization.[4] Women's clubs, on the other hand, originated as literary and intellectual gatherings. By the turn of the century the focus of these clubs shifted to activities directed toward social reform.[5] Through the informality of the quilting bee and the more structured women's club movement, women widened their experiences by sharing with and supporting one another. Women's participation in photography networks followed a similar pattern. In this unique art form women could become prominent and the women's support system proved a contributing factor toward this success.

The evolving photography network did not display formal organizational patterns as earlier or even contemporary associations often did. Neither were the interactions among women in photography related to political, feminist, or reform causes; they did not arise in response to any ideological debate. Rather, the photographic network involved women in an unstructured, voluntary arrangement which reflected the desire of women to participate in the arts and to encourage one another. Many of the women involved were friends who shared artistic interests, class backgrounds, and other objective sociological characteristics. These women, through photography, tested the bonds of domesticity, found a sense of sisterhood, and sought to establish their own creative identities. In their way, they were at odds with the prevailing middle class social expectations for women and this as much as their interest in photography defines them as a unique cultural group.

The presence of Frances Benjamin Johnston within the network acted as a catalytic force from the 1880s on; her career and her relationship with a number of professional and amateur photographers represented a crucial aspect of the nineteenth century support system in photography. These women, separated geographically and often isolated in small towns, communicated their desire for mutual encouragement. Learning of Johnston's exploits and achievements, as photographer, journalist, and international lecturer, in the pages of popular illustrated magazines, newspapers, and photographic journals, they corresponded with their celebrated colleague. Letters from Massachusetts, Nebraska, Mississippi, and New Jersey testified to a shared commitment to photography.

Johnston's contribution as counselor, friend, and critic encouraged the progress of many uneasy amateurs toward a more independent phase of their participation in photography. The interaction between Johnston and her amateur and professional colleagues worked because of Johnston's belief in what she perceived as women's inherent common sense, "patience, determination, taste and tact." Johnston's message to women, enunciated since 1891 in the pages of publications such as *The Ladies Home Journal*, *Demorest's Family Magazine*, and *The Press*, was only a part of a recognizable trend by which women were attracted to photography. Letters to Johnston and the articles and letters that appeared in contemporary periodicals provide evidence of the widespread articulation among women of their desire for sharing in the new technology and their burgeoning consciousness of themselves as creative women.

Johnston's position as focal point in this web of women photographers caused numerous writers and editors to turn to her for advice and information on many aspects of women's lives and photography. As a woman, for example, her advice was sought on appropriate subjects for a family magazine. As a woman photographer she was considered knowledgeable about distinguished American women. Even George Eastman sought Johnston's expertise for an article, "Women Who Use Kodaks," that promoted his company's product.[6] Clarisse Moore, a journalist as well as an amateur photographer who won awards for her camera work, not only wrote of Johnston's photography in "Women Experts in Photography" for *Cosmopolitan* in 1892, but also sought Johnston's comments on picturemaking. Publications such as *The Ladies Home Journal*, the *Women's Home Journal*, and publishers like Harper and Brothers solicited Johnston's recent photographs, her thoughts on the new medium, and her comments on women's potential in the growing field.

This closeness that existed between Johnston and the contemporary press enhanced Johnston's appeal to the mostly middle class women aspiring to be photographers. Her image as a woman from a prominent family who combined feminine virtues, an artistic sensibility, and an astute business sense was reported by newspapers and magazines. The media approved of Johnston, a woman who did not have to earn money but instead was depicted as one motivated by the purity of her artistry. "Miss Johnston," the *Brooklyn Eagle* noted in 1891, "is in circumstances of affluence and though she is proud of her earnings it is her love of work rather than necessity which sends her off at a moment's notice . . . "[7] *The Photographic Times*, a photography journal, similarly reported on the uniqueness of Johnston's achievement, her fine work, and deserved recognition, recording as well that Johnston was "by no means dependent on the money for remuneration for her labor."[8]

Johnston's hometown paper, *The Washington Post*, stressed her feminine qualities. Her slender, delicate appearance, and her fine quiet manners made her effectiveness as a business woman acceptable. In fact, the same *Washington Post* that enthusiastically endorsed Johnston's business activity ran the following rhyme mocking the changing roles of women:

> Yes, I like anything, in fact,
> In the shape of a man, said she,
> 'Ah' then, he said, 'how very fond
> of the new woman you must be.'[9]

Aspiring women photographers among the female readership found a role model in Frances Benjamin Johnston. Women, hesitant about being typed as "new women," found Johnston to have narrowed the gap between the private and public arenas without threatening convention or societal expectations.

Johnston established her reputation in the early years of her career (1889-1890's). At this time she became known for the variety of her undertakings and the verve with which she pursued these projects. Women photographers could view her work, for example, in *Demorest's Family Magazine*. For that publication, she photographed the Kohinoor mines in Shenandoah, Pennsylvania, a particularly rigorous and atypical assignment for a nineteenth century woman. Her work for *Demorest's* and other publications displayed her aptitude for photojournalism; other subjects included women workers in Lynn, Massachusetts, cadets at Annapolis, students at the Hampton Institute, and the magnificence of Yellowstone National Park.

As a photojournalist Johnston recorded images of great men and important events. These assignments continued to increase her reknown and enhanced her position as a popular and well known figure. She photographed Presidents Harrison, Cleveland, McKinley, Roosevelt, and Taft; she documented Admiral Dewey's return from Manila, the signing of treaties, the opening of expositions. Honors and awards accrued to Johnston. In 1904, for example, she received the prestigious French decoration, the *Palmes Académique*.[10] She was repeatedly asked to serve on photographic juries and invited to show her work internationally. Even the Boys Military Clubs of San Francisco presented Johnston with an honorary membership.[11]

But throughout her career, Frances Benjamin Johnston concerned herself with women's activities both in an out of photography. As a member of the Business Woman's Club of Washington in 1894, Johnston sought the companionship of other women. At the club's headquarters, in a space decorated with examples of members' art (including Johnston's own photographs of the World's Fair), Washington women discussed everything from business to babies. Beyond this, the club women participated in various activities that promoted and publicized members' achievements; an exhibit and sale of women's contributions to the Washington community and the preparation of a women's library for the women's building at the Chicago World's Fair indicates the type of club activity in which Johnston and her sisters took part.[12]

In 1900, Johnston secured her place as central to the women's support system in photography. In that year she organized an exhibit for the International Photographic Congress of the Paris Exposition comprised of 142 photographs produced by 28 American women whose subjects ranged from portraits and landscapes to flowers and documentaries.[13] Ellen Henrotin of the United States Commission to the Paris Exposition contacted Johnston in April of 1900. Henrotin noted the unique work of women photographers in America and asked for Johnston's participation.[14] Thus, with only six weeks before the scheduled event, Johnston used her wide range of connections to secure a selection of photographs and biographical data from the women photographers. She also contacted editors of photography journals for advice and suggestions as to whom to include in the forthcoming exhibition.

The show in Paris represented Johnston's sense of photographic history and women's place in it. Ten years before, in the summer of 1890, bearing letters of introduction to museum directors in Europe, Johnston studied available collections illustrating the history of photography for the Department of Photography of the United States National Museum. This early awareness of photographic history persisted and coincided in 1900 with her avowed belief in women's place in the field. In 1900, Johnston not only served as a delegate to the Paris Exposition but she also spoke there about women's achievements in photography while proudly showing the extraordinary group of photographs done by her female contemporaries.[15] The implications of the women's work and Johnston's role were noted in this country and in Europe. Johnston came to represent women photographers everywhere. Her status as a role model for numbers of women was enhanced. And her involvement with the Exposition led to Johnston's writing a series in *The Ladies Home Journal* on the subject of women photographers.

In 1901, Johnston edited the series for *The Ladies Home Journal* that included photographs by women and Johnston's descriptive text, "The Foremost Women Photographers of America."[16] She described women's accomplishments as represented by selected photographers whose work she had shown at the Paris Exposition. Earlier, in 1897, writing in *The Ladies Home Journal*, Johnston had emphasized the advantages of the new art, stating that, "Photography as a profession should appeal to women."[17] Now, through exhibition and publication, she could point to a wide range of professional quality work from Frances and Mary Allen's scenes of Massachusetts village life to the "daring and original" portraiture that reflected the intense personality of Zaida Ben-Yusuf. Within this spectrum, Johnston focused on Emma Farnsworth's poetic and romantic views of women and Eva Watson-Schütze's graceful, elegant subjects. Women from all over the country responded to the articles. The examples of successful women in the field coupled with Johnston's advice and encouragement evoked comments that indicated women's search for fulfillment. "I wish to do something," a Miss Ormsbee wrote plaintively from Nantucket, Massachusetts. She expressed her willingness to visit Johnston's studio at any time to discuss photography with her.[18]

Frances Benjamin Johnston's correspondence indicates the widespread extent of her reputation and the diversity of her correspondents. Women photographers writing to Johnston fell into three categories: professionals, dedicated amateurs, and fun-loving snapshooters. Professionals asked for advice regarding the progress of their careers and spoke of intense work loads; some expressed ideas on marriage and men, others merely exchanged items of gossip about friends or colleagues. Eva Watson-Schütze, for example, was a well known professional with career experiences similar to Johnston. Mary E. Allen, on the other hand, represented the serious amateur working in small town America, isolated from photography's centers, if not from the camera mania. Then, the exuberant "Kodakers," to whom photography was strictly a diversion, wrote to Johnston telling of gay outings enhanced by the camera.

Several of the professional women photographers who corresponded with Johnston were close friends as well as colleagues. In 1903, Gertrude Käsebier wrote to Johnston about their special relationship; she described "two women with a common interest."[19] The exchange between the photographers began in 1892, during the early years of their careers. Their professional and personal friendship intensified when in 1899 both were appointed to the jury of the second Philadelphia Photographic Salon. By 1905, an apparently companionable working relationship evolved; in that year both women were invited by the Royal Photographic Society of Great Britain to use the Society's dark rooms, library and other facilities during their stay in England. Johnston and Käsebier also traveled to Italy together. The two women and their cameras enjoyed "a beautiful time . . . taking all the curious and interesting things [they] saw." Their travels through Switzerland, France, and Italy included dinners with "Papa" Lumière and a visit with photographer, Baron de Meyer. Companionship and photography were integrated into the trip.[20]

Their letters express professional and personal matters. Käsebier asked Johnston for help in securing European connections for a photographic project on royalty and, in a more intimate vein, extended a cordial invitation to her friend: "I have a cottage at Newport, just out of town. If you need a rest come to me. You will be most heartily welcome. I cannot but think that good would come if we were to see each other more."[21]

Käsebier herself was highly esteemed as a photographer, well respected and admired by her peers. As a well known photographer, Gertrude Käsebier played her own part in influencing the experiences of women in the next generation of photographers. Imogen Cunningham became interested in photography after observing examples of Käsebier's work and on Käsebier's recommendation,

Laura Gilpin enrolled in the Clarence White School of Photography in New York.[22]

Eva Watson-Schütze, like Johnston and Käsebier, set up and maintained a public studio, which by nineteenth century standards, defined her as professional. In addition, her fine art training, high artistic standards, intense dedication to her craft, and the earned respect of colleagues gained for her the professional designation. The exchange of letters between Watson-Schütze and Johnston began in 1893 and reveals the developing friendship between them, a deepening relationship that coincided with the progression of the careers of both women. They shared several concerns of women photographers in turn of the century America and, at the same time, expressed an understanding of the vast artistic and business possibilities opened up by the camera.

As one who earned her living from photography, the issue of appropriate fees was important for Watson-Schütze. She confided to Johnston her concern that she would "startle" her friends with even a "slight" increase in charges which Watson-Schütze considered "small but formidable."[23] For Watson-Schütze the price hike was justified because of her hard work, long hours (often staying up until midnight), and illness suffered because of her rigorous schedule. This attention to business details marked letters from other women to Johnston. Mary Allen, for one, wrote from Deerfield, Massachusetts that she was "always in a quandry as to what is a market price"[24] for her work. Allen and Watson-Schütze turned to Johnston for counsel. Unfortunately Johnston's replies are unknown. One might expect, however, judging from her extensive correspondence with dozens of businesses and clients, that Johnston would have solved the dilemma much in the manner of Watson-Schütze. At times inattentive to deadlines, Johnston nevertheless consistently revealed an ability to manage her affairs to her advantage, displaying none of the nineteenth century woman's alleged reticence in the marketplace.

Many women writing from small towns or cities in far flung parts of the United States shared, in their letters to Johnston, the experience of being dedicated amateurs in nonurban locales. And, although professional women photographers wrote to Johnston and imparted aspects of their social and working lives, it was the women amateurs who particularly responded to Johnston's activities and to her art. Their status as women in photography was an interesting one, for without public studios they were not categorized as professonals by peers or clients. Usually working in home studios, often earning money through their photographic work as illustrators or designers, these photographers were still perceived as amateurs integrated into the approved domestic sphere. Their decision to work at home and their choice of subject matter, for example, fit in with accepted notions of women's activity. Many of Frances Benjamin Johnston's correspondents conformed to this pattern and their exchanges with Johnston express the manner in which home and work remained tied to traditional ways.

Mary and Frances Allen, photographers who lived in Deerfield Massachusetts, used their cameras while remaining within accepted boundaries. And Mary Allen, like several other women photographers, was a good friend of Johnston's, occasionally visiting the Johnston family at their house on V Street in Washington, D.C.[25]

Both sisters became photographers in 1890, producing what Mary described as "unconventional Portraiture and some landscape work."[26] These photographs were used for book and magazine illustrations. The sisters were not only photographers but former school teachers also active in the Arts and Crafts movement of the late nineteenth century, a center of which was located in Deerfield.[27] Dedicated to both photography and the revival of the traditional art of crewel stitch embroidery, the Allens maintained conventions while reaching out to the new technology of the camera. The Allens remained unmarried (like most of the women in the Deerfield crafts movement) yet they felt obligated to family and domestic duties. Photography and needlework meant that they could sustain their household connections while developing their creativity. Indeed, Mary Allen positively affirmed these home related activities for she could work "as leisure permits, without the interrupting [of] the family life."[28]

The Allens approach to photography embodied more of the conventional Victorian outlook than that of the emerging "new woman." They seemed most comfortable as amateurs within the domestic sphere. Their association with women's crafts affirmed this perspective. For the Allens, career represented more of what Mary called a "resource" than the total commitment it was for Johnston, Käsebier and Watson-Schütze. The Allens resolved the career/ family conflict within the nature of photography because it allowed the integration of family responsibilities with their photographic work. A home studio, not open to the public, and subjects derived from the intimacy of home and village life made this viable.

Through the network that revolved around Johnston, the Allens expressed their thoughts about photography and their connections to it. Mary Allen noticed, for example, the prevalence of cameras in Deerfield. She observed to Johnston, in the summer of 1898, that "there are so many cameras afield, ordinary pictures are cheap."[29] Allen's perception of the incipient changes to occur due to the profusion of amateurs' photographs was insightful. She displayed an awareness of her own status as a photographer within the context of the growing debates over professionalism and the claims of photography to be a legitimate art form.

Virginia Sharp, another serious amateur, also worked within the confines of a small town. She wrote to Johnston from Nantucket, Massachusetts expressing the common nineteenth century idea that a women's career must end upon marriage. And, up to a point, Sharp's life affirmed such a view. Her letters reveal the frustrations of a life in which the creative drive was close to being stifled.

Having studied drawing and painting both at the Art Museum of Boston and, for short periods, in Paris, Sharp married, had children and for a time the " . . . cares of a family put a stop to all art . . . "[30] In 1898, feeling that a return to "regular work" in painting was not compatible with her family responsibilities, Sharp " . . . took up photography to satisfy the longing . . . to do something in the art line." She confided to Johnston that she had little time to devote to her camera work but was, nevertheless, "very much interested in the biochromate printing and . . . always hoping for a better chance and more leisure."[31] Self-trained in photography, Sharp worked at home at her chosen craft, still fulfilling her home and mothering functions. Indeed, photography was acceptable for it helped to enlarge a woman's world by aiding her "mental, moral, and spiritual development."[32] Sharp, like the Allens, chose photography for the ease with which it coincided with home and family duties. For these creative women, photography transcended the spaces between art, family, and work without causing a loss of place in society's mainstream.

In the evolution of another photographic career, Mattie Edwards Hewitt made the transition from an amateur in the nineteenth century to twentieth century professional with the help of Frances Benjamin Johnston. Technical, social, and cultural changes occurring at the time affected the lives of women like Hewitt; camera improvements provided options and outlets while the middle class position allowed free time and the means to buy the latest in photographic equipment.

The photographic experience of Mattie Edwards Hewitt not only bridged the gap between nineteenth century amateur and twentieth century professional but also demonstrated Johnston's strong influence in the life of one of her female colleagues. A long time friend of Johnston and an amateur photographer living in St. Louis, Missouri, Hewitt lived far from photography's mainstream. The plight of such small city photographers was recognized by camera clubs and photography journals, both of which consistently advised members and readers of the benefits of organization and regular contacts among photographers. The burgeoning numbers of camera clubs in the United States in the late nineteenth century testified to the interest and needs of thousands of dedicated camera enthusiasts. Hewitt read this material and was inspired by it. She was encouraged as well by an article by Johnston in *The Ladies Home Journal*. Commenting on the high quality of Johnston's work, Hewitt also asked Johnston's opinion on the advisability of Hewitt's photographing the work in progress at the St. Louis World's Fair:

> Do you suppose any of the magazines or weeklys would want pictures of the World's Fair grounds, unfinished or the buildings in progress . . . Any advice you could give me will be appreciated.[33]

Hewitt solicited Johnston's help in other matters. In 1907, she asked Johnston to intervene with Lumière to obtain a position for Hewitt's photographer husband in the newly opened East coast office of the well known French photographer and scientist.[34]

At another time, Hewitt, geographically separated from Johnston, nostalgically recalled elements of that friendship longing for "a stein, and then a cig—and a nice chat"[35] with Johnston. However, months would pass without any response from Johnston. Hewitt, nevertheless, continued to uphold her end of the correspondence. She asked Johnston for suggestions for a home darkroom that was eventually built for Hewitt by her husband. He built a small darkroom for his wife, a space that Hewitt excitedly described in a letter to Johnston as "papered with terra cotta building paper, [it has] shelves galore, and large enough for two to work without quarreling."[36]

The Hewitt/Johnston relationship culminated in a partnership and the establishment of the Johnston-Hewitt Studio in New York City, circa 1913. At this time, Johnston's decision to specialize in architectural and garden photography and her need for darkroom and enlargement help coincided with Hewitt's desire to develop a professional career. During the early years of their association, Johnston assumed the central role. Johnston was the photographer, Hewitt was the darkroom assistant. Hewitt's dependence on Johnston is clearly suggested; Johnston's mentor-like presence looms in the background of Hewitt's burgeoning career as it shifted from small city amateur to New York City professional as Hewitt went on to develop her own interest in home and garden photography. Little is known about the dissolution of Johnston's and Hewitt's business association except that it ended on a bitter note in 1917.

Not only professional and serious amateurs wrote to Frances Benjamin Johnston. "Kodakers" from all over the country communicated their interest in the camera to her. Having read of and seen Johnston's work in the many periodicals available to them, women interested in photography freely shared their thoughts on the subject and questioned the reknowned photographer. Frances Benjamin Johnston's relationship with many of these female correspondents coincided with accepted nineteenth century social practices. Letters from younger women timidly requesting instruction or employment, and mail from less experienced photographers hesitantly asking Johnston for advice evokes reminders of the well-known closeness between the Victorian mother and her daughter. Historian Ellen Lagemann recognizes the "logical extension" of such domestic interactions to the vocational arena in her discussion of the lives of several successful women of the time.[37] Aspiring women photographers who wished to train or study in Johnston's studio frequently expressed a desire to enter into an apprentice arrangement with her in which Johnston, the expert, would direct their careers and nourish their insecure spirits.

Emily Mews' appeal for training in Johnston's studio resonates with the writer's feeling of respect for Johnston's position. Written after her courage faltered during an earlier visit to Johnston's studio, Mews tentatively proposed her plan to Johnston for an apprenticeship:

> I want very much to learn photography, or at least, to find out
> if I have any talent for it . . . Will you take me as a pupil . . .
> Would you be willing to give me as many lessons as you found
> convenient at whatever time best suited you . . . I hope you
> will not think it cheeky of me to ask you—and that you will
> understand I don't want to invade that inner sanctum of
> yours . . .[38]

Mews' hesitant tone is repeated in correspondence from other women seeking Johnston's tutelage. They defined a particular connection between themselves and Johnston. These generally younger, less experienced women were prepared to play the role of student to Johnston's mentor. Twenty-one year old Frances Barbour had heard of Johnston's reputation in photography and wrote to Johnston asking to be taken on as "a pupil—or apprentice—and as an assistant." "It would be," she wrote, "the greatest advantage to study under you." Barbour described herself as "very artistic and have done a good deal in watercolors, but recognize the possibilities in photography."[39] Like many of the other beginning photographers, Barbour appeared naive about photography.

Novices in the field, these women's letters often reveal a self-deprecatory tone. Miss I.W. Blake, writing from Connecticut, asked Johnston to examine "two or three photographs with the possible chance of being included in your 'Home Journal' list of women photographers . . . "[40] Concerned that Johnston might not think her work "worthy," Blake apologetically explains that she is "strictly an amateur." Mrs. Lottie M. Hamilton of Michigan similarly stressed her lack of expertise, describing herself as "an amateur of scarce a year's experience." Hamilton nevertheless sent Johnston four prints for inclusion in the *Journal* article. Because of her limited experience in photography, Hamilton's remarks are tentative and unsure. Probably, she suggested, her "pictures are not worth the least consideration." If, indeed that is the case, then Hamilton humbly assured Johnston that her "criticism would be kindly received . . . " instead.[41]

Women photographers echoed these requests for encouragement and technical advice in the pages of photography journals. These periodicals, so important to all photographers, served a particularly useful function for women in the medium. It was through this literature that a network of women communicating with other women became further definable. Professional and experienced photographers shared their expertise with beginners or devoted amateurs. Columns existed as regular forums for women from around the country to question women experts or relate their experiences as novices.

Elizabeth Flint Wade, a successful amateur, shared her experiences with others in *The Photo-American* series, "Amateur Photography Through Women's Eyes."[42] Wade described her progress from her hesitant steps with her camera to her eventual success as photographic illustrator of stories and poems and winner of several competitions. Wade encouraged other women: "What was begun as a diversion has now become a vocation, and my camera is a source of income as well as a source of pleasure and recreation . . . I believe there is no other vocation open to women in which so much pleasure and profit is combined with so little drudgery . . ."[43]

In still another of the series, Myra Albert Wiggins,[44] a specialist in photographing the vistas of the Cascades in her native state, Oregon, vividly described her mountaineering experiences with her camera strapped to a "sure footed cayuse." Adventurous, enthusiastic, and ultimately a prize winning photographer, Albert's escapades surely proved inspiring to homebound women seeking support for their unfulfilled ambitions.

Still another example of women's interactions through the pages of photography journals was the column edited by Adelaide Skeel, "Our Women Friends."[45] Skeel, a photographer, writer, and lecturer, presented a monthly forum in print that consisted of a "letters and questions to the editor" format which allowed a wide range of viewpoints, mostly from women. Technical queries ("Please explain the iridescent appearance of my plates") alternated with humorous anecdotes (*i.e.*, woman gains camera but loses boyfriend). More significantly, however, letters addressed to the editor tended to reflect the world of women and photography; college girls and housewives communicated the pains and joys of their struggle to master the new art form. Madeline V. wrote of cameras and their enthusiastic owners at the Vassar campus: ". . . when June comes, it is all sunshine and cameras and portrait making and picture taking."[46] Still other correspondents revealed insecurities and wrote to editor Skeel for support and understanding from other amateurs. "We are all enthusiastic on the subject of photography . . . but so

stupid . . . Please, somebody write and tell of her earliest begin-
nings and mistakes, and, of course, how she corrected them."[47]
Women responded to such cries for assistance and in so doing continued the developing network, so important to women's position in
photography.

The ambivalent attitudes in turn of the century America toward
women's involvement in the public sphere necessitated their
search for positive reinforcement of even moderate choices that
took them outside of the home. Participation in networks was one
way of facilitating women's activity in photography. Amateurs and
professionals benefitted from their correspondence with Frances
Benjamin Johnston and from the material for women published in
photography journals and other publications. Still another form of
association was available for women photographers. Membership in
camera clubs meant an association quite different from the sense of
sisterhood derived from the photography network. Yet, camera
clubs provided a positive experience that also enhanced women's
role in photography.

The Camera Club:
A Room of Her Own

The formation of camera clubs for amateurs and professionals
was consistent with the popularity of the camera and with the apparent nineteenth century impulse to organize one's social life.
Fraternal associations, patriotic organizations, and women's clubs all
fit this pattern. Bicycle clubs presented a popular contemporary example of this phenomenon; men and women of similar backgrounds and social interests organized for mutual support and "to
promote the broad and general interests of cycling."[48]

The clubs had enormous appeal for middle class men and
women who possessed the leisure and economic ability to participate in this activity. During the 1880s and into the early decades of
the twentieth century, for example, thousands of cycling enthusiasts
sought the association of others devoted to the sport. In 1897, the
League of American Wheelmen boasted 150,000 members.[49]
Members of this and smaller local clubs took their participation very
seriously. They elected officers, drew up a constitution, and usually
established comfortable club quarters, complete with meeting and
music rooms, and other spaces that encouraged socialization. Club

activities included outings, social events, and the awarding of trophies to winners of races and to proficient members. In 1897, the New York Athletic Club was considered the "largest and strongest" cycling club in the world. The club's urban location accounted, in part, for the eminence of its members and reputation. This club, like many others, was open to women who turned out to be enthusiastic and active members.

Camera clubs, like the bicycle clubs, sprang up across America in small towns, in large cities, on college campuses. The participation of women in this activity was evident; occasionally women formed their own clubs but more usually they joined with men. For women, the camera clubs represented, in part, the continued tradition in which women joined together for mutual support, encouragement, and to further particular interests. The presence of the informal networking between women photographers has been noted as has women's involvement in other female identified associations. There were, however, important differences between these forms of women's organizations and camera clubs.

The camera club was not specifically a woman's activity, like the quilting bee or the woman's club. Camera clubs were, in fact, male dominated and while active as exhibitors, women's position in the clubs was often at the forebearance of the male members. Proper "ladies," unlike the marginal artistic, literary, or career women, were generally accepted as members, if not for higher executive positions. Their treatment in the clubs was consistent with prevailing social practices observable in male/female relationships generally.

Within the clubs, women members were provided with their own space. They were assigned separate meeting rooms; women's exhibitions were arranged; special activities for female members were frequently set up. This kind of separation notwithstanding, however, women photographers, both professional and amateur, took advantage of the opportunities offered by the clubs to advance their photographic interests. Women heard lectures by prominent photographers, they used the darkroom, library, and laboratory facilities and, even more importantly, women received comments and criticisms from male and female colleagues when their work was exhibited. And, in the end, camera clubs, like women's clubs and networks, acted as vehicles to facilitate women's entry into the current of public activities.

Camera clubs flourished in the 1880s, one result of the enormous popularity of the camera. In 1885, amateur photographers numbered in the thousands. Photography as technology and art had become democratized. It emerged as one field in which amateurs could rank with professionals. The proliferation of amateurs along with the burgeoning of camera clubs called attention to the long standing differences between amateur and professional photographers. Indeed, the work of amateur photographers, often with the support of their camera club colleagues, was frequently judged as superior to that of professionals.

By 1885, amateurs had demonstrated their eagerness to go beyond mere snap-shooting. Instead, noted *Anthony's Photographic Bulletin*, "they are willing to work harder than our professionals . . . to disseminate freely the information they possess . . . "[50] Amateurs, by virtue of their time, dedication, and artistic integrity (unlike professionals they were untainted by the demands of the marketplace) were glorified by critics, journals, and the interested public. In 1884, an editorial note on the Royal Society Exhibition noted that the best photographs taken that year were by amateurs, although those images were not included in the exhibit. The English journal articulated the advanced idea that photography was an art and "perhaps the only one in which the amateur soon equals and frequently excels the professional in proficiency."[51]

Amateurs believed in their role and the camera clubs validated their self-esteem. These aspiring photographers felt protected within their clubs and were often reticent to display their work outside the acceptable (and respectable) confines of the camera club. Publishers recognized the hesitancy on the part of amateurs to allow reproduction of their work commercially. They urged amateurs to feel freer to "open their portfolios" to the magazines. Such activity would surely effect an improvement in their work. To prove such assertions, the examples of Gertrude Käsebier and Joseph Keiley were frequently cited.[52]

In the United States by 1885, amateur photography was described as "flourishing." *The Photographic Eye, The Photographic Times,* and *Anthony's Photographic Bulletin* were established as well respected, regularly published photography journals. In addition, a major exhibit of amateurs' photography was sponsored by the Society of Amateur Photographers in New York. Seven hundred prints were shown, including the work of women.[53] By 1895, women's participation as amateurs became increasingly apparent and significant. The Pittsburgh Amateur Photographers Society admitted women as members and the *New York Mail Express* wrote that, "the most beautiful photographs taken in this city are by a young lady."[54]

The debate that arose in the mid 1880s over the relative status of the amateur and the professional was, in part, a response to the perceived exploitation of photography for commercial ends. Charles Caffin, famed photography critic of the period, noted apparent interactions between clients and photographers that led to the erosion of arstistic standards; "photographers aimed to please the public, and the latter accepted their work as representative of the art at its best."[55] Caffin's dire observation that photography had fallen into "evil times" was shared by photography greats such as Alfred Stieglitz as well as the throngs of amateurs. By the 1890s both were committed to the belief that their work and place in photography was superior to the banality of the studio workers.

The appreciation of amateur work depended not only on the absence of a monetary exchange but also on the assumption that the amateur photographer's work was produced solely for the love of the art. The idea that artistic work created for money was of lesser quality presented a considerable dilemma for nineteenth century photographers. Stieglitz promoted this idea, rejecting Käsebier, White and Steichen when they started to depend on photography for a living.[56] Money, said Stieglitz, exerted a terrible influence in artists' lives obscuring the true creative spirit.[57] Stieglitz's consistent belief in "an idea bigger than any individual"[58] implied the integrity of the amateur as opposed to those who promoted their private, professional interests at the expense of pure expression.

Even Gertrude Käsebier, whose commitment to the professional life led to her rift with Stieglitz, continued to celebrate the possibilities inherent in the amateur status:

> the art of photography . . . will come through the amateurs. They are not hampered by the traditions of the trade, and are not forced to produce quantity at the expense of quality. They go at their work in a more natural, simple and direct way; and they get corresponding results.[59]

The high praise of amateurs only fed into the continuing debate over the relative merits and contributions of amateurs versus the professionals. Amateurs, claimed some, are ruining the established profession of photography. The amateur might be a free creative spirit but he or she did not approach the field seriously; too often the amateur treated it as an amusing diversion.

In rebuttal, amateur supporters asserted that instead of destroying the field, they had improved photography: "Has not the amateur been in the first rank, both as inventor and improver?"[60] The amateur/professional debate persisted into the twentieth century. After all, one who draws his or her income from photography, who is available to photograph anything or anybody at the whim of the client, could hardly be favorably compared to the individual who used the camera only for the joy and inspiration derived from it.

For women photographers the amateur/professional dispute had particular significance. The very word "professional" in the late nineteenth century context evoked negative images connoting qualities and experiences opposed to and in conflict with conceptions of womanhood. The definition of professional included education, training, payment for one's work, and a public role. It meant confidence, ability, and accomplishment in a chosen field. All of this contradicted a "lady's" position in the domestic arena in which paid labor for women was denigrated in her class, advanced education was often unavailable and unacceptable, and the so-called masculine traits of commitment, drive, and assertiveness were deemed totally inappropriate. Women were conceived of as dependent and for the overwhelming part, they accepted such a stereotyping. It was as camera club members, however, that women as amateurs and professionals could work in an atmosphere that was respectably middle class; members were carefully scrutinized for membership and within the club accepted gender roles prevailed.

Camera clubs can be traced back to the 1850s when camera enthusiasts identified the idea of "clubbing" as one which would benefit members at several levels. The professional/amateur split emerged in these early years; association promised to alleviate "petty jealousies" and the "malevolent aspersion of talent."[61] In an age of growing cities, commercialism and competition, the new field of photography seemed open to business opportunities and, even worse, to those who would trade artistic standards for "get rich quick" advantages. Camera associations uniting "the profession in one great philosophical body" would counteract the crass and vulgar elements of the chaotic marketplace. Indeed, by the summer of 1851, the New York State Photographic Association was formed, consistent with a growing movement toward association all over the United States. These new societies were founded both to protect their members and provide a collegial atmosphere. In addition to fraternity, a "chemical apparatus, and an embryo library"[62] were often available through the efforts of the clubs.

In the 1860s, exchange clubs were formed. Throughout the United States amateurs communicated with one another by mail. While the initial intention was an exchange of photographic prints, the clubs also served another function in the lives of these early amateurs. As expressed in 1863 by Oliver Wendell Holmes, himself a devoted amateur, the exchange clubs represented "a new form of friendship."[63] In addition to swapping scenic views, for example, exchange club members sent photographs of themselves in home or studio to one another thereby presenting an intimate perspective into another's life style. This rather short lived activity (it peaked between 1861 and 1863) is illuminating for the insights it provides for future photographic interactions and associations.

Camera clubs continued to expand steadily between the 1860 and the 1880s. In 1873, the evolving clubs were often credited for the photographic advancements of the period. The mutual sharing of the experience and experiments between professionals and amateurs through papers and exhibitions served to assuage the harsh suspicion and competition among photographers that marked earlier periods. *The Photographer's Friend* praised the photographic societies for providing an environment in which "persons all engaged in the same pursuit . . . [gave] their individual experiences for the benefit of the whole body, at the same time receiving from others the results of *their* experience."[64]

By the early 1880s, camera clubs formed and flourished in several major American cities; the Pioneer Amateur Photographic Club was formed in New York. Chicago, Boston, and Philadelphia were also the sites of new club organization.[65] Photographic journals, often published by the clubs themselves, discussed at length the advantages of association. In 1882, *The Photographic Journal of America* noted the clubs' historical connections by comparing past European guilds to contemporary American clubs. The medieval guildhouse represented some trade or calling and attempted to establish standards, control the quality of the work produced, and better the position of its members. *The Photographic Journal* report similarly perceived that the function of a camera club was to work for a common goal and toward improved relations among amateurs and between amateurs and society. The camera clubs were envisioned by their founders and members as establishing a "cordial feeling of sociability" for "the free exchange of opinions and experiences necessary to advance art and friendship among members."[66]

Even those in isolated small towns and rural areas benefited from clubs through the postal photographic club that emerged to satisfy the growing demands of amateurs in remote areas.[67] These photographers in out of the way places, feeling an obvious lack of contact with other camera operators, conducted various activities. Similar to the early exchange clubs of the 1850s, the postal clubs of the 1880s created a club album. Each month or two, a member sent a favorite print to the organizer who in turn mounted the picture in an album which was sent around to the various members for viewing and criticism. For many, the impersonal nature of the commentary was particularly helpful. This method of interaction between photographers reaffirmed the strong need for organization and communication in the period. Many women joined postal clubs. In 1893, *Cosmopolitan* reported that well-known amateurs Sarah Eddy of Providence, Emilie Clarkson of Potsdam, and Cornelia Needles of Philadelphia all participated in this form of club organization.[68]

Organizing and running a successful club was not a simple undertaking. Rather it required an enthusiastic organizer (or organizers) who would devote time to it and demonstrate a commitment to the club's establishment. Photographic journals eased the organizational process by suggesting guidelines for those interested in forming a new club. How to run the primary meeting, a sample constitution, program and publicity ideas, and technical advice were all aspects of club organization that were carefully presented. Significantly, an article in *The Photo-Beacon* recommended that membership be open to men and women. The journal reasoned that such a policy was "conducive to better order and social features can be planned more readily."[69]

Societies ranged from the very large club with its own rooms to those clubs that merely rented a single room for regular meetings. A big society like the Chicago Society of Amateur Photographers possessed an elaborate establishment. It boasted a darkroom with several developing sections, a washing room for plates and prints, and an enlarging room. A library and reading room that included more than fifty magazines and periodicals from the United States and all over the world, plus roomy and comfortable meeting rooms completed this thoughtfully planned club environment.[70] For the beginner who had worked alone with his or her new camera, grappling to master the technical details, the camera club meant a major change in his or her approach to photography. Prior to club membership the individual amateur often used a makeshift home darkroom. As a club participant, the hesitant beginner could rapidly become an accomplished camera operator.

The support engendered within the club was important to photographers for reasons other than communal opportunities. By 1900, photography was not generally recognized as a fine art, despite the efforts of Alfred Stieglitz and others. Many photographers, insecure because of the low regard of critics toward their medium, felt bolstered within the club where colleagues provided instruction, aid, and usually encouraging criticism. The functions of camera clubs were, in fact, to extend beyond internal club activities to the larger community. Discussons and lantern slide presentations were frequently given in hospitals, unions, and working boys' clubs.

Camera clubs were formed in almost every major city during the 1880s and 1890s. The usually affluent middle and upper middle class membership and the clubs' urban settings suggested an influential future in the arts. And perhaps nowhere was the cultural impact of the camera club more apparent than in the activitities of the Camera Club of New York (CCNY). This well-known and prestigious club, formed in 1896 by the merger of The Society of Amateur Photographers and the New York Camera Club, reaffirmed objectives similar to those of other clubs. The union of the clubs also meant the fusion of two differing approaches to photography. As amateurs, the Society members were perceived as being artistically pure. They lacked, however, the numbers and money to sustain its status. On the other hand, the New York Camera Club boasted of members and dollars but lacked the artistic talent to draw public recognition and respect.[71] The new combination produced dynamic change and a cultural impact on the art world:

> Those in the camera club began to feel the educative and
> regenerative influence of the talented amateurs, who freely
> gave of their experience. The latter in turn enjoyed the advan-

tages of a revenue which would permit them to take the practical and artistic steps necessary to every lover of
photography.[72]

The New York club was concerned with "the advancement of
the photographic art" and wanted to provide an atmosphere conducive both to the pursuit of photography and the cultivation of
"social acceptance."[73] Like other large metropolitan clubs it offered
many fine facilities for members. The whole floor of a building at
Twenty-Ninth Street near Fifth Avenue was divided into a general
reception room and lounge, executive offices, a library, a large
working space holding cameras, lockers, and twelve darkrooms and
a rooftop studio. Membership meant free use of the club's developing and printing equipment, lectures, demonstrations of new
techniques, weekly lantern slide evenings, exhibitions, smokers,
dinners, and access to the library.[74] Obviously these offerings enticed both the timorous beginner and the already dedicated photographer. From its inception the Camera Club of New York welcomed
women who, like the male membership, were eager to take advantage of the companionable spirit which pervaded the club premises.

By 1898, the Camera Club of New York was probably the most
prestigious of the amateur clubs in the United States. Both its location in New York City and the active participation of Alfred Stieglitz
as vice-president (1897) and as the chairman of the Publications
Committee set the New York club apart from local associations
throughout the United States and enhanced the club's reputation as
an innovative force in American cultural life. Theodore Dreiser was
intensely aware of Stieglitz's role in the New York Camera Club,
especially as related to amateur photographers. Dreiser wrote:

> His influence on development, is not so much understood as
> felt . . . He has no specialty and no limitation. In every branch
> in which amateurs have specialized and distinguished them-
> selves he has proved himself superior . . . His attitude toward
> the club has come to be the club's attitude toward the world.[75]

Camera clubs generally were envisioned as contributing to a
larger social role but Stieglitz's vision for the Camera Club of New
York was particularly grand. "I had," said Stieglitz, "a mad idea
that the club could become the world center of photography and

Emma Farnsworth, "Diana," c.1897, The Library Of Congress.

Eva Watson-Schütze, Untitled, [Child With Oak Fringe], c.1900, The Library of Congress.

Eva Watson-Schütze, Untitled [Woman With Lily], c.1903, International Museum of Photography at George Eastman House.

Mary A. Bartlett, Untitled [Young Woman Seated in Front of a Curtained Window], c.1900, The Library of Congress.

Mary and Frances Allen, Untitled [Two Women Gossiping], c.1900, The Library of Congress.

Virginia Prall, Untitled [Two Girls Reading], c.1900, The Library of Congress.

Alice Boughton, Untitled [Two Women Under a Tree], c.1910, International Museum of Photography at George Eastman House.

Gertrude Käsebier (attributed), "Gertrude Käsebier," c.1912, International Museum of Photography at George Eastman House.

Gertrude Käsebier, Untitled [Family Group], c.1912, International Museum of Photography at George Eastman House.

Gertrude Käsebier, "Blessed Art Thou Among Women," 1899, The Library of Congress.

Gertrude Käsebier, "The Manger," 1899, The Library of Congress.

Gertrude Käsebier, "The Picture Book," c.1899, The Library of Congress.

Alice Austen, "E. Alice Austen, Full Length With Fan," September 19, 1892, The Staten Island Historical Society.

Alice Austen, "Clear Comfort," c.1890, The Staten Island Historical Society.

Alice Austen, "Staten Island Ladies Club Tournament, Miss Cahill and Miss McKinley," September 28, 1892, The Staten Island Historical Society.

Alice Austen, "Bicycles and Riders-Staten Island Bicycle Club Tea," June 25, 1895, The Staten Island Historical Society.

Alice Austen, "Violet Ward and Daisy Elliott," c.1896, The Staten Island Historical Society.

Alice Austen, "Bathing Party On South Beach," September 15, 1886, The Staten Island Historical Society.

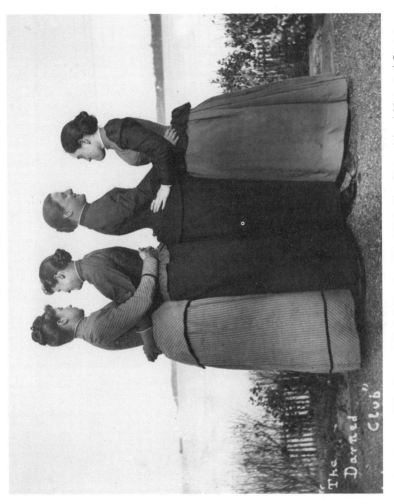

Alice Austen, "The Darned Club," October 29, 1891, The Staten Island Historical Society.

Alice Austen, "Trude and I, Masked, Short Skirts," August 6, 1891, The Staten Island Historical Society.

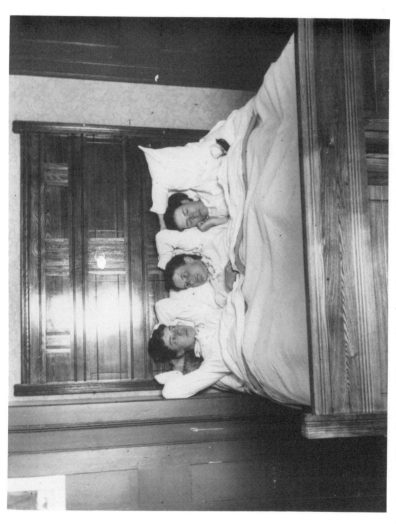

Alice Austen, "Mrs. Snively, Julie, and I in Bed," August 29, 1890, The Staten Island Historical Society.

Alice Austen, "Julia Martin, Julia Bredt, and Self Dressed Up as Men," October 15, 1891, The Staten Island Historical Society.

Alice Austen, "Trude Eccleston's Bedroom," October 16, 1889, The Staten Island Historical Society.

Alice Austen, "Ground Floor Bedroom, Undated," The Staten Island Historical Society.

Frances Benjamin Johnston, "Self Portrait," c.1896, The Library of Congress.

Frances Benjamin Johnston, "Self Portrait," c.1905, The Library of Congress.

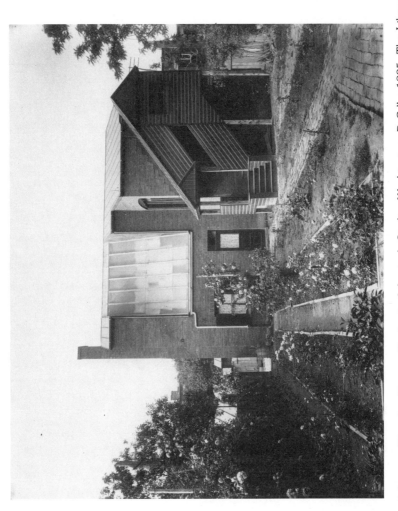

Frances Benjamin Johnston, "Exterior, Frances Benjamin Johnston's Studio, Washington, D.C." c.1895, The Library of Congress.

Frances Benjamin Johnston, "Woman Worker, Lynn, Massachusetts," c.1895, The Library of Congress.

Frances Benjamin Johnston, "Working Girls of Lynn, Massachusetts," c.1895, The Library of Congress.

Frances Benjamin Johnston, "Student Orchestra," Hampton Album, 1899-1900, The Library of Congress.

Frances Benjamin Johnston, "Carpentry Class," Hampton Album, 1899-1900, The Library of Congress.

Frances Benjamin Johnston, "Alice Roosevelt in White House Conservatory,"
1902, The Library of Congress.

Frances Benjamin Johnston, "Inauguration of President McKinley," 1900, The Library of Congress.

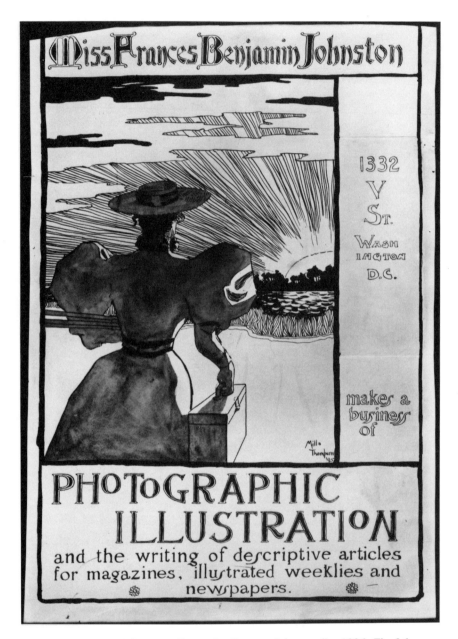

Mills Thompson, "Advertising Poster for Frances Johnston," c.1896, The Library of Congress.

Anne Brigman, "My Self," 1920, International Museum of Photography at George Eastman House.

Anne Brigman, "Incantation," c.1905, International Museum of Photography at George Eastman House.

Anne Brigman, "Soul of the Blasted Pine," 1908, International Museum of Photography at George Eastman House.

Anne Brigman, "The West Wind," 1915, International Museum of Photography at
George Eastman House.

eventually create a museum . . . "[76] Of course, in the case of the Camera Club of New York, Stieglitz's plan was, to a large extent, realized; the club and its journal, *Camera Notes*, came to exert a particular influence on the world of photography. *Camera Notes*, under the editorial guidance of Stieglitz, enunciated an aesthetic which embraced pictorialism as the photographic equivalent of painting. Through the pages of *Camera Notes*, the Camera Club of New York became known by photography adherents throughout the world. Critic Sadachiki Hartmann described the quarterly as "the most ambitious club publication in existence; there is no art magazine in this country which could compete with *Camera Notes* in its distinctive and peculiar make-up."[77] The journal's position and influence remained secure at least until Stieglitz's resignation as vice-president in 1902.

Because of its prestigious status and leadership role in the world of photography, the club's attitudes toward women are significant. Throughout the pages of *Camera Notes*, the wide-ranging nature of women's participation becomes evident; women contributed to club life as exhibitors and lecturers. They are listed as fellows and associate members. But women do not appear as officers.

Periodic exhibitions of women's work by the Camera Club of New York recognized the ability of these photographers. In November, 1899, for example, showings of prints by Zaida Ben-Yusuf and Frances Benjamin Johnston were held at the Camera Club of New York. Ben-Yusuf had exhibited successfully in London in 1898. Now her work was favorably received in New York. Ben-Yusuf's portraits and genre studies evoked positive comments by critic, William H. Murray, who predicted a promising future for her.[78] Frances Benjamin Johnston participated in the same exhibition. Murray emphasized her portraiture ability and her talent for reproducing subjects in a natural, unaffected style.[79]

In 1900, Gertrude Käsebier became a member of the Camera Club of New York, testifying, in part, to her artistic connections to Stieglitz as well as to the status of the club itself. Prior to her actual joining, Käsebier's prints were exhibited in its galleries and excited great interest. According to Joseph T. Keiley, Käsebier's work represented "the largest and most remarkable collection of excellent and artistic portraits ever shown in this country."[80] Keiley, a photographer himself, was an editorial associate for *Camera Notes*, a critic, and a close friend of Stieglitz. He appreciated Käsebier's innovative approach to portrait photography and compared her unique style to the conventional portraits of the period in which sitters were stiffly posed in stage-like settings. In another review of Käsebier's photography, painter Arthur K. Dow emphasized the painterly qualities in her work and commented as well on Käsebier's artistic training and her awareness of fine art.[81]

In 1900, *Camera Notes* reported Käsebier's acceptance into the Linked Ring.[82] Käsebier was the first woman to be so honored by the estimable London club, an elite group of amateur photographers. Steiglitz made important contacts through the Linked Ring and the British club's membership exerted a crucial influence upon his theories on photography. Gertrude Käsebier's election to that society was significant for it recognized Käsebier's accomplishment without any reference to gender. In fact, the account in *Camera Notes* credited the Ring with turning from earlier more traditional attitudes by welcoming a woman to its ranks.[83]

The evolution of Käsebier's career is evident through the pages of *Camera Notes*. From the onset of her membership in 1900 to the last edition of the journal under Steiglitz's supervision in 1902, Käsebier's life as a pictoral photographer is depicted. In July, 1899 "The Portfolio of American Pictorial Photography" exhibited the work of the most esteemed pictorialists of the day.[84] Gertrude Käsebier's work was included, as was the work of other women— Emilie Clarkson, Mathilde Weil, and Emma Farnsworth. Then in July, 1900 a special achievement of Käsebier's was highlighted in *Camera Notes*. At the London exhibit of that year, the work of thirty Americans was shown—thirteen of whom were women. English critic Child Bayley described Käsebier's photographs as "talented," her work "always artistic," although the work of other female participants did not fare as well.[85] Gertrude Käsebier's participation in subsequent London exhibits between 1899 and 1902 plus showings in Glasgow and other European cities and in the United States attest to Käsebier's enlarged reputation and the support of the Camera Club of New York.[86]

Although Gertrude Käsebier dominates the pages of *Camera Notes* as its most prestigious woman member, other women participated in club functions and exhibits. The names of many women appear on the membership roster published regularly in *Camera Notes*.[87] Most of these names, unknown today, were respected and honored by their contemporaries. Emilie Clarkson, for example, an early (1897) contributor to club activities had her work exhibited widely, was awarded medals for her photography, and received accolades from members and other viewers. She was noted as one of 23 contributors (and the only woman) to the club's "First Public Exhibition of Lantern Slides" in 1897. In that same issue of *Camera Notes*, Clarkson's photograph "Mother and Child" was published.[88] In subsequent issues, the scope of Clarkson's work burgeoned and demonstrated the intensity of involvement and the quality of work produced. Clarkson, notable in the early issues of *Camera Notes* as the rare female contributor, is joined by numbers of women members as the journal evolved.

Like Clarkson, Emma Justine Farnsworth's photography appeared regularly in *Camera Notes*. Farnsworth, an amateur photographer since 1890, had been trained as an artist and used that background in her poetic and romantic genre and figure images. Farnsworth decried her "lack of nervous strength" which prevented her from devoting the needed "energy and patience . . . to realize one's ideas in an artistic attempt with a camera."[89] Yet, in spite of her self-perceived limitations, Farnsworth exhibited extensively in the United States, Canada, Europe, and India.[90] In addition, she participated actively in the activities of the Camera Club of New York. Her photographs highlighted the November, 1898 meeting; members commented on the diversity of her subjects and her poetic and artistic temperament. Farnsworth was also the subject of the second "one man" show at the club in 1898, after having successfully shown her work at the Berlin Salon in the same year. Although Alfred Stieglitz did not include Farnsworth's photographs in his collection, he implicitly supported her work by endorsing her shows at the Camera Club of New York and abroad during the years of his leadership.[91] Indeed, the special nature of the Camera Club of New York was due in large part to Stieglitz's continued participation. For aspiring women and men photographers, Stieglitz's presence was particularly effective. The club exhibits allowed amateurs to demonstrate their work which at times was commented upon by Stieglitz. Isabel Churchill Taylor's portraits of children, and women were favorably reviewed by Stieglitz, who felt that the photographer showed "delicate feeling and refinement, at the same time showing a decided talent for pictorial treatment . . . "[92]

The clearly defined positive attitudes toward women found in the Camera Club of New York may have set precedents for clubs throughout the United States. However, the urbanity of New York City and the evolving modernist notions of Stieglitz did not always prevail elsewhere.

Nevertheless, the numbers of women amateurs on the photographic scene made it necessary for camera clubs to determine policies toward women members. Although generally they accepted women as members, the attitudes of the clubs regarding women photographers did not always reflect consistent or clearly formulated policies. The enthusiastic welcome of some clubs contrasted with the hesitant responses of others. *The Photographic Journal of America* encouraged membership for those "ladies" who were "successful and enthusiastic photographers."[93] A small room would, in fact, be set aside for the sole use of these women. In 1885, the Pittsburgh Amateur Photographer's Society emphatically stated at a meeting that "the fair sex" was eligible to join the club. In addition, the society admitted women as members assuring them that "there are no difficulties in the way that cannot be surmounted by any young woman of intelligence and possessed by artistic tastes and instincts."[94]

Confusion, however, was apparent in the official policy as expressed by *The Amateur Photographer*. Initially the journal encouraged the inclusion of "the photographic Eve" in the "Amateur Photographers Paradise" and acknowledged that "lady" photographers had "contributed such charming work."[95] Despite the interesting Garden of Eden metaphor, *The Amateur Photographer* eventually sent out mixed messages to its readership. In 1885, large numbers of membership applications reflected the enormous popularity of the camera. Small numbers of female candidates, however, caused the women applicants to be kept in suspension until they were numerous enough to warrant the expense of a special room to be arranged for their use. If enough women did not apply for club membership by a specified date, then women on the waiting list would be considered inelgible. The "problem" of women's membership necessitated the formulation of a special resolution: Women's names were placed on a waiting list to be submitted at a later date for the decision of a general meeting.

However, the policies of most clubs toward women tended to coincide with a more positive attitude. The numbers of fervent women amateurs encouraged the Chicago Camera Club to establish a "ladies section." The organizational meeting held by these women members was aided by the expertise and experience of male members. These men were apparently unconvinced of their female colleagues' ability to forumlate their own auxilliary; the inexperienced women, on the other hand, asked for the advice of their male associates. Therefore, the club secretary guided the women through their first meeting by helping to establish specific by-laws requested by the women. He arranged for the same constitution as followed by the main body and arranged for male members to provide technical assistance for the women's section. The "ladies" group would decide on their meeting times, set their own fees, and plan the order of business for future sessions.[96]

In the 1880s and into the 1890s the idea of separate facilities for women continued to prevail. The clubs tended to consider women as subordinate members of society and expected them to fulfill traditional familial and domestic duties. It was not surprising, therefore, in the 1880s and 1890s to discern a pattern of separate women's spheres within the photographic societies. Female members in most clubs automatically meant separate rooms for meetings, exhibits, and the possibility of special lectures and classes. A class in photography instruction for women was started at the Chautauqua School of Photography;[97] in clubs exhibition sections were devised for "lady photographers" who produced their photographs "without any assistance."[98] Contests for women amateurs encouraged the trend toward a separate sphere for women in camera clubs and classes. The Herald Tribune, for example, offered a prize for the best photograph by a woman and The Ladies Home Journal in the 1880s and 1890s similarly enticed women to enter special contests sponsored by that magazine.[99]

Not only were special rooms set aside for women members of camera clubs but women were expected to behave in a prescribed lady-like fashion. In the Los Angeles Camera Club, for example, women organized and met regularly for Saturday afternoon tea. Dressed in afternoon costumes and hats and seated beside a daintily laid out tea table, women sipped tea from china tea cups. An occasional male visitor would be welcomed.[100]

At the convention of the Professional Photographers Society of New York in 1906, the largest meeting in the group's history, women and men were often separated on special evenings. On the night of the men's smoker, for instance, Jessie Tarbox Beals was one of three women who escorted a group of forty women to the theater. At the after theater supper at the Astor, the president and president-elect detached themselves from the smoker to call on the women's party. Separate women's facilities were also evident at the Boston convention of The Photographers Association of America in August, 1905. Here the association pointed with pride to the establishment of a Ladies Entertaiment Committee to formulate plans to provide diversions for attending women. A special reception room for the women's use was provided.[101]

Women's relegation to rooms of their own in many clubs freed males to retain a men's club atmosphere. In 1890 the Camera Club of New York numbered 72 members, 12 of whom were women. These women generally contended with a male dominated atmosphere which included smokers on its social calendar, events which resonated maleness and most certainly discouraged women's attendance by the name alone. At the Friday lantern slide exhibits cordiality and sociability were promoted and moderate smoking allowed.[102] In light of nineteenth century customs and mores one wonders at the number of women whose attendance might be discouraged by such practices.

The idea of separate facilities for women existed as a part of the guiding principle behind camera club organizations. While clubs were at pains to stress women's abilities, assignment to separate areas reflected the general nineteenth century belief in keeping women in their proper place. In 1884, the Philadelphia Camera Club noted the numbers of woman amateurs and commented on the quality of that work.[103] Despite this reality most clubs were tentative about permitting women to participate equally in all club activities. Special exhibition classes were designated as open to lady photographers. These showings of women's work attracted attention and "in those fair amateur artists the gentlemen were said to have found rivals difficult to compete with." Exhibition classes for women were, in fact, seen as an inventive means of inducing the many women photographers to "come out of their shell" at exhibitions.[104] It was believed that women's assumed inherent traits of modesty and retirement would restrain them from showing their work publicly.

At the Philadelphia Exhibition in 1886, four classes for "ladies" were organized. The Philadelphia club proudly boasted of their idea which, except for a similar show sponsored in 1885 by the London Stereoscopic Company, no such opportunity had ever been provided to encourage amateur women exhibitors. The women's photographs were comprised mostly of figures, flowers, animals, and landscapes; they were described as "neatly arranged" and "on a level with the work of an ordinary amateur." Despite the subdued tone of the critics, however, the exhibits were deemed a success or at least "a most interesting feature" and a wider representation of women for the following year was encouraged.[105]

By the 1890s some change was apparent. Separate classes persisted in certain clubs, but women exhibiting with males slowly became an accepted practice. In 1899, The Old Cambridge Camera Club of Massachusetts and the Camera Club of Pittsburgh were among those that included women exhibitors. The Pittsburgh club's female participants, in fact, included women of considerable reknown; Amelia Van Buren, Eva L. Watson-Schütze, Emma L. Fitz all showed their work, and Mathilda Weil's photograph, "The Magic Crystal" attracted particular attention.[106] And these developments were becoming the rule rather than the exception. All over the country, women became important contributors to club exhibits. Frances Benjamin Johnston, for instance, regularly showed her prints. In March, 1899, her exhibition at the Boston Camera Club drew praise: "The posing, lighting, and selection or absence of accessories, showed a taste that amounted to genius," proclaimed *Photo-Era*.[107] The Boston club, in fact continued to demonstrate its appreciation of women's talents by awarding first prize at its annual exhibit that year (1899) to Emma Fitz's photograph, "Morning Service." Fitz, active as a photographer since 1897 and a member of the Boston Camera Club, won numerous awards for her genre pictures.[107]

In 1900, the *Photo Beacon* voiced a sentiment apparently shared throughout photographic circles. In an article describing the Chicago salon, the Beacon expressed the belief that women exhibitors had indeed earned "the laurels in the salon both in quantity and quality." Käsebier's portraits were represented as were several usually "pleasing" prints by Eva Watson-Schütze. Frances Benjamin Johnston's work was deemed "out of the usual," Weil's described as "humanly interesting." Alice Austin of Boston, the Misses Clark and Wade, Virginia Prall, and Virginia Sharp were among the participants.[109]

The general attitude of the camera clubs toward women evolved from the hesitancy of the 1880s to one of acceptance. In fact, it was the very presence of the American camera clubs that not only encouraged women to join their ranks but also provided the instruction and facilities essential for learning and developing the craft.

Catherine Weed Ward expressed high priase for the camera clubs in the United States and pointed out the generally restrictive nature of the English associations which rarely provided darkroom facilities for members. Floride Green, an American portraitist, remembered the positive nature of her experiences with the California Camera Club. There, the free exchange of ideas among members and the technical knowledge gained proved invaluable throughout her career.[110] Green's favorable alliance with the California Club affirms an aspect of the western clubs that seemed to particularly encourage female members. Reports from the Pacific Coast Camera Club indicated the involvement of women, while in *Camera Craft*, a photographic monthly from San Francisco, women were consistently presented as active members. The officers of the California Camera Club in May, 1900-April, 1900, included women as recording and corresponding secretaries. The Oregon City Camera Club also listed women officers.[111] This contrasted with the Camera Club of New York experience. The East Coast club could boast of the participation of well-known women photographers but could not point to women as club officers.

The emergence of camera clubs was not an isolated occurrence. Rather it coincided with the general middle class response to the results of industrialization and urbanization perceived by many as a threat to both individual creativity and to the maintenance of traditional human values. In this century of enormous changes, men and women often drew together with others of similar vocational and avocational interests to assert a burgeoning consciousness of themselves as a distinct group with a shared ideology. Photographers' surge toward organization whether as amateurs or professionals was akin to other nineteenth century activity; lawyers, doctors, teachers, social workers, and business people were among those with specialized occupations who found a commonality and a support system in association.

This impulse toward organization, whether among teachers, doctors, cyclists, or photographers implied a desire to better the nature of their work or leisure activities and to express a professional standard and a measure of accomplishment. Association proved to be a means of identifying with others of similar abilities while developing a sense of optimism in the face of society's seemingly chaotic growth and weakening standards. In such an environment, membership in a vocational association meant continuity and the establishment of a comprehensible system of values. The camera clubs, part of the country-wide network of clubs and associations, reflected a nineteenth century phenomenon. In this case, the photography clubs celebrated art, community, and the creative individual.

Camera clubs played a pivotal role in easing women's entry into photography. The clubs provided facilities often unobtainable by the amateur or even by the new professional. The club offered a meeting place where photographers of varying degrees of expertise could share experiences and exhibit their work. Women of the late nineteenth century were probably attracted to the camera club much in the same way they were to the women's club movement of the period. Like the women's clubs, camera clubs stressed culture and community service and offered women opportunities to connect with other women of like minds. The open membership policies of most clubs, the genteel surroundings, and the special facilities for women present in many clubs undoubtedly encouraged women's activity as photographers and as camera club women.

5

Alfred Stieglitz
and Women of the
Photo-Secession

At the turn of the century a group of photographers, known as the Generation of 1898,[1] decisively affected the evolution of photography in America. These photographers, all members of the Photo-Secession, included such photography greats as Gertrude Käsebier, Clarence White and Edward Steichen. Significantly, each maintained a particular association with Alfred Stieglitz, the moving spirit behind the Secessionist ideology. Other photographers, however, lesser known today but prestigious and respected in 1898, belonged to this special generation. These photographers were women and their membership in the Photo-Secession and their relationship with Stieglitz abetted their entry into the fine art of photography. At the same time, these women within the Stieglitz orbit

enhanced their own personal identities and furthered their professional and artistic standards as well.

In 1902 Alfred Stieglitz recognized the artistic capabilities of the
camera and so established the Photo-Secession to elevate photography to the same plane as painting and sculpture. Through their
new perceptions of photography, the Secessionists hoped to probe
below the banality and superficiality of the images being produced
by the traditional or "old-fashioned" photography of the day. Even
more importantly, they enjoined Secessionists to empathize with the
underlying spirit of the movement. A possibly apocryphal anecdote
was often repeated to illustrate the difficulties of defining the new
photographic outlook. At the 1902 opening of the exhibit,
"American Pictorial Photography Arranged by the 'Photo-
Secession,'" Gertrude Käsebier asked Stieglitz, "What's the Photo-
Secession? Am I a Photo-Secessionist?" Stieglitz replied "Do you
feel you are?" "I do," stated Käsebier. "Well that's all there is to it,"
rejoined Stieglitz.[2]

The Photo-Secession found its physical and spiritual home in
the Little Galleries at 291 Fifth Avenue. Here, from 1903 to 1917,
photographers and other artists gathered cult-like around the
patriarchal figure of Alfred Stieglitz. There was nothing about the old
Fifth Avenue brownstone between Thirtieth and Thirty-First Streets
that signified the unique impact it was to have on the history of
American cultural life in the twentieth century. The three rather
small rooms that comprised the home of the Secession were unpre-
possessing: Muted shades of olive, gray, and natural burlap decorated the walls and woodwork. The subdued decor, however, belied
the dynamic forces at work here. Against the calmness of the background a modern aesthetic emerged. This dynamism and vitality
which inspired so many throughout the art world, emanated from
the soul of the Photo-Secession, Alfred Stieglitz. Stieglitz was by
1903 an internationally recognized photographer. He could usually
be seen before a new photograph or painting expounding to his
devoted followers on subjects that ranged from esoteric discussions
on art to concern over the plight of the artist in America's changing
scene.

The various rooms presided over by Stieglitz functioned as
home-like environments for numbers of famous and obscure artists.
These spaces comprised havens in which Alfred Stieglitz dispensed

protection and advice to his "children." He passed on his aesthetic ideals, speculated on and criticized their work, and held forth on almost every intellectual issue of the day. As founder and artistic inspiration of the Photo-Secession Stieglitz assumed a paternal role in his relationships with members of that group. To his adherents, Stieglitz was seer, prophet, teacher. They sought and found in him "forces of vitality, love, and faith." 291 emerged as both a place and an idea of "freedom of expression through cooperation" and Stieglitz became "the man through whom the ideas functioned."[3]

In appearance Stieglitz looked the part of the venerable patriarch; his shock of whitening hair and large moustache complimented his dark eyes and intense expression. His affectation of wearing black capes further enhanced his dramatic image. He managed to combine the charisma of a cult figure with the dignity of a Victorian father.

But Stieglitz's "fatherliness" went beyond appearances. As head of the Photo-Secession, he exerted control over the activities of its photographer members. To belong to the Secession was both an artistic honor and an act of faith. Stieglitz, as revered leader, provided his followers with a refuge from what he perceived to be the chaos and philistinism of the outside world. In return he expected that loyalty to the ideals of the Photo-Secession and 291 must exist first in the hearts of his followers.[4] For most, 291 did represent "a haven in a storm,"[5] "a home," "a place."[6] Harold Clurman described 291 as a "protective association" where artists "healed their wounds by looking at the lovely and exciting images that Stieglitz showed them and listening to the ecstatic words that Stieglitz spoke which soothed and lulled them."[7] Stieglitz encouraged the young Paul Strand to think of 291 as his home.[8]

If a father's role is, in part, protection of his brood, Stieglitz lived up to that expectation. Dorothy Norman remembers that "protection" was a primary concern of Alfred Stieglitz.[9] Stieglitz acted out the patriarchal role, perceiving himself as an authoritative but benign presence, expressing the patience and exasperation of any parent. Stieglitz admitted, in fact, that 291 represented for him "a big family in which the children have grown up." And like any slightly bemused father, he added, "of course it is all very interesting and stimulating, but at times it is trying beyond words."[10]

Photo-Secessionists often identified themselves as belonging to a large, close family. Photographer Cornelia Sage, at the close of an exhibit in Buffalo, sensed the unusual closeness emanating from the Secessionists. "I felt," she said, "as though the members of the Secession were all long lost brothers and I am glad to have found them."[11] This sentiment was similarly expressed by Anne Brigman on her visit to the Little Galleries in 1910.

Stieglitz's mentor status affected the lives of many women photographers. At a time when few in the art world understood the fine art implications of photography, the approval of Stieglitz was particularly meaningful. For female art photographers the association with Alfred Stieglitz is reminiscent of the traditional woman artist's experience with a learned, experienced male. This early twentieth century example, however, proved to be quite unlike the mentor/student relationships of the past upon which so many women painters had relied.

Germaine Greer in *The Obstacle Race*[12] focuses on the role of the male mentor in the lives of women artists. She argues that this relationship has been crucial to women's success (or lack of it) as painters in Western societies. The male advisor might be a husband, father (or other male relative), lover, or friend. Until the late nineteenth century, association with the male mentor represented one way for a talented, ambitious woman to acquire art training. This art education was otherwise unavailable to aspiring women artists within the male dominated art academies. However, Greer notes "common patterns of female subjugation"[13] in these relationships; many of these female painters failed to assert "an independent artistic personality."[14] Within such a structure it is usually difficult, Greer suggests, to distinguish between the work of the women and their male relative or lover. The women fail to create an art style for themselves, tending instead to replicate that of their male mentors.

Nineteenth century photography, however, represented a truly modern art form in which unlike painting, women participated in great numbers and with an ease that helped to define the new art as very different from the more traditional pursuit. In the world of the camera the presence of the male mentor meant a positive experience for women photographers.

Alfred Stieglitz, mentor to dozens of female photographers, was egocentric, domineering, dictatorial. He was also sympathetic, kind, and willing to stand up for any of his loyal Secessionists. Women were taught by Stieglitz; they were advised and encouraged by him; women were welcomed into his elite inner circle. But late nineteenth century and early twentieth century women were neither psychologically nor artistically subjugated by him. Gertrude Käsebier, in fact, openly rebelled against him; Anne Brigman developed a mystical, symbolist style removed from the modernist evolution of her mentor; Eva Watson-Schütze remained firmly feminist and independent minded. And, although difficult to differentiate between male and female photographic imagery, the women's work, nevertheless, did culminate in a special view of their world which could mean the romantic, sensual visions of Brigman, the fair, genteel women of Watson-Schütze, or the elite society that surrounded Frances Benjamin Johnson.[15]

As a mentor, Stieglitz played an influential part in the artistic and personal experiences of many women. In 1919, Alfred Stieglitz wrote to Anne Brigman that for him universality existed in the shape of women.[16] Indeed, looking back it seemed that women had always been important to Stieglitz. William Innes Homer speculates that Stieglitz's Jewish background helped to formulate his perception that women were the true generators of life. Yet, despite Stieglitz's acknowledged love for women, he believed himself unworthy of their reciprocal feelings.[17] Perhaps this accounts, in part, for Stieglitz's life long devotion to women as artists and as the subjects of his own work.

Intimate data remains scarce about Alfred Stieglitz's early life. It is tempting therefore to resurrect boyhood memories to explain the mature Stieglitz's treatment of women in his artistic and personal circles. Did young Alfred's lovesick admiration for a beautiful friend of his mother's foreshadow his later behavior? That tall, dark-haired, white-skinned beauty caused the young Stieglitz intense anguish and heartache.[18] He later looked back ot his boyhood "crush" and identified those feelings as "the same as that in which all love, like art is rooted . . . " A great romantic, Stieglitz admitted that he had "always been in love."[19]

These special feelings for women might also have derived from his response to his mother, Hedwig Werner. Born in Germany, she was warm, outgoing, and cultured.[29] Like her German born husband, Edward, she loved the arts, music, and literature and both rejected the coarseness and materialism they observed in so many areas of late nineteenth century life. Both parents encouraged a spirit of freedom and hospitality in their home—a feeling that Alfred Stieglitz was to later recapture within his New York City galleries.

Stieglitz consistently demonstrated a clear-cut belief and commitment to women in the arts. The first issue of *Camera Work* highlighted the work of Gertrude Käsebier; Gertrude Stein's first writings published in America appeared in *Camera Work*; the first nonphotographic exhibit at the Little Galleries was the work of a young, relatively unknown painter, Pamela Coleman-Smith. Stieglitz's own photographs of women glow with the photographer's involvement with women's experience. One only has to examine Stieglitz's prints of the body, hands, and face of Georgia O'Keeffe to understand the expression of intimacy which to Stieglitz meant the equivalent of involvement with life itself.[21]

Alfred Stieglitz exhibited his faith in women photographers. "The women in this country," he wrote to Frances Benjamin Johnston in 1900, "are certainly doing great photographic work and deserve much commendation for their efforts."[22] These were not idle words. By 1900, Alfred Stieglitz as vice-president of the Camera Club of New York and as editor of *Camera Notes* had welcomed women to the membership in the camera club and had published women's work in the pages of that journal. In future years he was to become even more actively involved with women artists as their mentor and as the artistic inspiration of 291.

The contacts between a number of women photographers and Alfred Stieglitz served to make photography more accessible to them. For some the Stieglitz connection meant an intense learning experience, for others the association meant an exhibit of their recent prints or a critical comment on a photograph displayed at a camera club event. For still others, like Gertrude Käsebier, knowing Stieglitz meant intellectual ferment, personal conflicts, and finally revolt. For most, however, Stieglitz represented an artistic genius and confidante. He emerged as one who encouraged their art while transmitting the Stieglitz faith in artistic integrity.

Stieglitz believed in the creative spirit and this view encouraged no gender distinctions. Photographic work to Stieglitz meant art that "gives evidence of individuality and artistic worth, regardless of school, or contains some exceptional feature worhty of consideration."[23]

Most returned Alfred Stieglitz's guidance with personal loyalty to him and a belief in the concepts of 291 and the Photo-Secession. Mary Devens of Cambridge, Massachusetts, was a member of the Secession and a protégée of photographer, F. Holland Day. She was considered a talented newcomer by her peers in photography[24] and was encouraged as well by Stieglitz. Devens expressed her loyalty to Stieglitz. On the occasion (1902) of Stieglitz's resignation from *Camera Notes*, Mary Devens was outraged. "You have given so much time and thought to the magazine and done so much to raise the standard of photographic work that any change in its administration seems more than ungrateful."[25] Her appreciation of Stieglitz's efforts to maintain photographic standards was reiterated in subsequent correspondence. She noted, in fact, the decline in the quality of *Camera Notes* after Stieglitz's departure. A Fellow of the Photo-Secession and a subscriber to *Camera Work*, Devens complimented Stieglitz on that publication which she considered "a marvel of good taste and good work."[26]

Other women with relationships to Stieglitz were grateful for his support. Rose Clark, for example, who was capable of going "down into the depths" due to the burdens of work and the problems with her associate, Elizabeth Wade, felt Stieglitz's encouragement at such times to be revivifying.[27] In the midst of her fatigue and hard work, Alice Boughton eased her pressures by confiding in Stieglitz.[28]

Elizabeth Beuhrmann, a New Yorker with society connections as well as contacts in the arts (Haviland, Cassatt, Van Vechten) was also encouraged by Alfred Stieglitz. In 1904, Beuhrmann was elected to the Associateship of the Secession and by 1909, Stieglitz's criticism affirmed her new efforts. "You have certainly made decided progress," he wrote. In addition, he exhibited three of her photographs at the National Arts Club and considered Beuhrmann among the up and coming young photographers whom he was watching closely.[29] For Beurhmann, Stieglitz ranked as one of photography's "top-notchers."[30]

Like Beuhrmann, Sarah Sears came from a wealthy background. A society woman from Massachusetts, Sears appreciated Stieglitz's help and criticism of her work. Stieglitz arranged to have Sears' photographs exhibited in various shows. Sears, a firm believer in the tenets of the Photo-Secession, regularly contributed money to that cause; 50 dollars at a time was not unusual.[31]

The experience of Landon Rives, still another young woman with a society background, illustrates Stieglitz's active role as mentor to a talented woman amateur. Not quite 21 years old in 1905, Rives, like many of her female colleagues in photography, had studied drawing and painting before becoming seriously interested in the camera. At first, Rives dabbled in photography; she photographed the domesticated animals on her family's estate in Castle Hill, Virginia, captured her favorite view of the surrounding countryside, and had her friends sit for informal portraits. These subjects coincided with traditional perceptions appropriate and appealing to women amateurs of the period.

It was at the Camera Club of New York, however, that Rives made particular progress in her photographic efforts. The New York club with its extensive physical facilities and the camraderie provided by its members encouraged amateur photographers. In Rives' case, the personal tutelage of Alfred Stieglitz proved significant. Stieglitz, a member of the club and well known for his encouragement of dedicated photographers, took Rives under his wing by providing both technical advice and personal validation. Indeed, Rives' abilities improved so rapidly that even her family gave in and reluctantly supported her burgeoning photographic career.[32]

Rives' career presents an interesting example of how class and an appropriate mentor could positively affect a woman's progress in photography. As a rich and charming young Southern woman, Rives was helped by her family and friends in the establishment of her Fifth Avenue studio in New York City. Her portraits included images of Southern society figures like Charles Dana Gibson and Mrs. Henry Havemeyer. In addition, Rives' sister, Amelie, the Princess Troubetzkoy, expressed unequivocal support for her relative. Amelie's husband, Prince Troubetzkoy, a well known society portrait painter, similarly encouraged his sister-in-law's efforts. Landon Rives herself predicted that this early family patronage would be replaced, as her career and reputation expanded, by a completely professional clientele derived from the general public.[33]

In contrast to the rather predictable career of Landon Rives, Gertrude Käsebier emerged as a strong-minded woman in her relationship with Alfred Stieglitz, a woman willing to provoke Stieglitz if necessary. And, indeed, in 1912, Käsebier rebelled against Alfred Stieglitz by resigning from the Photo-Secession. In refusing to give in to what she perceived as Stieglitz's willfulness or to compromise her own artistic beliefs, Käsebier broke from the 291 circle.

The relationship between Alfred Stieglitz and Gertrude Käsebier was a complex and often uneasy one. It began in mutual trust and admiration. During the early years of the association, Käsebier cared deeply for Stieglitz and in fact inscribed the back of a portrait she had taken of him that he was "the only man [she] ever loved."[34] Stieglitz demonstrated respect for Käsebier's work as early as 1898. In that year he acknowledged Käsebier as among five most promising photographers at the Philadelphia Salon. By 1899, at the time of the Second Philadelphia Salon, Stieglitz was convinced of Gertrude Käsebier's merits as a qualified juror for that exhibition. For that jury, he suggested Käsebier, Day, and White—three photographers he envisioned as "the new photographic triumverate."[35] Stieglitz's continuing recognition of Käsebier's talent was very meaningful to her as an aspiring photographer who understood Stieglitz's high standards and expectations. In 1902, he featured Käsebier's photogravures in the first number of Camera Work. Subsequently, he exhibited her work at the Camera Club of New York, in other photographic exhibits, and in portfolios of "American Pictorial Photography." Gertrude Käsebier became a member of the governing council of the Photo-Secession in 1902. Käsebier and Stieglitz seemed linked in a collegial relationship in which both found common ground about photography. Like Stieglitz, Käsebier believed in photography as an art equal to painting and sculpture.[36]

However, it became apparent that the two personalities were doomed to clash. Käsebier was often outspoken and frank and she disagreed frequently with Stieglitz on aesthetic questions. A strong personality himself, Stieglitz often had difficulty dealing with Käsebier. Indeed, Stieglitz's stewardship of the Secession though lauded by most was sometimes described by critics as disdainful, an attitude that led to quarrels with even his most faithful colleagues. In addition, others were heard to complain about his testiness and dogmatic behavior. Clarence White, for one, became alienated enough from Stieglitz to eventually resign from the Photo-Secession.[37] In 1907, Käsebier joined the Professional Photographer's Association of New York, an act that infuriated Stieglitz, who interpreted it as an insult to the Secession. Baron De Meyer, a photographer and good friend of Käsebier, attempted to heal the widening breach between the two. To Stieglitz, he described Käsebier as "poor old mother Käsebier," in other words, an aging, sick woman out of control over her behavior and deserving Stieglitz's forgiveness.

The actual Käsebier/Stieglitz falling out, however, had roots not only within the nature of their personalities but also in the intensity of their growing artistic differences. This became quite obvious around 1907. Käsebier had embarked upon portrait work—much to the distaste of Stieglitz. And, although always adhering to a standard of excellence, Käsebier was determined to integrate commercial goals into her professional life. She had by that time devoted herself almost exclusively to her portrait business. Stieglitz, on the other hand, remained adamantly opposed to any sort of commercial photography. Observing Käsebier (and Clarence White, as well) deriving incomes from photography enraged Stieglitz who equated such work with the rampant cheap commercial output he observed all over New York. To him, Käsebier's involvement with her portrait photography was at the expense of pure art. From her perspective, Stieglitz's public utterances about her behavior appeared unfair and dictatorial. She began to notice his flaws more clearly and went so far as to denounce Stieglitz as "hot air."[38] Joseph Keiley might have lauded Käsebier's work as "artistic creations"[39] and others might have estimated Gertrude Käsebier as the foremost photographer of the period[40] but Stieglitz persisted in his disapproval.

Käsebier objected to Stieglitz's demands for artistic accountability to himself and to the Secession. Did every photograph have to be up to exhibition standards?, she wondered. "Has our medium reached a phase where an account of our mentality must be rendered, not only that but our spirituality, our very being is on trial?"[41] Stieglitz's criticisms of Käsebier's artistic vision were cutting. He persistently attacked her adherence to the soft focus and romantic images of pictorialism at a time when he was increasingly drawn to the aesthetics of modernism.

Frustration with the deteriorating relationship caused Stieglitz to resort to sexist language in an attempt to explain what he perceived as Käsebier's irrational behavior. She was, after all, "a queer creature" and he tried in a letter to Keiley to explain Käsebier in the context of all women for "like all women . . . what might seem cold to you, may simply mean . . . diplomacy and getting even on her part."[42] Nevertheless, the Käsebier/Stieglitz controversy does not seem explainable on sexist grounds. Rather, their struggle emanated from professional, aesthetic, and personal differences. Stieglitz's treatment of the women in his circle had always been based on respect for their talent and their commitment to 291. His relationship with Käsebier lapsed when, in his eyes, these factors eroded.

By 1909, Käsebier appeared ousted from the top echelons of the Photo-Secession. At that time of reorganization, Käsebier was not elevated to Fellow of the Directorate.[43] In 1912, she cancelled her subscription to *Camera Work* and resigned from the Photo-Secession without any formal explanation to Stieglitz. Despite their apparent personal and professional differences, Stieglitz could not comfortably accept her resignation without a definitive statement admitting that she was "no longer in sympathy with the Secession's work nor belief in its aims and activities."[44]

Anne Brigman's relationship with Alfred Stieglitz comes closest to the traditional male mentor/female artist conception. From 1903 (the inception of 291) to 1941 (just a few years prior to Stieglitz's death) Brigman and Stieglitz established a remarkable interaction apparently devoid of the negative aspects in many mentor/student relationships that Greer depicts. Perhaps distance had something to do with this. Brigman wrote to the New York City based Stieglitz from her home in Oakland, California; the two only met at the time of Brigman's visit to New York in 1910. Their relationship consisted primarily of an intense correspondence initiated by Brigman in which Stieglitz expressed consistent support and encouragement for Brigman and her work. She responded with warmth, affection, loyalty, and respect. Advice, openly asked for by Brigman, was freely given by Stieglitz.

In 1903 Anne Brigman exhibited one of her prints, "A Soldier of Fortune," in the Third San Francisco Photograph Salon. The exhibition included as well a traveling exhibit of Photo-Secession art that displayed the work of Steichen, Stieglitz, and Käsebier. Brigman was fascinated by the work of these photographers. With apparent naiveté, she wrote to Stieglitz praising the Secessionist showing and included samples of her own photography. In this 1903 letter she enthusiastically recounted her "pride and pleasure" in *Camera Work*, especially with Käsebier's "The Manger" and Stieglitz's own "Hand of Man." "Both are," wrote Brigman, "so intensely human; both are so radiant with soul."[45] Brigman's admiration for the work of the Photo-Secession was obvious and this feeling resonated throughout future contacts with Stieglitz. Stieglitz responded positively to Brigman's enthusiasm for the Secession and to her photography. She became his adoring disciple and devoted friend.

The 1903 show proved propitious; that same year, shortly after their correspondence began, Brigman was made an Associate of the Photo-Secession. Anne Brigman's links to Alfred Stieglitz, the man and his movement, meant support, encouragement, and the evolvement for her of a creative aesthetic.

Perhaps no woman in the Stieglitz circle expressed her faith in him and loyalty to the Secession more emphatically than Anne Brigman. In 1904, Brigman declared her belief in Stieglitz's fairness and dignity. In return, she described herself as "loyal to the core."[46] Four years later, in response to Stieglitz's ousting from the Camera Club of New York due to political infighting, Brigman came to her mentor's defense. She expressed understanding of his excesses of ambition and drive: "I know . . . that he is ambitious for the cause he is furthering with all the intensity of his heart and hands, and if he has been aggressive it's because his standards are so high that the majority can't come up to it."[47] Disclaiming any charges of hero-worship in the esteem she felt for Stieglitz and 291, Brigman lauded his spirit, likening it to "the Flat Iron Building . . . breasting the winds of heaven."[49]

The contact for Brigman ended for the most part her self-described isolation on the West coast. She had periodically reflected upon her "great distance from the scene of the action."[40] Feeling herself to be the only Secessionist in California intensified these feelings of separateness and her cries from the California wilderness seemed to draw Alfred Stieglitz closer to her. She was frustrated by her contacts with Western practitioners noting a "lack of kindred spirits." Brigman described West coast photographer Dassonville as "a queer freaky chap" and Laura Adams Armer as a "sweet" but "colorless character" from whom Brigman derived little support. Arnold Genthe, who was to teach Dorothea Lange, appeared remote to Brigman who perceived Genthe as "very teutonic, and in with rich customers . . . "[50]

It is interesting that Brigman failed to connect with Arnold Genthe. Genthe lived in the San Francisco area from 1896 to 1911. He hobnobbed with the Bohemian elite of the area—writers (Jack London, for one), painters, and opera singers were among his friends. Genthe's life style corresponded to Brigman's; both wrote poetry, acted in local theatre productions, and both continuously sought outlets for their creative expression. In addition, Genthe was an enthusiastic supporter of Alfred Stieglitz and the Photo-Secession. Genthe's photographs were included in Stieglitz's own collection. And, like Stieglitz, Genthe always expressed an affinity for women. Dorothea Lange described her teacher, Genthe, as a man who sincerely "loved women, understood them . . . "[51] Lange, in fact, learned a great deal from Genthe. However, despite Genthe's association with the Photo-Secession, his reputation as a teacher, his Bohemian lifestyle, and his concern for women, Brigman apparently remained untouched by Genthe's influence.

Brigman did admit to some contacts with the photographic community in California. She admired Doctor H. D. D'Aray as a fine technician but decried his lack of concern with pictorialism. She felt too that Emily Pitchford was a "dandy woman" whose portraiture work was highly respected by Brigman. But the few friends in California photography notwithstanding, a gulf existed for Brigman until her connection with Stieglitz and the work of the Photo-Secessionists at 291.

At the outset of her relationship with Stieglitz, Brigman established the student/mentor dynamic. In describing herself to Stieglitz as a "stumbler" whose "soul is afire with enthusiasm" while at the same time extolling the precepts of the Secession, Brigman no doubt ingratiated herself with the renowned photographer. She reinforced their roles even further by describing herself as Stieglitz's "Western disciple"[52] and the Little Gallery as "the promised land."[53]

The role models of Stieglitz, Käsebier, Steichen and White provided the photographic inspiration for Brigman. At the same time these idols also served to frustrate her efforts. She expressed these feelings in a letter to Stieglitz: " . . . if you could only understand how I've worshipped before its [Camera Work] wondrous beauties and then gone way to my grim printing, fired with zeal and then the blessed prints would not yield what my soul demands."[54]

Brigman finally met Alfred Stieglitz face to face in 1910—seven years after they first began their friendship-by-mail. Before meeting Stieglitz in New York, Brigman admitted to difficulties in her work. She complained that, "It was almost like squeezing blood from a turnip . . . I tore my long brown hair and gnashed my . . . teeth."[55] The forthcoming New York visit increasingly came to promise artistic inspiration and personal fulfillment.

The long visit introduced Brigman to Stieglitz and to the women and men of 291 who Brigman knew only through their published photographs. The trip turned out to be an exhilarating experience for Brigman. She looked forward to it with some trepidation, likening herself to "a poor little leaf that is drifing toward a great whirlpool that is going to swallow it."[56] This hesitancy appears in

Brigman's reluctance to have Stieglitz mount a one woman show of her work. Brigman had long fantasized about the possibility of such an event and expressed that dream to Stieglitz on past occasions. In 1907, for instance, Brigman's determination to have a show of her own conflicted with her anxiety over that eventuality. If the one woman show did not transpire she would "wear crepe or a sad sweet smile."[57] Stieglitz, however, did not deem her ready for an exhibit at that time. By 1909 when a visit to New York City was in the offing, Stieglitz finally encouraged a showing of her work. But Brigman now shied away from being compared with "all the great ones who have been in the field much longer." She went on to admit, "It's the swell head probably—for I've had much praise from you and others and I need taking down."[58] Her insecurities about her work and position in the world of photography continued to surface. Just prior to coming to New York, Brigman confessed to having "cold feet" regarding a show of her own[59] and requested that Stieglitz postpone such an event indefinitely. As it turned out, Brigman never did experience a one woman show in Stieglitz's galleries. However, the self-deprecating tone that crept into many letters before the 1910 visit to New York fades eventually. The impact of the meeting with Stieglitz and the Photo-Secessionists affected a substantive change in Anne Brigman's attitudes toward herself and her work. Anne Brigman's own prophecy that in New York she would "find so many friends and new joys, and progress so much"[60] proved to be fulfilled.

For eight months in New York she absorbed the vitality of the environment that was 291; her consciousness was aroused by "the vital current . . . running swift and steady."[61] In addition, she learned specific photographic techniques. Clarence White taught her the intricacies of platinum printing, a process that she had found difficult to master.[62]

Even more importantly, the Eastern visit reaffirmed for Brigman her belief in herself as "a woman, simple and honest."[63] She felt the Photo-Secessionists reciprocated these feelings. The camaraderie that she experienced with Stieglitz and those at 291 provided Brigman with professional friendships she had not found in California. They in turn were intrigued by what they saw as a "strange, foreign California tone" in both Brigman and her photographs.[64] Brigman, whose photographs invoked mystical images of the wild Sierra landscape surely must have appeared something of the friendly alien to the New York Secessionists.

About a year after Brigman's Eastern sojourn, she looked back to the exhilarating days with Stieglitz and his circle. She still retained the headiness of her stay and remembered "the glow of light . . . that is the Beauty that the gray haired Vagabond speaks of."[65] She periodically evoked the time spent in the rooms of 291; the grays, browns, and dull greens of that space haunted her and proved to be inspirational in the following years. Most of all, Brigman felt even closer to Stieglitz. A photograph taken of Stieglitz by Brigman became for her "a thing of beauty and a joy"; she enjoyed gazing at his "satyrical smile" captured in the print hanging on a wall in her small garden studio.[66]

Brigman used the past experiences to bolster her spirits when they flagged. Tiredness and discouragement dissipated when Stieglitz wrote. The Stieglitz mystique was powerful enough to conjure up, even through letters, fond thoughts. Almost like a lover she recalled Stieglitz's restless pace, his voice with its "odd, delightful staccato," and other of his quirky habits. Brigman's reminiscences took on a bittersweet tone as she recalled: " . . . the little room is quiet and softly lighted. I was very happy there . . . I grew—and growth through pain is a marvelous thing."[67] New York repeatedly surfaced in photograph-like images—the blossoming dogwood of Bronx Park, the arbutus of Long Island, a corner at 291—all combined to tantalize Brigman in California even while she felt continued personal development in her everyday life.[68]

Brigman's intensified feelings about herself are evident in the years following the East coast visit. In 1910 she left her husband in order to work out her own future. Then in 1911 an exhibit of 150 of her prints in Oakland inspired Brigman to evaluate and sort out her diverse and sharply etched experiences of the year before. She recognized those events as part of a "terrifically formative place"[69] in her life. She stood, in effect, outside of herself and confronted the unusual "shaping" she had gone through and attributed much of this to Stieglitz and his "great heart." Indeed, two years later she could still write: "I can see all the place. I always loved the yellow light in the little ante room . . . the book cases and curves that took on a medieval glow, and there were queer pictures on the table . . . there's a tree outside of the east window that looks like a walnut . . ."[70]

Brigman acknowledged the 1909-1910 period as a turning point—a time of emerging self assurance and confidence in her artistic ability. Once apologetic about her work and tentative about showing it to Stieglitz, she could, by 1912, state that "I've come to the place where I'm glad and unafraid to send you my work."[71] And her personal growth continued. In 1915, Anne Brigman, exuding confidence, set up her own version of a Photo-Secession exhibition at the San Francisco Exposition. Francis Brugière, a photographer and friend was her partner in this venture. Brigman expressed enthusiasm over the prospect of such a show, a joint idea of hers and Brugière. Brigman sought Stieglitz's approval for the exhibition which he bestowed happily. The idea, he wrote, was "capital . . . By all means go ahead."[72]

Throughout their relationship, Stieglitz proved of inestimable value to Brigman's career in photography. In publishing Brigman's work in *Camera Work* and including her photographs in 291 shows, Stieglitz encouraged criticism from Secessionists and other viewers. Joseph Keiley's enthusiastic review of Brigman's work in the Member's Exhibition at the Little Galleries in 1908 gave Brigman praise that she considered "simple, comprehensive, and understanding . . . "[73] A year later her work was published in *Camera Work*. Brigman was exuberant in her thanks to Stieglitz. "You have," she wrote, "out Brigmaned-Brigman, the reproductions are perfect."[74] Yet it was crucial to Brigman to hear the comments of others. An intense worker, she perceived her photographs through "maternal eyes"[75] and required objective criticism. Stieglitz himself usually provided the comments that validated her work. In 1919 he finally made Brigman a Fellow of the Secession, a designation that deeply moved her for she had coveted such recognition since 1910.

In addition to publishing and promoting her photography, Stieglitz was usually lavish in his praise. Even while offering criticism it was laced with expressions of encouragement and a belief in his protégée's potential. In 1915, for example, Stieglitz made these comments:

> Some of the new prints from the old plates are not quite as rich as they might be. They are a little 'thin' and so lose in power. But taken all in all you show a tremendous step forward

technically. A greater command of your medium, some
knowledge of how to do what you want to do. The spirit remains as pure as ever.[76]

The successful teacher/student relationship established between Alfred Stieglitz and Anne Brigman rested on several
elements. First was the unfaltering faith in one another. To Anne
Brigman, Stieglitz always remained a "steady old friend." He remained for her "clear-sighted, so rudely honest-so merciful . . . "[77] He
enjoined her to be herself when she was tormented by feeling in-
ferior to Steichen or Käsebier.

Stieglitz was steadfast in his feelings toward Brigman. Often
referring to himself as "the Old War Horse"[78] he presented himself
as patient, respectful, and concerned about Brigman's life and work.
As a mentor, Stieglitz had high expectations for his disciple.
Brigman attributed her winning the struggle to Stieglitz's unfaltering
standards.[79]

In addition to his role as advisor to Brigman on artistic matters,
Alfred Stieglitz also handled much of her professional and business
affairs. Brigman admitted to Stieglitz that she was not a business
woman and was quite direct in soliciting his aid. "Can you," she
asked, "give me an idea what Eastern magazines pay for high class
photography? . . . I'm so far away from these things that I don't
know what fair prices are."[80] Brigman was delighted when her
older, more experienced mentor took over the management of such
details. Brigman's deference to Stieglitz from the inception of their
friendship encouraged a "take charge" attitude in him. Indeed,
Stieglitz clearly stated his managerial intentions: "Don't let any
publishers beat you down. You must get a fair price for your things.
Of course, I know how difficult this is, when you are so many thou-
sand miles away. So to make a start and to make it easy for you I
shall be perfectly willing to undertake the work for you."[81]

And, over the years, Stieglitz did obtain the proper treatment
and financial remuneration for Brigman. He served as mediator in
an ongoing dispute between Frank Crowninshield, publisher of
Vanity Fair, and Anne Brigman. Brigman, feeling that she was
neither getting a fair price nor the right consideration from Crowninshield, asked Stieglitz to intercede in her behalf. Stieglitz, she explained to Crowninshield, would act as "a middle man." To
Brigman, Stieglitz existed as a very special intermediary, a friend

who "gave me my soul in photography,"[82] one whose judgment she valued and trusted above all others.

Brigman's dependence on Stieglitz in business matters is evident throughout their relationship. Not only did Stieglitz handle Crowninshield, but he acted similarly with Houghton Mifflin, Sidney House, and others. He entered her work in competitions such as the Wanamaker in 1913; Stieglitz arranged for the exhibition, publication, and sale of her prints; he gave advice on fees and pricing.

The male mentor/female student relationship became revitalized in the Brigman-Stieglitz association. Theirs evolved as a friendship that included mutual respect, shared feelings, dedication to work, and faith in the guiding principles of the Photo-Secession. Stieglitz's position of power in the art world could have been demoralizing for Brigman. Instead her desire for personal autonomy and her ability to derive strength from the Stieglitz connection worked to develop her sense of self as well as an understanding of and commitment to her art. And her association with Stieglitz and 291 meant an end to her artistic isolation in California.

For Brigman and the other women in his circle, Stieglitz and the Secession presented the only alternative to the banal, commerical photography that they rejected in favor of pictorialism. To them, Stieglitz embodied artistic standards, integrity, creativity. Accepted as peers, they particpated actively and enthusiastically in this artistic milieu, recognizing that Stieglitz and 291 represented their only access to the world of art photography. With Stieglitz's encouragement, they exhibited and published their photographs and frequently took part in the Camera Club of New York as associates and fellows.

In their relationship with Stieglitz, these photographers did not display the signs of women's subjugation historically found in the work and lives of women artists.[83] Rather, these women art photographers found in their link to Alfred Stieglitz still another means of transcending the restrictive Victorianism of the nineteenth century. The women of the Photo-Secession took on the aspect of the "new woman" at the turn of the century. Yet they could not resist several backward glances at the domestic world they were leaving behind.

6

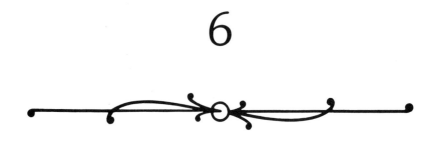

Female Visions as Social History

Women photographers working in the late nineteenth century and early twentieth centuries internalized distinct aspects of middle class cultural and social values of the period and projected this ideology into their photography. The ideals of the cult of true womanhood alternated with Progressive expectations in the iconography of women photographers. In these ideologies the true woman of the nineteenth century was expected to bear many children, be a loving mother, perform expected domestic and wifely duties. She was, in fact, the cornerstone of the late nineteenth century value system that professed a commitment to traits of diligence, faith, individualism, and a trust in moral advancement. In this sense, women of the middle class were essential to the development of the Progressive ideal.

By the late Victorian period, the woman with a camera fit easily into such a structure. The woman photographer usually maintained a refined and genteel stance; her photography enhanced rather than denied her role in shoring up family autonomy. Pictures of family groups signified harmoniousness and representations of females as mothers celebrated woman's place while images of sisters and female friendships affirmed nineteenth century notions of women's delicate nature, their tenderness, and their purity. In other words, during this period, women's photography, like their art, came to correspond with the bourgeois patriarchal ideology that emphasized separate spheres for women and men.

Most women's photography provides evidence of their attempts to express pictorially the essence of the domestic and feminine. The cult of true womanhood that defined a distinct and special sphere for women pervaded photography just as it effected women's participation in other art forms and prescribed women's place in various professions. It was in their domestic space that women's essential feminine nature was to be realized and, indeed, these womanly obligations were assumed to be "divinely ordained."

The expectations for women expressed in the cult of true womanhood fit in naturally with accepted art styles and subject matter—flowers, portraits, genre scenes, and motherhood were particularly appropriate in the world of Victorian women.[1] The ideal of femininity conjured up images of nature which in turn led to a tradition of nineteenth century female imagery that enhanced such a connection. The flower, for example, emerged as a metaphor for women, and a woman artist painting flowers was therefore perceived as remaining true to her natural womanly instincts. Flowers, like women, were decorative, sweet, fragile, and vulnerable.

In addition to floral associations, women were, of course, inextricably linked to the states of motherhood and domesticity. Indeed, established women photographers described their early encounters with photography as being closely associated with domestic subjects. Gertrude Käsebier's entry into photography was admittedly connected to children and home. Käsebier related that, "After my babies came I determined to use the brush. I wanted to hold their lovely little faces . . . so I went to an art school . . . But art is long and childhood is fleeting . . . so I chose a quicker medium."[2] Similarly, Mattie Edwards Hewitt began her photography career by reproducing scences around her own home—the barnyard chickens, the cat, and the dog seemed appropriate beginning subjects.[3]

Photographer Mary Scott Boyd advised other women amateurs of the many available photographic subjects around the house; children and "all the well-known places about the house, all the pets . . . and the favorite trees and shrubs,"[4] provide wonderful domestic settings. Boyd's audience consisted of women like herself who with babies, a home, and all the trappings of the middle class life style, demonstrated a commitment to their homes while still yearning for a cultural outlet that would enhance their lives.

At the turn of the century, middle class Americans were particularly proud of their possessions and homes. A man's home became not only his castle but his hobby as well and he spent much of his free time attending to the house and its surroundings. For women, home was to be their special, full time sphere of influence and activity. Women furnished and decorated this space in a manner that would enhance the family's status as well as their moral and Christian behavior. Noting this phenomenon, *The Professional and Amateur Photographer* in 1902 advised women photographers to consider home photography as a potentially lucrative specialty.[5] The implications for women as natural keepers of the home were apparent and indeed photographers like Frances Benjamin Johnston, Mattie Edwards Hewitt, and Jessie Tarbox Beals, devoted many years to home and garden photography. In "The Garden Photographer," an article by Jessie Tarbox Beals, she described women as "natural makers and lovers of gardens"[6] and advised women to take up garden photography. Beals and Johnston promoted this aspect of photography for women with its obvious affinity for the feminine.

Beatrice Tonneson devoted much of her work to the reproduction of home interiors; many of her clients sought to have themselves photographed while surrounded by their possessions and proudly furnished rooms. Tonneson recognized that this work was properly suited to a woman's special experience: "Women's admitted facility in homemaking ought to make her particularly successful. Her quick eye should be able to catch the gentle attitudes, the graceful groups of mother and children in the moment which will most appeal to the heart of the beholder."[7] For Tonneson, the woman photographer played a significant part in preserving images of family and hearth for far-away relatives. Through this choice of subject matter, women photographers became closely identified with the feminine, a trait that in the public mind meant subordinate to and lesser than as related to gender and art.

In certain ways the photography journals and other contemporary literature contributed to this perception by pointing to the affinity of women photographers for special subjects—women, children, flowers, social elites. Of course, male photographers photographed similar subjects; many of Clarence White's images are of women as are those of Alvin Langdon Coburn. But for most women amateurs and for many women professional photographers, these subjects comprised the bulk of their work. In photographing women, children, and genre subjects women photographers displayed their conservative orientation, for these images generally celebrated women as beautiful and ornamental or as glowing maternal or mythical figures. In so doing, these photographers did not attempt to supercede the established cultural norms or to formulate a radical outlook. Rather, these women perceived themselves as particularly well-equipped to handle specialized themes and integrated into their work the expectations of the still persistent cult of domesticity.

The oeuvre, for example, of the women photographers in Frances Benjamin Johnston's Paris exhibition of 1900 reveals that most exhibitors asserted a specific photographic interest in women, children, flowers, or genre photography. Fannie Elton, for instance, a professional photographer from Cleveland kept away from what she described as "odd, freaky, things" and instead determined to "stick close to nature."[8] Alta Belle Sniff loved photography and worked with two female assistants in Columbus, Ohio. She regarded photography as "a women's vocation in every sense."[9] The Allen sisters often photographed genre scenes and Mrs. Nelson Crowell exhibited her pictures of children and flowers in shows sponsored by the Camera Club of San Francisco; Mrs. Crowell was a society portraitist who specialized in photographing children.

Emma Justine Farnsworth whose work was included in the Johnston collecton usually chose beautiful women and charming children to photograph. From Albany, Farnsworth strove for softly focused effects. She usually emphasized the fine features of her sitters. Drapery was carefully arranged and light artfully used to highlight special details. In "Diana" (1897), for example, the young woman's face and elegantly garbed upper torso are set off from the shadowy wooded background. "Diana" is manifestly feminine. Her large, dark eyes, beautifully formed nose, well proportioned mouth, and ethereal expression epitomized a nineteenth century standard of beauty.

Eva Watson-Schütze, colleague of Johnston, Photo-Secessionist and outspoken against her photography being evaluated as "women's work," nevertheless often photographed women and children and wrote about this interest. In a 1904 article for *The Photographer*, "Portraits of Children," Watson-Schütze professed a special understanding of youngsters. "If," she wrote, "we recognize what is the essential character of a child, we shall come to require in the portrait . . . those qualities that agree in nature with the great works of art which we accept as our standards."[10] In her remarks Watson-Schütze expressed a view that sees in children a means for developing an elevated artistic vision.

Other women were attracted to women and children as subjects and their photography sought to preserve idealized roles. Beatrice Tonneson's body of work reveals that her subjects were usually women and children.[11] Tonneson celebrated the beauty of her sitters feeling it her responsibility to impart this quality through the photograph. In photographing a young woman with a lovely forehead but a receding chin, Tonneson arranged her to look down into a book to obscure her inadequate feature. In still another study, Tonneson emphasized the beautiful arms and hands of the subject. This facility toward innovative poses that would favor the sitter is derived, according to an 1897 Godey's article, from a female instinct for beauty and an "artisitc eye."[12]

Mary Bartlett of Chicago, an active and productive amateur, belonged to the Chicago Lantern Slide Club and the Chicago Camera Club as well as the Photographer's Society of Chicago. She won a grand diploma in photography at the Vienna Salon of 1891 and earned special awards at a Chicago exhibition in 1889.[13] Yet, despite these successes, Mrs. Bartlett remained close to home with her large family and was inspired by domestic environments. Bartlett's work emphasized studies of children, especially young girls. Her untitled portrait of a young woman seated before a curtained window (circa 1900) possesses a painter-like quality. The young woman's face is in profile, her body posed at a three-quarter angle. Her expression is pensive—she stares through the softly draped window. The sitter's legs are crossed under her full skirt, hands are crossed in her lap. This young woman is of modest demeanor, is lady-like and thoughtful. Bartlett has relied on techniques using light and shade to achieve an almost sculptured look in the folds of the girl's skirt and the curtains. A diffused light pervades the whole photograph.

Other pictorial categories seemed appropriate for women in photography. As in painting, genre studies existed as generally popular fare for visual representation by nineteenth century artists. Female photographers found this subject especially accessible. These sentimental, modest domestic scenes provide insights into women's world at this time. Scenes of everyday life might include women engrossed in household chores, the antics of favorite pets, or scenes on a quiet farm. By contemporarly standards these were worthwhile images that confirmed societal values. Essentially conservative, this photography reminded viewers that traditional ways still existed in the midst of an increasingly urbanized and industrial world.

Women amateurs reproduced scenes of ordinary life that recalled the satisfactions of simple pleasures or the joys of a fast disappearing rural lifestyle. Photographer Elizabeth Flint Wade wrote frequently of her experiencess as an amateur photographer. "My subjects are chosen mostly from country and domestic life . . . " explained Wade in *The Photo-American* (1894).[14] The photographs often told a story and were easily adapted to the illustration of articles and stories. A tale is spun in the two photograph series, "Where Ignorance is Bliss." The first image presents two cats—a kitten and its mother—atop a white clothed table set for a meal. They are about to sample the food. A glass of milk and a plate of food are set out. An empty chair is ready for a presumably hungry occupant. A floral patterned screen in the background provides some decorative interest in an otherwise simple composition. In the second photograph, a young man blissfully unaware sits down to eat and drink from the same dish used by the cats. In this homely pictorial anecdote, the photographer tells a simple, amusing story with little concern for aesthetic effects. The domestic setting, the playful antics of the cats, the naive young diner fit into a popular genre that Wade and other women found to be well received by an audience that responded to its unadorned humor and evocative mood. More than a simple visual essay, these photographs reflect a bourgeois sensibility that sustained those values.

Sarah Jane Eddy, a photographer from Rhode Island, like many amateurs belonged to camera clubs, exhibited her work, and won prizes for her photography. Eddy specialized in images of children, animals, and flowers. "Contentment," a photograph included in Frances Benjamin Johnston's Paris exhibition, exemplifies another interpretation of genre photography. A farm woman sits in a corner of a rustic room with a bowl in her lap. She peels potatoes.

Her hair is softly pinned up in a bun. She is dressed simply in gingham. A cat sits on a hassock at the woman's feet; the animal is content in a pool of sunlight that streams through two open windows. Baskets, gourds, and other familiar country objects surround the farm woman imparting an air of coziness. Outside, hazy sunlight plays on leaves seen through the open windows. This is a studied grouping of easily recognized figures and objects. The city dweller might take special nostalgic comfort from the comfortable details of the photograph. Contentment here means simple tasks in plain surroundings performed by a country woman with inner strengths.

Mary Paschall's "Picking Geese" is part of a series taken between 1898 and 1900. This picture recaptures another rural task that again evokes memories of a simpler way of life. A farm family in a barnyard corner pluck geese together and find in this prosaic task a special kind of satisfaction. Paschall, Eddy, Wade and other women photographers explored the pleasures inherent in a life-style removed from the chaos of urban existence. In these modest genre photographs women, home, and family in rural settings symbolized for many a haven in the midst of the unpredictable fluctuations of modern life. Women photographers seemed naturally suited to maintain such memories.

Woman as mother was a particularly appealing theme in photography as in other arts. In the history of American art, the motherhood theme can be traced to the early decades of the nineteenth century.[15] Creative women found inspiration for this subject within their own experiences and in the lives of other women. The subject's obvious accessibility made it relatively popular. In this context, gender becomes especially meaningful because of the relation between social ideology and the artists' personal lives.

"Mother and Child" by Adelaide Hanscom reminds the viewer of a Mary Cassatt painting. Hanscom, a West coast pictorialist, used a painterly style through which she not only evoked memories of Cassatt but also created a sentimental quality in her work. To critic Sidney Allen, Hanscom's "Mother and Child" was a "very strong picture,"[16] almost a masterpiece. Allen, a demanding critic, no doubt appreciated the fine pictorialist attributes of Hanscom's work but probably responded as well to the mother/child imagery.

The work of Gertrude Käsebier particularly reveals the late nineteenth and early twentieth century attitudes that glorified motherhood. In the 1880s when Käsebier commenced her artistic career, the cult of true womanhood still persisted as part of the social ideology. By the turn of the century these beliefs in the instinctual nature of mothering existed concomitant with the Progressive notions of educated motherhood that stressed an insightful, rational approach to maternal duties.[17] President Theodore Roosevelt believed that the truly "womanly woman" who bore many children would reverse the period's tendency toward "race suicide." Roosevelt and other Progressives perceived in the increased flood of immigrants to the United States, the declining birth rate among white middle class women, and in the activities of feminists a serious challenge to American values and to the stability of the American family.[18] Other observers also recognized the power of women in the home; home, the realm of women "was the most impressive experience in life."[19] Women's role as mothers assumed an exalted purpose. Special government agencies and legislation, mothers clubs, and college courses were among the ways Progressive-minded women could better their own families while improving society as a whole. The congressional designation in 1914 of an annual Mother's Day stands as further evidence of the country's preoccupation with the mother's significant role. Even feminist reformer Charlotte Perkins Gilman spoke about the important position of Mother. Gilman perceived the essence of women to be "first, last, and always . . . a dutiful and affectionate mother."[20]

Käsebier, herself a mother and grandmother, valued these roles. The relationship between herself and her children was a close one. Indeed, it has been noted that Käsebier put off her own art training and photographic career until her children were teenagers and less likely to feel any adverse effects due to their mother's decision to pursue a profession in mid-life. In 1907, Käsebier told an interviewer, "I am now a mother and a grandmother, and I do not recall that I have ever ignored the claims of that nomadic button and the ceaseless call for sympathy, and the greatest demands on time and patience. My children have been my closest thought."[21]

Käsebier expressed her intense feelings about motherhood in her photography believing, like other pictorialists, that one's life experience is inextricably bound to one's art. She stated such views emphatically: " . . . it is impossible to understand people unless you understand life. You see through experience."[22] Käsebier utilized this pictorialist philosophy to make her mother/child photographs particularly meaningful.

She began her motherhood photographs around 1898. The series was not preconceived but rather evolved casually as she photographed family and friends. Käsebier's children and grandchildren sat for her frequently. Friends Frances Lee and Beatrice Baxter Ruyl appear in the well known photographs "Blessed Art Thou Among Women" and "The War Widow." Photographer Clarence White, his mother, and his wife and children are represented in other portraits as are Mrs. Alfred Stieglitz and her daughter. In her motherhood series, Käsebier displayed the nineteenth century regard for women as the mothers, the moral agents, and the educators in American society. This is in keeping with other American women artists who celebrated the intimacy of the domestic environment and the classic subject of mother and child. Lilly Martin Spencer, for example, painting in the mid-nineteenth century, concentrated on domestic genre scenes and Mary Cassatt, the renowned American impressionist, found inspiration for the bulk of her work in the mother/child imagery.

Käsebier's concern with the mother and child theme was quickly noted by viewers. After one of the first public showings of her work at the Philadelphia Salon of 1899, a critic wondered if a man could have taken such pictures. No, he answered rhetorically for " . . . only a woman whose being vibrated to joy of a mother's love . . . the magic of love has made them live . . . photography is no mere trade to her; it is a passion that absorbs her life."[23] An extremely successful and well regarded professional photographer, Gertrude Käsebier revealed an especially moral perception in her work. By glorifying women as mothers, Käsebier not only confirmed the dominant nineteenth century belief in women as spiritual and nurturing but she also played out her own personal commitment to that role for women.

Critic Giles Edgerton noted the links between Käsebier's temperament, her life, her imagination, her humanity, and her art; her "need of expressing what had been experiences."[24] In the motherhood photographs, Käsebier translates both her emotional responses to her children and her experience as a mother to the work itself. "Real Motherhood," a portrait of Käsebier's daughter and granddaughter, is an example of the interaction between photographer, subjects, and Käsebier's perception about herself as parent. The personal intimacy inherent in this image evoked an intense response from Käsebier:

While posing my daughter there suddenly seemed to develop between us a greater intimacy than I had ever known before. Every barrier was down. We were not two women, mother and daughter, old and young, but two *mothers* with one feeling; all I had experienced in life that had opened my eyes and brought me in close touch with humanity seemed to well up and meet an instant response in her, and the tremendous import of motherhood which we had both realized seemed to find its expression in this photograph.[25]

The photographer's emphasis here in picture and text is on the sacredness of motherhood and in this case the doubleness implicit in the role.

"The Manger," one of Käsebier's most popular and well known photographs was shown at the Philadelphia Salon of 1900. It was one of the most acclaimed pictures at the exhibition; a print sold for one hundred dollars, an unheard of amount for art photography at that time. "The Manger" depicts a madonna-like figure clothed in a long, full-cut white dress. A pale gossamer veiling drapes her hair and entire figure. The woman gazes down at the infant she holds closely on her lap. Her face is obscured by shadow. She sits in a corner of a barn, her body illuminated by the light that streams in through a window above the mother and child. Beyond the lighted corner, the rest of the barn is in gloomy darkness. The photograph is overtly sentimental and Käsebier's painterly style that obscures detail contributes to this feeling. The picture is suffused with a religious feeling. In it motherhood is elevated to its most unequivocal level. The image evokes spirituality, peace, tenderness, intimacy, love. There is an explicit universality in the darkened face. The easily understood symbolism is further underlined by Käsebier's titling the photograph, "The Manger."

In "Blessed Art Thou Among Women" Käsebier is again concerned with the mother and child relationship. Here she has photographed two figures—one apparently a mother and the other a young girl about ten years old. They stand framed in a doorway. The mother is an elegant woman dressed in a long, pale, billowing gown. She inclines toward the child and rests her right arm on the youngster's shoulder. The woman appears to be speaking to the child who, dressed in a prim black dress with bow and white collar, stares unblinkingly ahead. The dark dress of the girl contrasts with the soft, paleness of the mother's costume. The mother appears sophisticated and confident; she speaks—perhaps offers advice—to her young daughter. The child accepts her parent's words quietly yet at the same time appears worried. Her gaze is too intense, her mien overly somber expressing a maturity beyond her years.

The mother here is the Progressive's educated mother—a knowing woman in whom the emotional and the rational come together. She has inherited the precepts of the nineteenth century cult of true womanhood and has tempered that ideology with acquired insights of the turn of the century.

Käsebier used women as subjects in other contexts as well. Like other photographers (and painters) she frequently placed women in dusky or misty outdoor environments. In these landscapes, heavy with atmosphere, the form of a solitary woman is usually diffused in an undefined light. The woman in "The Sketch" (1899) and the woman and child in "The Picture Book" (circa 1899) evoke feelings of nostalgia and melancholy reflection. The subject matter and the photographic technique combine in these mood pieces as in the motherhood imagery to symbolize the beauty and sentiment of life and mirror as well the photographer's own emotions.[26] Käsebier and other pictorialists who sought to effect such responses experimented to achieve this atmospheric tone; one means, for example, was to photograph the subject through a piece of gauze placed on the lens itself.

By utilizing these techniques and in her attraction to the subjective landscape, Käsebier placed her artistry within a recognizable tradition. Called tonalists, these late nineteenth century photographers and painters were inspired by all that was private and personal in nature. In doing so their work became closely linked to nineteenth century perceptions. Käsebier's own vision that encompassed women as nurturers, beautiful but passive children, and the landscape as sublime counteracted those aspects of her contemporary world that were committed to the values of the marketplace. Instead she evoked a time and a place that was a spiritual haven to counter an increasingly troublesome modern age.

The photographs of Gertrude Käsebier, as described above, as well as the images produced by Alice Austen, Frances Benjamin Johnston, and Anne Brigman represent examples of the ways in which women used photography to define and explain their worlds. There is a considerable gap between Käsebier who sought to preserve the wonder of motherhood in the face of feminist activism and contemporary fears for family coherence and Anne Brigman whose photography expressed a clear-cut rebellion against middle class conventions. In between, Frances Benjamin Johnston worked within the confines of market demands. She usually projected a Progressive vision yet occasionally used the camera to mock traditional norms. Alice Austen tread somewhere on the edge; on the surface she reproduced genteel Victorian scenes while simultaneously dropping clues that spoke of unexpressed sensuality and female self-imaginings.

On a "fine day" in 1892, on a shady piazza, Alice Austen took her own picture. This self-portrait, like an autobiographical essay, reveals a great deal about the subject. Conceived, taken, and printed by Austen, the photograph is very much her own formulation and perception.

At first glance, Austen appears to be seated in a wild, jungle-like setting. A second look, however, confirms a very different reality. She is leaning not against a rough tree trunk but rather rests upon an ornately carved wooden chair. Emerging from the seemingly overgrown background is a lush fern, a plant that flourishes in a delicately ornamented urn resting on a carved plant stand. The ground is covered not by moss and underbrush but by an intricately patterned oriental rug. The wilderness in the background belongs to the well-kept grounds that surround Clear Comfort.

Austen is dressed in a festive gown. She might be costumed for a party, yet it is somewhat out of place in the outdoor setting. The dress is covered with a delicate floral pattern. The lace neckline is modestly scooped to reveal just a curve of neck and shoulders. Puffed short sleeves, an hourglass waistline, and a flounced hemline flatter the sitter. No wonder that Austen described the dress as her favorite.[27] She wears long white gloves and holds a fan. Austen's expression is serious. Her dark eyes are dreamy and soulful. Sitting on her porch, surrounded by carefully tended house plants and by furniture that suggests Victorian middle class comfort, Austen at 26 years old appears very much a young woman concerned with the details of her environment. Clothes and accessories, hairstyle and furnishings testify to her place in the world.

The picture itself departs from much of contemporary portraiture. The formally dressed woman in the outdoor setting differs from the studio portrait in which the sitter was overwhelmed by potted palms, heavy draperies, and other theatrically derived props.

The bulk of the photographs of Alice Austen describe her middle class world of the late nineteenth to early twentieth century. Austen, who died in 1952, left behind no written record of her life on Staten Island—no diaries or letters provide personal insights or commentary about this photographer. Instead, Austen's legacy is in pictorial form, a vast array of images of her daily life, friends, family. And although Austen's photographs largely depict the private experience of a Victorian woman's home and social life, she also included her perceptions of certain public events; she witnessed and recorded the Chicago Exposition and viewed Dewey's arrival in New York; she photographed immigrants in New York and black workers in Annapolis; she preserved in pictures many of her travel experiences in Europe and the United States. Whether at home on Staten Island or in a European country, Austen's vision was distinctly shaped by her experience as a woman who came of age in Victorian America. The Alice Austen of these photographs is, however, not a provincial—she demonstrated interest in life outside the Staten Island world. She was fascinated with workers and immigrants, with presidents and peddlers. Austen loved to travel and her shots of the Netherlands and France indicate such an interest.

The photographer Alice Austen is hard to categorize. She was a contemporary of Stieglitz, Steichen, and Käsebier but she was neither a pictorialist nor a Photo-Secessionist. Austen's work is devoid of the influence of tonalism, symbolism, or impressionism, found, for example, in the work of Käsebier and Brigman. Neither was Alice Austen a casual "snapshooter." Clearly, her work reflects a professional attitude evident in her high artistic standards and her total commitment to the medium. She would seem to fit most naturally into the large group of women amateurs who photographed their domestic environments, for Austen did indeed concentrate on her personal surroundings. Yet, unlike these female contemporaries, Austen does not romanticize that world. Her direct approach differs considerably from the work of those women amateurs who sought to sentimentalize their women's sphere.

Austen's record of her family, her home, and her friends reveal as much about Austen as about the people and places of that late nineteenth century world. Hers was a traditional Victorian female perception that integrated the social ideology of the period as

Austen celebrated the private domestic sphere. Woman's place existed within the framework of home, family, close friends. At Clear Comfort, Austen could isolate herself from the chaos of the outside world. Austen, aware of the encroaching forces, preserved the quality of her ritualized existence. In a sense, the camera enabled her to protect this world from obliteration.

Austen's love for her home emerges from her many photographs. She records interior spaces from living room to bedrooms to the front porch. These pictures evoke a sense of timelessness. Clear Comfort in the 1880s existed as a charming Victorian two-story cottage. Three gabled windows poke through the long, gently sloping roof. The windows and roof line are decorated with the "gingerbread" detail of the period. Japanese wisteria and Dutchman's pipe vine almost cover the ground floor of the house. A verandah, shaded by the vines and the roof overhang, runs the length of the house. Tall, leafy trees, carefully tended shrubbery, and smooth lawns enhance the appeal of the house. The sky seems eternally clear and the sun shines brightly on Clear Comfort. Another photograph of the Austen house taken in mid-winter, shows the house covered with snow. The trees and bushes are bare, the lawn is hidden under the snow. The house itself is a dark shape nestled cozily in the icy landscape. But this is not an ominous wintry image. Instead it is a scene reminiscent of an illustrated picture book or fairy tale.

In other images of the family home, Austen focuses on the carefully and beautifully landscaped grounds. The well tended paths, gardens, trees, and shrubs dominate the space. Photographs of Clear Comfort in the springtime present a truly ordered environment in which nothing can go wrong. All who live here seem to be protected from the realities of the heartless world beyond.

Austen's photographs have become more than a visual diary of her remembrances of a privileged world. They are historical documents that present the style and fashion of a past era. Here are insights into middle class society that dispel certain widely held notions about women's activity while at the same time they feed our modern fantasies about "the good old days."

Austen's photographs of her friends and herself at play suggest the presence of many leisured hours. The images are particularly interesting as they pertain to women's leisure. These women do not merely sit in shady corners doing needlework. Rather, they play tennis, ride bicycles, go swimming, boating, and bowling. They attend dancing classes and gym classes, drive carriages, go horseback riding. They travel extensively. All attend a variety of social events— musicales, teas, costume parties, and picnics. Women joined in all these festivities. The photographs depict young women cavorting, dressing up, and generally having as much fun as the men. Indeed, Austen's record of the Staten Island social life presents a reality that is removed from the prescriptive ideology of the period. Images of women on the tennis courts or at the local bicycle club, for example, do not coincide with the observations of Dr. Arabella Kenealy who deplored physical activity for women.

> The spectacle of young women, with set jaws, eyes strained
> tensely on a ball, a fierce battle-look gripping their features,
> their hands clutching some or other implement, their arms
> engaged in striking and beating, their legs disposed in coarse
> ungainly attitudes, is an object lesson in all that is ugly in action
> and unwomanly in mode.[28]

In fact, much medical literature of the period prescribed only "passive exercise" for women in fear that more strenuous exercise detracted them from their "efficient function, and beauty of body and mind."[29] Austen's photographs question such prevailing contemporary views. The Staten Island women must surely have been aware of the negative medical attitude toward cycling yet they clearly ignored the dire warnings of the doctors.

The Staten Island women played tennis. Indeed, they engaged in competitive play. In 1892, for example, Austen photographed a tennis tournament sponsored by the Staten Island Ladies Club. Her photographs of sisters Grace and Ellen Roosevelt winning a match and of other women players on the courts provide evidence that young, middle class women were not heeding the advice of the medical establishment and others who warned women of the hazards of play and particularly of competitive involvement. Austen photographed several scenes of her friends on the tennis courts.[30] The women, dressed in long skirts, crisp shirts, hats, and even an occasional bustle, seem equally at ease playing with men or among themselves on the grass courts of private homes or at the local tennis club.

Bicycling was another sport for women that was viewed skeptically by many doctors. Although some in the medical profession encouraged bicycle riding for women as a cheap, safe, and accessible exercise, many others decried the sight of the woman cyclist. Some, for instance, saw the sport as another means to separate women from the domestic sphere; others perceived it as leading to immodest and immoral behavior because of the dress reforms women adopted for comfort and safety while riding. Even more disturbing to some physicians was the conviction that the sport encouraged the habit of masturbation.[31] These dire concerns seemed largely ignored by Austen and her set, many of whom were active and enthusiastic bicyclists.

On Staten Island one could belong to the local bicycle club. There, Austen photographed her friends who heartily endorsed the latest fad. Sportily attired men in caps and knickers and women in skirts and gibson-girl blouses, each had his or her own safety bike. In an 1895 photograph of the Staten Island Bicycle tea, eighteen members line up with their vehicles for Austen's camera. All appear serious and intense. They are ready to set out along the rough Staten Island roads on one of their regular jaunts.

Interestingly, Austen's good friend Violet Ward actually compiled a book on cycling for ladies for which Alice Austen did the illustrations.[32] In these photographs the radical bloomer costume is worn by Daisy Elliott who posed for many of the how-to-do-it pictures. The full bloomers that end below the knee and the high, laced flat heeled boots evoked intense comments by some observers. Such dress, they declared, led to promiscuity and immorality in American society. Bloomers and divided skirts, wrote E.D. Page, made women appear ridiculous.[33] Apparently, however, Daisy Elliott, a gymnastics teacher, and Violet Ward, the intrepid bicyclist, were immune to such comments. Elliott, attired in the latest bloomer outfit, smartly demonstrates proper cycling procedure and etiquette abetted by a business-like Ward.

Other of Austen's photographs depict her friends and herself at other forms of recreation. Swimming parties were popular. Young men and women in bathing costumes posed for Austen at the Staten Island shore. In a group picture of Staten Island's South Beach in 1886, Austen became part of the photograph, controlling the cable release once she was in place.

These images of well-to-do Staten Island residents involved in light-hearted leisure activities evoke a past time and place. They differ in certain respects from other of Austen's photographs that reveal a more introspective and psychological dimension. In her role as a photographer who was also a woman, Alice Austen provides glimpses into a private world that she shared with her female friends. Austen is particularly interested in women's special relationships with one another.

Austen's photograph of her friend Trude Eccleston and herself taken in 1895 in Trude's bedroom could only have been taken by a woman.[34] They appear at first to be twins, so close are the details of their appearance. Great pains were obviously taken to present an approximation of a double image. The two young women face each other. Each wears a short, simple white petticoat and a white mask that covers the upper part of the face; both women hold cigarettes loosely in their mouths. Each with one arm akimbo, their dark hair long and loose, each wearing identical black ribbed stockings and sensible shoes, they appear part of a surrealistic vision.

There are several features of the photograph that mock conventional Victorian mores. Appearing in underclothes that reveal many inches of leg is a flagrant denial of a fashion tradition that decreed modesty and decorum for women. Indeed, a sense of the erotic pervades the photograph, so removed is it from the conventional imagery. The cigarette, of course, was taboo for women in the 1890s; women could be arrested for smoking in public at this time. Long flowing hair might be appropriate for the heroine of a romantic stage play but hardly acceptable for 26 year old women. No wonder Austen has masked Trude Eccleston and herself. The two young women act up guilessly and guiltlessly before the camera. It seems that the very presence of the camera permits such behavior. The fact that the photographer is a woman allowed for an unrestrained atmosphere in which to act out their usually controlled attitudes toward society. Despite the seemingly relaxed environment that existed on Staten Island, the two women chose a private moment to express satire and sensuality unavailable through other means.

Another lighthearted pose that poked fun at middle class convention is apparent in Austen's 1890 photograph of Miss Sanford and Mrs. Snively, "two respectable residents of Bennington, Vt." Here, two mature looking women in proper afternoon attire—hats, summer suits, pinned up hair—cavort on a lawn in late afternoon. Supposedly put up to such antics by Austen and her friend, Julia Martin, the subjects of the photograph hike up their skirts in a mock jig to expose black stockings and glimpses of petticoats, hardly appropriate behavior in that small town setting. That evening, Austen photographed "Mrs. Snively, Julia, and I in Bed." This is an intimate scene. Julia appears to be asleep. Mrs. Snively is in between the two younger women; she is awake but looks dreamily off to the side. The young Alice Austen makes no pretense at being asleep. She leans her head back on her folded arms; her eyes are bright as she stares into space, seemingly absorbed in her thoughts. The large wooden bed frames the three women who are together yet separate. This unusual photograph reveals once again the private world of women as recorded by Austen. This bedroom is a special place closed to all except an "insider" like Austen, the trusted friend and photographer.

Then on a fall day in 1891, Austen and two female friends dressed up as men for one of Austen's pictures. The three assume poses they interpret as typical of the social minded young men of their set. Austen herself, on the left, stands with legs slightly apart, thumbs in vest pockets. She holds a fake cigarette. Julia Bredt is seated with one leg crossed; she leans back confidently. Julia Martin stands at the right. She attempts to glower from under a furrowed brow. Leaning forward, hands in front pockets, she strikes a pseudo-intimidating stance. The three wear hats, vests, and have acquired moustaches for the occasion. These are self-conscious men given to affectation. The women laugh at themselves and poke fun at the young men's gestures of manliness and dash. And, in a period when gender roles were being questioned, Austen evinced her confusion with such arbitrary divisions.

Austen rejected the studio in favor of the garden, the parlor, and the bedroom. The success and appeal of her photographs lie in the uninhibited approach of the photographer, unfettered by studio conventions or painterly standards. The candid qualities of the work and apparent lack of artifice reflects too the sitters' sense of comfort with the photographer and her camera.

Austen's interest in room interiors and the details of these domestic spaces continued to express her woman's experience. She, of course, did not work and spent most of her life within the limits of Staten Island. In her photographs Austen depicted that sphere. Austen's photograph of her friend, Trude Eccleston's bedroom taken in 1889, presents a young woman's personal world rarely seen by those outside her innermost circle. Here, an intricate yet delicately patterned floral wallpaper serves as background for

Trude's collection of watercolors, drawings and other carefully arranged momentoes. A mirrored oak dressing table is charmingly
cluttered with small items—a pincushion, a framed picture, a dainty
basket, tiny boxes, souvenirs of dances and travels. Victorian lamps
that frame the chest have been put to use to display other hanging
treasures. The intimate corner is furnished with a wicker chair and
sewing basket, patterned rugs, printed footstool, flowered curtains.
Although in 1889, Trude Eccleston was a young woman in her early
to mid-twenties, the dainty atmosphere of this corner seems to
belong to a much younger inhabitant. Austen and her camera have
opened the bedroom door to allow a glimpse of a very personal
space.

Austen photographed other bedrooms of her family and
friends. "Betsy Strong's Bedroom" (1892) resembles a parlor except
for a corner of the bed that protrudes into the lower right space of
the photograph. This room has a strong Victorian character filled as
it is with a carefully arranged profusion of objects that nevertheless
exude a special charm. The room reflects Betsy's femininity and her
personal interests. Travel mementoes mix with dance cards; an array
of prints and photographs suggest the occupant's taste and social experiences.

Still another picture offers a peek at a corner of Alice Austen's
own bedroom. Books, framed pictures, china plates, baskets, and
vases fill this part of her room. Again, the heavy patterns of the wallpaper and table covers serve as a background for Austen's artfully
arranged belongings. Austen's room lacks the girlish note present in
Trude's and Betsy's rooms. Here, books dominate the corner, pictures are framed and hung to suggest a permanent arrangement.
Austen's room is not readily identifiable as belonging to a Victorian
woman. Instead, this could represent a male environment of the
period.

Each room that Austen photographed exhibits the decisive im-
print of its owner. The spaces have in common the period's emphasis on the decorative and the ornate. Yet the rooms exist as
microcosms of the world of women living in the late nineteenth century. By attending carefully to the memorabilia and artifacts, the
viewer becomes aware of the women's burgeoning sense of who
they are.

The world of Frances Benjamin Johnston contrasted in many
ways with the private, well-defined space that Alice Austen inhab-

ited. A professional photographer with public studios in Washington, D.C. and later in New York City, Johnston established a wide range of personal and professional contacts. Her role in the women's network, Johnston's associations with the high echelons of the Washington government and social strata assured Johnston a much more public experience. Despite the obvious disparities, however, Johnston manifested a photographic perception essentially as Victorian and middle class as that of Austen. In addition, both women evinced a clear interest in photographing women. Unlike Austen, Johnston's work is not the intimate, feminine perspective of the Staten Island photographer that was characterized in part by young women at play and views of feminine interiors. Instead, Johnston's photographs of women defined the gender in more public terms, whether in Washington society, as celebrities, or as factory workers.

The body of the camera work of Frances Benjamin Johnston includes not only women but also photographs of blacks, native-Americans, workers, social elites, and special historical events and personalities.[35] These images are more varied than those of most of her female colleagues. Johnston's photography, however, does not define her as muckraker, social housekeeper, or radical femininst. However Progressive-minded she appears, Johnston, through her photography, emerges with a middle class consciousness similar to that of other female photographers.

In an attempt to decipher Johnston's perception of herself in her bourgeois world, it is instructive to examine two of several self-portraits. These photographs project a dual consciousness that takes into account her middle class upbringing as well as her willingness to reject certain prescriptions of that class. Which image of the photographer represents the real Frances Benjamin Johnston?

On the one hand is the Victorian matron posing for a pensive portrait. Seated in an ornate chair, almost overwhelmed by her large plumed hat and full collared fur jacket, Johnston, her head resting on one gloved hand, gazes with a sideways glance at the camera. Hat, gloves, fur, and afternoon dress all attest to her well-to-do social position. Her outdoor clothing, worn for the sitting, suggests her active life. The quiet moment of the photograph is just that, an interlude in an otherwise hectic day. The portrait, despite its outwardly conventional look, departs somewhat from the traditional studio view. The angle from which Johnston confronts the camera differs from the usual frontal image of the late nineteenth century. The side-long perspective emphasizes one half of the sitter's body, leaving the other part to disappear into the dark, shadowy background. This technique accentuates Johnston's face with its enigmatic, slightly amused expression. Within the limits of this studio photograph, Johnston manages to promote the impression of a genteel, respectable woman who, nevertheless, can still smile at herself.

This conventionally derived image is confounded by the informal setting and symbols of rebellion present in another self-portrait taken around 1896. Here, contrary to social and photographic conventions of the time, Johnston poses herself in profile surrounded by the arts and crafts type furnishings and personal memorabilia in her Washington, D.C. studio. The sitter strikes a defiant air; Johnston poses with a casually held cigarette in one hand and a beer stein in the other. Her dark-stockinged legs are crossed to reveal a white petticoat. Her blouse and skirt and perky cap further enhance the informal pose. This appears a deliberate attempt to startle the viewer by arranging three signs of inappropriate Victorian behavior for women in the one photograph—smoking, beer drinking, and exposing shapely legs. Johnston pokes fun at contemporary social conventions that restrict women's behavior.

In addition, Johnston chooses to pose before the fireplace, in effect to "claim the hearth," indicating feelings of independence and self-assertion. Surrounding her is an accumulation of evidence of her rich, adventurous, and successful life; artifacts from her travels, photographs of friends and colleagues all decorate a very intimate corner of the photographer's studio.

In these portraits, Frances Benjamin Johnston plays out pictorially the internal dilemma that confronted so many women of her generation: the rebelliousness and urge toward non-conformity conflicted with the need to live up to the expectations for Victorian womanhood. For her own part, Johnston was unconcerned with the apparent ambiguities in the two portraits. She accepted the middle class identification that included for her close family attachments, a genteel social life, and economic well-being. But the role was not so ingrained that she could not in 1896 satirize such a position. Johnson never had to make a definitive choice between middle class gentility and the bohemian avant-garde. She remained unself-consciously the genteel Victorian. Photography, however, gave

Johnston the means to occasionally confront the limitations of her society. In her unconventional self-portrait, for example, she took an opportunity to play at being rather outrageous.

In certain ways, Frances Benjamin Johnston embodied traits that defined her as a Progressive woman. As a woman of the middle class with the education, social position, leisure, and secure economic position, she found a socially accepted outlet for her energy and ambition. Jane Addams, a woman from similar social class and background to Johnston's wrote in *Twenty Years at Hull House* of the need for women to have something to do, an opportunity to "restore a balance of activity . . . where they might try out some of the things they had been taught."[36] Addams, of course, finally directed her energies to the settlement house. This indeed became a way for many Progressive women to use their education to affect turn of the century society as "mother" to the poor population of the city. Frances Benjamin Johnston did not become a Progressive reformer. However, her photographs of black students at Hampton and Tuskegee, her images of women factory workers and male mine workers display a Progressive interpretation of her world.

Ideas of change and the impulse toward reform were pervasive in 1900 and affected American political, cultural, and social life. This mentality was apparent, for example, in the muckraking journalism of Ida Tarbell and Upton Sinclair. The photographs of Jacob Riis were in this tradition; with his camera, Riis revealed the squalor and poverty in the urban ghettoes. These images touched the public feeling of "responsibility, indignation, and guilt."[37] Johnston's photographs of workers and minorities found another response in the public imagination.

A view that combined the Progressive with the Victorian emerges in Frances Benjamin Johnston's photographs of women workers. Fulfilling an assignment for *Demorest's Family Magazine*, Johnston recorded the working experience of women in a Lynn, Massachusetts shoe factory.[38] Large numbers of women had been employed in the shoe factories of Lynn since 1750. Indeed, since the 1830s these women had established a tradition of organizing and striking that culminated in a history making strike in 1860 that in turn led to the founding of the first national union of women workers in 1869.[39]

There is no doubt about Johnston's belief in the dignity and humanity of the factory worker: the intrinsic character of the

American worker emerges through the photographs. Johnston accepts these women as workers with a right to participate in the work force. Despite this outlook, Johnston's representation of the worker does not fall into the social documentation tradition of Jacob Riis and Lewis Hine. A look at Hine's photographs of women workers taken around 1907 reveals his intense social consciousness. Hine set out to expose the injustices and evils of industrial America and these effects on the work force. His intention is to foster sociological change. In Hine's pre-war images of working women, he records them at work. These women, unlike Johnston's subjects, are actually shown on the job. Hine's camera surprises them in the course of the long, arduous work day. Their expressions reveal fatigue and boredom. Hair straggles into their eyes: aprons are torn, pinned, soiled.

In contrast, Johnston's workers could be models depicting appropriate dress and behavior on the job. Here, Johnston's pictures resonate with her Victorian sensibilities. The photographer presents what her middle class public expects and desires to see. The women of Lynn are well-dressed. Their hair is smooth, their eyes are clear. Aprons are crisp, blouses and skirts tidy. Bonnets are flowered and perch jauntily on unbowed heads. In one photograph, a group of workers leaving the factory appear ready to pour tea for family or friends or browse in a downtown shop. These women are benign and content; no thought of strike clouds their thinking. The photograph suggests the Victorian ideal of womanhood; although they are hard at work during the day, these women will still fulfill the expectations of domesticity when the factory job ends. In the more likely instance that the young women are unmarried, they were expected to be pleasing and unharried enough to attract a suitor. Indeed, Johnston comforted herself with the observation that even though the women might earn as little as three dollars per week, their home lives were comfortable and secure.

Nineteenth century Victorians approved and applauded Johnston's photographs of working class men and women and blacks; they saw in these images a record that was acceptable to their class sensibilities. In the photographs that documented student life at the Hampton Institute[40] they were presented with diligent young black men and women who evidently accepted the middle class credo of hard work, religion, and character. The Hampton Institute that Frances Benjamin Johnston recorded in 1900 remains suffused in a romantic aura far removed from the harsh reality of the life faced by most black Americans at the time. There is no senseless racial violence here—no lynchings, no peonage, no urban poverty, no despair. Rather, the viewer is charmed by an environment that celebrates home and family learning. Pretty, neatly dressed women learn dressmaking and sketching. Boys gain carpentry and agricultural skills. Both men and women attend classes in arithmetic, geography, and American history. At the completion of his or her studies, the Hampton graduate might live in a white-painted, two story house complete with porch and tidy lawn, a far cry from the cabin of slavery days that Johnston also depicts in this collection of photographs. The message is clear—hard work, cleanliness, and vocational skill will raise the untutored, unskilled black to middle class respectability in true Horatio Alger-like fashion.

Johnston's carefully arranged pictures of life at Hampton shows young blacks participating in very "proper" pursuits. Serious young men strike a pose for a football team portrait. The campus-like surroundings could be at a New England school attended by white middle and upper class students. The Hampton football players are handsome, serious men, all casually yet carefully arranged by the photographer in the manner of any contemporary team portrait. In fact, only their dark skins distinguish them from Ivy League athletes. Similarly a representation of the "Indian" orchestra presents another group of young students seated on wide wooden steps holding musical instruments—violins, cello, bugle, drums. Dressed in immaculate uniforms, their hair carefully parted and their expressions intense and determined, these young musicians, like the athletes, present an appealing picture of young manhood.

Women are depicted in a like manner. They wear white starched blouses, aprons, pinafores, or tailored suits. When outdoors they add a perky bonnet atop their carefully arranged hairdos. These are pretty, serene women who diligently participate in their varied classes that range from history to sewing. These young women will graduate from Hampton prepared to teach other motivated black students or to run their own respectable middle class households.

The Hampton Institute series was taken in 1900, just five years after Booker T. Washington's speech at the Atlanta Exposition encouraging American blacks to "accommodate" themselves to white society. Well-received by whites in the North and South, Washington's remarks eased the nation's fear of a potential threat from the free black population striving to find places in a generally hostile and racist white America.

The young men and women that Johnston photographed at Hampton (and later at Tuskeegee) represented no problem at all to white society. Johnston's photographs were exactly what the white middle class wanted to see. The black subjects of her photographs celebrated the appropriate Victorian virtues and values of home, family, and tradition. Well-behaved, regimented, these men and women observed American holidays and were shown in proper Victorian settings. The black family was photographed, for example, at a white-covered dining room table—father is seated at the head with mother facing him and three decorous children seated primly and properly in between. Paintings decorate the walls, rich woodwork and bibelots add to the comfortable surroundings.

These Hampton students are far from the negative stereotype of blacks held by many in the nineteenth century of black males as slothful and lustful and black women as licentious or simple-minded. By presenting her version of diligent, respectable blacks, Johnston not only revealed the middle class nature of her own assumptions and expectations but presented white America with a portrait of a black population who ascribed to the prevailing ideology of both Victorian Americans and Progressive reformers. Both mentalities are clearly expressed in the series that demonstrate the Hampton students imbued with the impulse toward social progress and moral uplift. For reformers, educators, and administrators this portrait of the reknowned black educational institution documented what vocational training and moral teaching could accomplish.

Johnston's photographs of celebrities, socialites, and special events comprise a record of another strata of society. Yet, despite the disparity in subject matter, the impact that these images impart relates to the series on black students and women workers. Here is a history of individual accomplishment. The self-made man is represented by Andrew Carnegie, the Scottish immigrant who became an American millionaire. The inspirational figures of Booker T. Washington and George Washington Carver are included in this portfolio. Born into slavery these black men, through diligence and hard work, became leaders of their race. Mark Twain, the quintessential American writer and Joel Chandler Harris, one of the country's most beloved authors are among Johnston's subjects. The great woman is represented as well: Susan B. Anthony is pictured as very old but dignified by her accomplishments. The Theodore Roosevelt family in its various poses confirmed familial values of American society. The American public could smile at the antics of the Roosevelt children and take pride in the elegant beauty and independent spirit of Alice Roosevelt. These portraits of renowned Americans reinforced American ideals of greatness. They affirmed the Victorian conviction that the poor, the worker, the black, or the immigrant could, through sincere efforts, rise not only to middle class respectability but also attain celebrity status.

Anne Brigman is one of the few women photographers of this generation—working from the 1880s into the early twentieth century—who in her life and work manifested a radical vision. Brigman lived an idiosyncratic lifestyle that included separation from her husband, Martin Brigman, a love of the outdoors, and attempts at various forms of self-expression. In addition, she utilized the traditional language of romanticism to express her revolutionary belief in woman's freedom to follow her own destiny.

In selecting the camera to vent her creativity and her passion, Brigman believed herself to be acting in an unconventional manner for her times. She perceived the camera as outside the "prescribed mediums and methods of academic lore."[41] Contemporaries, she observed, thought the camera "a despised, a rejected thing." Yet Brigman found that this device enabled her to expand her visualization of nature and the human figure. The camera became to Brigman a "beloved thing" that gave her "a power and abandon that [she] could not have otherwise."[42] Her photographs became to her "important allegories" in which she could reveal her most personal responses to the natural wonders of the Sierras.

Brigman did not simply reproduce the natural outdoor environment that she loved so much and in which she found personal pleasure as well as inspiration. She used the scenic beauty of the California mountains to create the essence of romanticism. Inspired by her loving, intense, and intimate contact with this region, Brigman produced work that expressed her artistry as well as a moral statement.

The form and content of Brigman's photographs puts them into the artistic context of nineteenth century romanticism in America. The roots of this movement can be traced as far back as the seventeenth century in Europe from whence it evolved into a formal movement that peaked in the first half of the nineteenth century. By the later nineteenth century, however, though no longer solidified, it continued to exist in the form of the artist's personal vision. This artistic perception stressed the place of imagination and instinct over reason and relied on a special iconography to express its emotional and passionate content. Abstract patterns of storm clouds, for example, might heighten a mournful landscape in which moonlight played upon a nude (usually female) figure. Other lonely outdoor settings would be suffused in a melancholy yet sensual atmosphere shaped by the contrasting of gloomy blacks with light efects.

Anne Brigman was part of this romantic movement in art and literature that envisioned "the emancipation of slavery, the reclaiming of erotic life as part of human nature, and the reclaiming of nature itself."[43] Olive Schreiner, Margaret Sanger, Charlotte Perkins Gilman, Paula Modersohn-Becker, and Elizabeth Browning are some women who discovered in the romantic framework a particularly effective mode to impart their feelings and ideas. The American novelist, Kate Chopin, also manifested this romantic vision in her writings. The common romantic theme of the sea is a primary symbol in Chopin's novel, *The Awakening*, in which the heroine finally drowns herself.[44] Images from nature similarly pervade Brigman's photography and her passionate conception of female freedom.

Brigman's photographs of the nude posed in spectral wooded settings have little connection to the elegant mothers of Käsebier, to Austen's genteel Staten Island women, or to Johnston's glamorous celebrities. Brigman's ethereal nudes, perched in gaunt branches or beside mystical deep running mountain streams impart the photographer's concern with woman as a free spirit unencumbered by clothing or conventionally structured settings. Brigman's struggles to seek her own destiny resonate in these images. The expression of emotion and inner feelings was crucial to Brigman's art. Interestingly, this kind of romanticism was implicit in the work of most members of the Stieglitz circle. To Brigman, as to these other photographers, the subject matter attained significance only if it expressed the emotions of the photographer. This was accomplished through their selections of subject matter and enhanced by their printing methods.

"Soul of the Blasted Pine" taken by Brigman in 1909 represents many of her photographs that depict the nude female figure in a natural, outdoor setting. The figure here stands beside a great fallen tree atop a mountain slope. Turbulent storm clouds fill the big sky. The woman's head is flung back; her left arm is out-stretched, reaching toward the heavens. Her shape is, in fact, tree-like. The landscape is dark and threatening, yet a glimpse of white clouds lightens the image and the mood. The woman is not despair-ing. She is part of nature and will respond to its changes and challenges. Her extended reach toward the breaking clouds is full of meaning. In most of Brigman's nature/figure studies such a symbol of spiritual uplift is present whether in the guise of a physical move-ment (*i.e.* woman's uplifted arms), a clear white stream, a sparkling transparent bubble, or elongated branches.

Brigman placed her subjects within a primeval landscape. The turbulent skies, the threatening cliffs, the wildness of the trees all could be elements of a primitive time. Art historians have identified similar proclivities in nineteenth and twentieth century painting. Albert Pinkham Ryder, Edwin Dickinson, Marsden Hartley, and John Marin, for example, evoked such imagery. But while these art-ists were concerned with broad symbolic, albeit emotional state-ments, Brigman narrowed her message to a personal one that linked her to women's struggles for emancipation and growth.

A favorite way for Brigman to assert her feelings photograph-ically was to use the primeval landscape as a background for the female nude. She was one of the few nineteenth century women photographers to consistently employ the female nude in her work. Victorian morality restricted most women artists and photographers from approaching nudity in their imagery. Yet male photographers, just as male painters, frequently used nude women as subjects. Steichen, Demachy, White, Stieglitz and others produced studies of the female nude. Their work, in fact, resembles stylistically the nudes done by Brigman. Like Brigman, these male photographers were pictorialists and Photo-Secessionists; their work was affected by the symbolist and romantic traditions. In comparing the photo-graphs of the men and Brigman, however, significant differences surface. Steichen's nudes, for example, are not placed in natural outdoor settings; they were photographed in the studio. The women in these images are bent over. Their faces are hidden and their backs are often to the camera. Instead of the free spirit evoked by Brigman's women, Steichen's images recall interpretations of a disgraced Eve.

Robert Demachy's photograph, "Struggle" (1904) is of a nude woman in a struggle to overcome or hold back a wave of enormous strength and proportion; the figure will be engulfed by this monstrous force. Symbolist and pictorialist in tone, the study pictures woman about to be conquered rather than challenged by nature. Woman is not, as in Brigman's work, at one with nature. Neither does the Demachy subject find liberation in the oceanic onslaught.

Still other male photographers photographed nude women. In C. Puyo's "Nude Against the Light" (1906) a child-woman with flowers in her hair poses seductively. This model is indoors, seated before a large multipaned window. Puyo presents a male fantasy far from Brigman's subjects who strive for physical and personal emancipation.

Clarence White and Alfred Stieglitz did an experimental series of photographs to test lenses and printing materials. This group of images included many nude studies. Artistically executed, these photographs are not concerned with the intense expression of liberation that infuses Brigman's work.

The work of Austen, Johnston, Käsebier, and Brigman has been specifically cited here to suggest new readings of their photographs. Most women photographers lived and worked within the prescribed domestic traditions and adhered to a middle class ideology that implied morality, restraint, and order. Yet each followed some independent form of behavior that symbolized a personal kind of rebellion. In their particular rejection of some aspect of mainstream behavior, each was emboldened by the camera. Indeed, photography became, in effect, a part of the household. It allowed them to stay in touch with domesticity while establishing themselves as artists. Certainly, as creative women in the late nineteenth and early twentieth centuries, they were asserting their willingness to overturn certain preconceived traditions and roles. As Victorian women their subject matter was often delineated by the persistence of the cults of true womanhood and domesticity. As photographers and artists they could glorify certain aspects of the system (as, for example, Käsebier did in her motherhood series), satirize it (as Austen did), or even express a more extreme vision in the manner of Anne Brigman. But all women photographers of this period accepted photography's challenge and in so doing found a means to transcend the limitations of nineteenth century domesticity.

Through their work and their lives, women photographers exemplified in many ways a new type of woman of the period—the professional woman. Single, educated, committed to their work, financially independent yet attracted to a woman's culture, the lives of women photographers paralleled those of women in other professions. Their choice of photography made the professional life somewhat easier, however. The dilemma over career and marriage, for example, was often avoided; women photographers were able to pursue a career without necessarily leaving the domestic environment. Even for amateurs the camera gave women the chance to experiment with an example of the new technology while affirming domestic values in the pictures they took. If indeed every age needs an image, then the late Victorians found their reflection in the photography produced by the women of that period. And, for the most part, the women photographers confirmed the prevailing societal view in their work.

It becomes obvious that women established a significant presence during the early years of photography. As professionals, as amateurs, and as artists they contributed a body of work to American culture. As middle class women they were connected to the experience of many others like them who began breaking the social restraints imposed by Victorian morality and ideology. The lives and work of female photographers provide insights into what constituted the reality for creative, productive women of the period. In light of these factors, how does one account for the absence of these nineteenth century women from the history of mainstream photography? Photography was, of course, dominated by men. Thus, women appropriated the camera to relate their special experience. They utilized the technique, style, and technologies of men. Indeed, women used the men themselves when necessary. Women art photographers took advantage of the possibilities offered by Alfred Stieglitz and many amateur and professional women photographers broke into photography through their photographer husbands.

In addition, the relationship of women photographers to the dominant culture emerged as distinctive. Women artists have always been considered marginal members of society. Female photographers, however, were doubly marginal for they were women artists in an art form that was itself peripheral. Because of this status, women photographers created a special language for expressing themselves, a form of self-representation in which their pictorial work remained inseparable from their class and gender. To be sure, these images must now be carefully decoded to arrive at the nineteenth century attitudes and ideologies they represent. The imagery they produced linked them to the domestic and this apparently diminished their role in photography and eroded the judgement of their artistic contribution. The twentieth century art world that came more and more to celebrate the concepts of modernism, looked down upon an art that continued to be rooted in pictorialism and dedicated to nineteenth century domestic ideals and Progressive values.

Despite the judgement of the dominant culture as it evolved with the turn of the century, women managed to make their experience in photography a positive one. They used domesticity, art, and technology for their own needs. In so doing they defined themselves as women who were independent rather than idiosyncratic, rebellious but not radical. Theirs were small revolts that expressed a desire to enlarge their domestic environments. For each women who picked up and used a camera, it meant a step toward becoming a different kind of woman.

The story of this first generation of women and photography is one that tells of the interaction between changing attitudes toward domesticity, modern technology and the presence of a new kind of leisure that rearranged home responsibilities. In the end, women photographers generally honored family expectations but not without taking an occasional swipe at the prevailing ideology. Remember, for example, the playful poses of Alice Austen and friends and Frances Benjamin Johnston's self-portrait.

Underlying the debates over the nature of photography and concerns over women's role in the profession was a theme that connected the dominant belief in true womanhood with the improved technology and social ideologies of the new industrial age. Here was an alliance between women and technology that encouraged not the feminization of photography, implying a lowered status of the art, but instead related photography to the social changes of its age. Not usually feminists, these women photographers nevertheless expressed themselves as women through their remarkable imagery. In articulating and transmitting these common experiences they connected themselves to the essence of the feminist tradition in America. In this process they essentially cleared a path for women's involvement in photography in the nineteenth century and thereafter.

Notes

Introduction

1. See Janet Malcolm, *Diana and Nikon* (Boston: David R. Godine, 1980) for an insightful commentary on this golden age from the perspective of a photography critic.

2. An exhibition of women's painting, "Women Artists, 1550-1950," appeared at the Brooklyn Museum, October-November, 1977. Photography exhibitions have recently featured the work of women. Note, for example, "Recollections: Ten Women of Photography" at the International Center of Photography, September-November, 1979. Germaine Greer's *The Obstacle Race* (New York: Farrar, Straus, Giroux, 1979) stands as a groundbreaking work on women artists in Western painting. Greer's feminist interpretation sheds new light on a long ignored historical tradition of woman painters.

3. Beaumont Newhall, *The History of Photography* (New York: The Museum of Modern Art, 1964, 1982).

4. William Welling, *Photography in America* (New York: Thomas Y. Crowell, 1978).

5. See, for example, Robert Taft, *Photography and the American Scene* (New York: The Macmillan Company, 1938). More recent literature includes Arnold Gassan, *A Chronology of Photography* (Athens, Ohio: Handbook Company, 1972).

6. These books include: Ann Novotny, *Alice's World* (Old Greenwich, Connecticut: The Chatham Press, 1976); Pete Daniel and Raymond Smock, *A Talent for Detail* (New York: Harmony Books, 1974); Alexander Alland, Sr., *Jessie Tarbox Beals, First Woman News Photographer* (New York: Camera/Graphic Press, Ltd., 1978).

7. Anne Tucker, *The Woman's Eye* (New York: Alfred A. Knopf, 1976).

8. Ibid., p. 1.

9. Greer, *The Obstacle Race*, p. 6

10. See, for instance, Charlotte Strieffer Rubinstein, *American Women Artists* (New York: Avon Books, 1982). Rubinstein's book includes women artists from Native-Americans to feminist artists of the 1970s and 1980s. It is important because it tells the reader that women were indeed there. As a broad overview it has its limitations, however.

11. See Linda Nochlin, "Why Have There Been No Great Women Artists?" *Art and Sexual Politics*, eds. Thomas Hess and Elizabeth Baker (New York: Collier Books, 1973, 1975).

12. Mary Walsh in *Doctors Wanted: No Women Need Apply* (New Haven and London: Yale University Press, 1977) provides a clear explanation of the problems faced by women desirous of entering the medical profession. Also, see the more recent book by Regina Markell Morantz-Sanchez, *Sympathy and Science: Women Physicians in American Medicine* (New York: Oxford University Press, 1985).

13. For examples of this photography see *Camera Work* published by Alfred Stieglitz from 1903 to 1917. Also see the Joseph Byron Collection of photographs at the Museum of the City of New York.

14. Malcolm, *Diana and Nikon*, p. 3.

Chapter 1

1. Nancy Tomes and Joan Jacobs Brumberg in "Women in the Professions: A Research Agenda for American Historians," *Reviews in American History* (1982), pp. 275-296, discuss the notion of an historical "fit" as applied to the feminization of certain professions.

2. "Kodak Advertisements," *The Photography*, II (December 3, 1904), p. 90.

3. See letter from Eva Watson-Schütze to Francis Benjamin Johnston, 1897, Francis Benjamin Johnston Collection, Manuscript Division, Library of Congress.

4. Peter G. Filene, *Him, Her, Self: Sex Roles in Modern America* (New York, London: Harcourt, Brace Jovanovich, 1974, 1975), Chapter One.

5. See Karen Blair, *The Clubwoman as Feminist* (New York, London: Holmes and Meier Publishers, Inc., 1980) for details on the clubwoman. Filene, *Him, Her, Self* also deals with this subject.

6. Filene, *Him, Her, Self*, p. 24.

7. *Statistics of Women at Work 1900* (Washington: Government Printing Office, 1907), Unpublished Information Derived from 12th Census: 1900. Also, see Mary Roth Walsh, *Doctors Wanted: No Women Need Apply* (New Haven and London: Yale University Press, 1977).

8. Filene, *Him, Her, Self*, p. 31.

9. Hilda Smith, quoted in Filene, *Him, Her, Self, p. 26*.

10. See Jane Addams, *Twenty Years at Hull House* (New York: Signet Classic, 1960). Also see Joyce Antler, "After College What? New Graduates and the Family Claim," *American Quarterly* 32 (Fall, 1980), pp. 409-434 for an insightful discussion of this dilemma faced by many nineteenth century women.

11. Other decorative arts included shell work, wax modelling, paper mosaic.

12. Crafts made by women (including quilts) have recently been exhibited in major museums and galleries. Note, for example, the exhibition at the Whitney Museum, "American Folk Painters of Three Centuries," (February 26-May 13, 1980).

13. These descriptions of photography can be found throughout the literature of the period. See, for example, Catharine Filene, *Careers for Women* (Boston and New York: Houghton Mifflin Company, 1920), p. 63; Mrs. M.L. Rayne, *What Can a Woman Do?* (Detroit, Chicago, Cincinnati, St. Louis; F.B. Dickerson and

Co., 1884), p. 126; M.A. Root, *The Camera and the Pencil* (New York: D. Appleton and Co., 1864), pp. 37-39.

14. "Early Days of Amateur Photography," *Anthony's Photographic Bulletin* 120 (1889), pp. 146-148.

15. William Welling, *Photography in America* (New York: Thomas Y. Crowell Company, 1978), p. 56.

16. Amy S. Doherty, "19th Century Women Photographers," *The Blatant Image* 1(1981), p. 24.

17. Welling, *Photography in America*, p. 56.

18. Robert Taft, *Photography and the American Scene* (New York: The MacMillan Company, 1938), p. 134.

19. Welling, *Photography in America*, p. 91.

20. Emma Freeman of Humboldt, California, for example, managed her husband's studio during his absences. After their divorce, Emma successfully ran the photography business. One of her special projects was doing portraits of women. Also see, "Story of a Woman's Help," *The Photographic-Art Journal* 8 (June 1, 1888), pp. 85-86.

21. The wet plate process was used in the early days of photography. A collodion emulsion that included iodide potassium coated the glass plate. The plate was then sensitized at once with silver nitrate and, while still wet, put in the camera. Experiments in 1855 and 1860 led to the development of the fast gelatin silver bromide plate. These plates were quicker and simplified the printing process. This technique was especially significant because it led to the instantaneous photography of the 1880s. See Taft, *Photography and the American Scene*, for further details.

22. Taft, *Photography and the American Scene*, p. 208.

23. This innovative camera also possessed an improved method of controlling exposure which meant that in addition to diminished bulk, the new device produced more successful images.

24. "The New Photography," *The Photographic Times* (1880), p. 79.

25. Mary Thomas to M. Carey Thomas quoted in Edith Finch, *Carey Thomas of Bryn Mawr* (New York: Harper, 1947), p. 49.

26. Beaumont, Newhall, *The History of Photography* (New York: The Museum of Modern Art, 1964), p. 129.

27. Welling, *Photography in America*, p. 285.

28. Emerson quoted in Newhall, p. 97.

29. See Beaumont Newhall for details of this debate. Also Weston Naef, *The Collection of Alfred Stieglitz* (New York: Viking Press, The Museum of Modern Art, 1978) for a good explication of aesthetic debates in photography during this period.

30. Giles Edgerton, "The Lyric Quality in the Photo-Secession Art of George Seeley," *The Craftsman* 14 (Apr.-Sept. 1908), p. 303.

31. Joseph Keiley, "Philadelphia Salon-Origin and Influence," *Camera Notes* 2 (January, 1899), p. 39.

32. See Chapter VI, this volume, "Female Visions as Social History," for a closer analysis of this question.

33. Robert Atwan, Donald McQuade, John W. Wright, *Edsels, Luckies, and Frigidaires* (New York: Dell, 1979), p. 2.

34. Kathryn Weibel, *Mirror, Mirror* (Garden City, New York: Anchor Books, 1977), p. 149.

35. Singer, Charles, *A History of Technology* vol. 5 (Oxford: Oxford University Press, 1958), p. 560.

36. Atwan, *Edsels*, p. 124.

37. Carl W. Ackerman, *George Eastman* (Boston and New York: Houghton, Mifflin Company, 1930), pp. 52-53.

38. Reese V. Jenkins, *Images and Enterprise: Technology and the American Photographic Industry (1839-1925)* (Baltimore and London: Johns Hopkins University Press, 1975), pp. 116-117.

39. Walter Dill Scott quoted in Weibel, *Mirror, Mirror*, p. 155.

40. Frank Presbrey, *The History and Development of Advertising* (New York: Greenwood Press, 1968), p. 360.

41. Jenkins, *Images and Enterprise*, p. 112.

42. In 1888, George Eastman's "primer" on the Kodak announced that "today photography has been reduced to a cycle of

three operations: 1-Pull the String, 2-Turn the Key, 3-Press the Button."

43. See, for example, *The Ladies Home Journal* of the period, 1884-1890.

44. Presbrey, *History and Development of Advertising*, p. 367.

45. Welling, *Photography in America*, pp. 285, 321.

46. "The Camera Girl," *The Photo-American* 11 (October, 1900), p. 320.

47. "The Deadly Kodak Girl," *The Photographic Times* 21 (October 16, 1891), p. 581.

48. E.S. Turner, *The Shocking History of Advertising* (New York: E.P. Dutton, 1953), p. 185.

49. *Kodakery* published by Eastman Kodak Company, September 1913-August, 1923.

Chapter 2

1. *Statistics of Women at Work* 1900 (Washington: Government Printing Office, (907), Unpublished Information Derived From 12th Census: 1900.

2. Hersey, Heloise, "The Educated Woman of Tomorrow," *The Outlook* (August 1, 1903), p. 841.

3. "Woman and Business," *The Century* 23 (1881-1882), p. 954.

4. "The Day of the Clever Woman," *The Critic* 544 (July 23, 1892), p. 49.

5. Catherine Filene, ed., *Careers for Woman* (Boston and New York: Houghton Mifflin Company, 1920).

6. M.L. Rayne, *What Can a Woman Do?* (Detroit, Chicago, Cincinnati, St. Louis: F.B. Dickerson and Company, 1884), p. 3.

7. Joyce Antler, *The Educated Woman and Professionalization: The Struggle For a New Feminine Identity, 1890-1920* (Ph.D. Dissertation, State University of New York at Stony Brook, 1977), pp. 85-86.

8. Julia Ward Howe quoted in Karen J. Blair, *The Clubwoman as a Feminist* (New York: Holmes and Meier, 1980), p. 131, fn. 56.

9. Blair, *Clubwoman as Feminist*, p. 51.

10. "The Day of the Clever Woman," *The Critic* No. 544 (July 23, 1892), p. 49.

11. "Women and Their Work," *The Outlook* (October 1, 1904), p. 257.

12. "The Return of the Business Woman," *The Ladies Home Journal* (March, 1900), p. 142.

13. *Anthony's Photographic Bulletin* (1884), p. 171.

14. William Welling, *Photography in America* (New York: Thomas Crowell Company, 1978), p. 291. The *Chicago Sun* also noted that the fad had come to stay. See, for example, Carl Ackerman, *George Eastman* (Boston and New York: Houghton Mifflin Company, 1930), p. 87.

15. "Photography for the Girls," *Photographic Times and American Photographer* 17 (August 24, 1888), pp. 404-405.

16. "The New York Exhibition of Photographs," *Photo-American* 10 (January, 1898), p. 84.

17. "World's Photography Focuses," *The Philadelphia Photographer* 17 (September, 1907), p. 49.

18. "Items of Interest—Empress as Expert Photographer," *Photo-American* 17 (September, 1907), p. 77.

19. "Royalty's Exhibit," *The Professional Photographer*, 3 (Feb., 1898), p. 74.

20. Alan Thomas, *Time in a Frame* (New York: Schocken Books, 1977), p. 84.

21. Joseph T. Keiley, "The Philadelphia Salon," *Camera Notes* 2 (January, 1899), p. 115.

22. Arnold Genthe, *As I Remember* (New York: Reynal and Hitchcock, 1936), p. 261.

23. *The Professional Photographer* 4 (May, 1899), p. 209.

24. Marion Foster Washburne, "A New Profession for Women," *Godey's Magazine* 134 (February, 1897), p. 127.

25. J. Pitcher Spooner, "Only a Photographer," *Photographic Mosaics* (1899), p. 54.

26. Mary McPhail, "Anne Brigman," *San Francisco Examiner* (November 23, 1924), n.p.

27. F. Holland Day, "Art and the Camera," *Camera Notes* 1 (October, 1897), p. 22.

28. See, for example, the advertising in *The Ladies Home Journal* from the mid 1880s on.

29. Alice Hughes, *My Father and I* (London: Thornton Butterworth, Ltd., 1923), p. 181.

30. "A Woman's Success as a Photographer. *The Amateur Photographer*, 2 (December 5, 1884), p. 142.

31. Elizabeth Flint Wade, "The Camera as a Source of Income Outside the Studio," *Photographic Times*, 24 (June 8, 1894), p. 358.

32. Clarisse Moore, "Women Experts in Photography," *Cosmopolitan* 14 (1893), p. 584.

33. "The Camera Has Opened a New Profession for Women," *New York Times* (April 20, 1912), p. 12.

34. Ibid.

35. Ibid.

36. Mary Patten, "The Photographer," in Filene, *Careers for Women*, p. 72.

37. J.H. Parsons, "Women as Photographers," in Rayne, *What Can a Woman Do?* p. 127.

38. "Now Then Try It," *Photographic Mosaics* (1888), p. 313.

39. Hughes, *My Father and I*, p. 111.

40. See Catherine Weed (Barnes) Ward's several articles written from 1890-1891.

41. Rayne, *What Can a Woman Do?* p. 127.

42. Jessie Tarbox Beals, "The Garden Photographer, in Filene, *Careers for Women*, p. 216.

43. Mary C. Bisland, "Current Topics of Interest to Women," *The Illustrated American* (December 31, 1892), p. 698.

44. Edward Mott Woolley, "The Best Paid Occupations for Women," *Every Week* (August 9, 1895), p. 15.

45. Weston Naef, *The Collection of Alfred Stieglitz: Fifty Pioneers of Modern Photography* (New York: Viking Press, A Studio Book, The Metropolitan Museum of Art), p. 100.

46. Robert Smuts, *Women and Work in America* (New York: Columbia University Press, 1959), p. 25.

47. Heloise E. Hersey, "The Educated Woman of Tomorrow," *The Outlook* (August 1, 1903), p. 841.

48. "Women and Their Work," *The Outlook* (October 1, 1904), p. 257.

49. "Amateur Photography—A Woman's View of the Art of Which Her Husband is a Devotee," *Wilson's Photographic Magazine* 27 (February 1, 1890), p. 259.

50. Louise P. Yellott, "Some Experiences of a Martyr," *Photo-American* 9 (July, 1890), p. 259.

51. Julia Crane, "That Horrid Photography," *Photographic Mosaics* (1891), p. 91.

52. Welling, *Photography in America*, p. 297.

53. F.M. Somers, "The Ladies—and How To Deal With Them," *Photographic Mosaics* (1895), p. 260.

54. A. Lee Snelling, "More Art and More Women Wanted in Our Art." *Photographic Mosaics* (1895), p. 120.

55. Ibid.

56. Mrs. A.D. Waterbury, "A Menu Hint to Housewives," *Photo American* 3 (April, 1897), p. 311.

57. "Women's Work in Photography," *The Photographic Times and Amateur Photographer* 17 (March 18, 1887), p. 127.

58. *Photographic Times*, 21 (June 19, 1891), p. 299.

59. Hersey, *The Outlook*, (October 1, 1904), p. 841.

60. "Gossip," *The Photographic Art Journal* (March, 1851), p. 188.

61. M.A. Root, *The Camera and the Pencil* (New York: D. Appleton and Company, 1864), p. 26.

62. Ibid.

63. Ibid., p. 27.

64. Julia Margaret Cameron, "Annals of My Glass House," *Photography in Print*, ed., Vicki Goldberg (New York: Simon and Schuster, 1981), p. 186.

65. See, for example, Barbara Welter, "The Cult of True Womanhood," *Dimity Convictions: The American Woman in the Nineteenth Century* (Athens: Ohio University Press, 1976), for a fine analysis of the perception of women during the mid-nineteenth century.

66. Root, *Camera and the Pencil*, p. 26.

67. "Studio Stories," *The Photogram* 4 (February, 1906) pp. 266-267.

68. "Prominent Photographers of The Year," *The Professional Photographer*, 4 (February, 1899), p. 48.

69. "Studio Stories," *The Photographer* 4 (November 21, 1965), p. 53.

70. H.P. Robinson quoted in Beamont Newhall, *The History of Photography* (New York: The Museum of Modern Art, 1964), p. 104.

71. Frances Benjamin Johnston, "What a Woman Can Do With a Camera," *The Ladies Home Journal* (September, 1897), p. 7.

72. Rayne, *What Can a Woman Do?* p. 126.

73, Margaret Bisland, "A Home Photographic Studio," *The American Amateur Photographer* (October, 1890), pp. 384-385.

74. Joyce Antler, "After College What?: New Graduates and The Family Claim," *American Quarterly* 32 (Fall, 1980), p. 410.

75. *The Craftsman* (1907-1908), p. 75.

76. Ibid., p. 157.

77. Antler, "After College What?" p. 430.

Chapter 3

1. In *The Positive Image* I discuss women photographers who are white and from the middle class. It is important to note that black women played a significant role in the history of photography. In *Viewfinders: Black Women Photographers* (New York: Dodd, Mead and Company, 1986), Jeanne Moutoussamy-Ashe describes the experience of black women photographers from 1839 to 1985. From the south as well as from large cities, these women were usually educated and often from the middle class. Many learned photography from photographer husbands.

2. Jill Conway, "Women Reformers and American Culture, 1870-1930," *Our American Sisters*, eds. Jean Friedman and William Slade (Boston: Allyn and Baum, 1976), p. 306.

3. Sondra R. Herman, "Loving Courtship or the Marriage Market? The Ideal and Its Critics, 1871-1911," *Our American Sisters*, p. 235.

4. Roberta Frankfort, *Collegiate Women* (New York: New York University Press, 1977). See section on Alice Freeman Palmer.

5. Charlotte Perkins Gilman, *The Living of Charlotte Perkins Gilman* (New York: Harper Colophon Books, 1885, 1963).

6. Blanche Weisen Cook, "Female Support Networks and Political Activism: Lillian Ward, Crystal Eastman, Emma Goldman," *"A Heritage of Her Own*, eds. Nancy Cott and Elizabeth Pleck (New York: Simon and Schuster, 1979), pp. 412-444.

7. M.F. Washburne, "A New Profession for Women," *Godey's Magazine* 134 (February, 1897), p. 124.

8. Letter from F.D. Todd (editor, *Photo-Beacon*) to Frances Benjamin Johnston, June 5, 1900, Frances Benjamin Johnston Collection, Manuscript Division, Library of Congress.

9. Patricia A. Palmieri, "Patterns of Achievement of Single

Academic Women at Wellesley College, 1880-1920," *Frontiers* 1 (Spring, 1980), pp. 63-67.

10. Letters between Anderson Johnston and Frances Benjamin Johnston, July 7, 1900 and August, 1905, Frances Benjamin Johnston Collection, Manuscript Division, Library of Congress.

11. Letters from Mrs. Johnston to Frances Benjamin Johnston, August, 1905 and June, 1907, Frances Benjamin Johnston Collection, Manuscript Division, Library of Congress.

12. See Anne Novotny, *Alice's World* (Old Greenwich, Connecticut: The Chatham Press, 1976), for biographical details on Alice Austen.

13. Palmieri, *Frontiers*, (Spring 1980), p. 7.

14. Novotny, *Alice's World* p. 60. In the nineteenth century, women in intimate relationships with other women were often lesbians. Austen was in all probability a lesbian. Ann Novotny in "Alice Austen's World," *Heresies 3, Lesbian Art and Artists* (Fall, 1977), pp. 28-32, refers to Gertrude Tate as Austen's lover noting as well that Tate's family was appalled at her decision to move in with Austen in 1917. The same article refers to the likelihood that Frances Benjamin Johnston was also a lesbian "although her private life remains hidden behind a veil of Victorian manners."

15. Mary Ryan, *Womanhood in America* (New York: Franklin Watts, 1979), p. 142.

16. Lillian Faderman in *Surpassing the Love of Men* (New York: William Morrow and Company, 1981), describes the "Boston marriage," a late nineteenth century phenomenon, as "a long-term monogamous relationship between two otherwise unmarried women. The women were usually feminists, New Women, often pioneers in a profession. They were also very involved in culture and social betterment, and these female values . . . formed a strong basis of their life together." p. 190.

17. Washburn, *Godey's* (February, 1899), p. 124.

18. See Palmieri, *Frontiers*, (Spring, 1980), for a more extensive discussion.

19. Karen Blair, *The Clubwoman as Feminist* (New York, London: Holmes and Meier, 1980), p. 59.

20. Personal unpublished notes of Mina Turner, daughter-in-law of Gertrude Kasebier.

21. William Innes Homer, *A Pictorial Heritage: The Photographs of Gertrude Käsebier* (University of Delaware and Delaware Art Museum, 1979).

22. Blair, *Club Woman as Feminist*, p. 15.

23. William O'Neill, "Divorce in the Progressive Era," *The American Family in Social-Historical Perspective*, ed., Michael Gordon (New York: St. Martin's Press, 1973), pp. 251-266.

24. See this volume, Chapter VI, "Female Visions as Social History," for further discussion.

25. Therese Thau Heyman, *Anne Brigman* (Oakland Museum, 1974), p. 8.

26. Ibid., p. 6.

27. Anne Brigman, *Songs of a Pagan* (Calswell, Idaho: The Caxton Printers, 1949), p. 34.

28. Jessie Tarbox Beals quoted in Alexander Alland Sr., *Jessie Tarbox Beals* (New York: Camera: Graphic Press, 1978) p. 75.

29. Ibid., p. 65.

30. Herman, *Our American Sisters*, p. 238.

31. "A Woman Worth Knowing," *The Photographic Times* 21 (May 29, 1891), p. 261.

32. Letter from Catherine Weed Ward to Frances Benjamin Johnston, April 25, 1905, Frances Benjamin Johnston Collection, Manuscript Division, Library of Congress.

33. Carolyn Heilbrun, "Hers," *New York Times* (March 5, 1981), p. 33. Professor Heilbrun offers some interesting insights into successful marriages when both partners are successful.

34. "Martin Schütze," *New York Times* (July 21, 1951), p. 19.

35. Jean F. Block, *Eva Watson-Schütze: Chicago Photo-Secessionist* (University of Chicago Press, 1985).

36. Joseph T. Keiley, *Camera Work* (1905), p. 25.

37. Letter from Eva Watson-Schütze to Frances Benjamin Johnston, 1893, Frances Benjamin Johnston Collection, Manuscript Division, Library of Congress.

38. Thomas Woody, *A History of Women's Education in the United States* vol. 2 (New York, Lancaster, Pennsylvania: The Science Press, 1929), p. 143.

39. Washburne, *Godey's* (February, 1897), p. 24.

40. Block, *Eva Watson-Schütze*, p. 2.

41. Ibid.

42. For further details see Toby Quitslund, "Her Feminine Colleagues," *Women Artists in Washington Collections* (University of Maryland Art Gallery, 1979).

43. Nancy Hale, *Mary Cassatt* (Garden City, New York: Doubleday, 1975), p. 32.

44. Ibid.

45. Germaine Greer, *The Obstacle Race* (New York: Farrar, Straus, Giroux, 1979), p. 317-318.

46. For a good first hand description of the Fleury studio see Cecilia Beaux, *Background With Figures* (Boston and Newport, s.d., 1930).

47. Clarisse Moore, "Women Experts in Photography," *Cosmopolitan* 14 (March, 1893), p. 580.

48. Frances Benjamin Johnston, "What a Woman Can Do With a Camera," *The Ladies Home Journal* (1898), p. 7.

49. Catherine Weed Barnes, "Women as Professional Photographers," *Wilson's Photographic Magazine* (1891).

50. Ward also had training in chemistry and recommended this knowledge for the well prepared photographers.

51. Käsebier described the antiphotography attitude in her art teachers. See Gertrude Käsebier, "Studies in Photography," *Photographic Times* 30 (June, 1898), pp. 269-272.

52. Ibid.

53. Ibid., p. 270.

54. Letter from Virginia Sharp to Frances Benjamin Johnston, June 13, 1900, Manuscript Division, Library of Congress.

55. "A Lady Amateur," p. 118.

56. Jane Addams, *Twenty Years at Hull House* (New York: New American Library, 1910, 1961), p. 61.

57. "A Lady Amateur," *Photogrpahic Times* p. 117.

58. John S. Haller and Robin M. Haller, *The Physician and Sexuality in Victorian America* (New York: W.W. Norton and Company, 1974), p. 37.

59. "A Lady Amateur," p. 117.

60. *Photographic Times* 20 (May 30, 1890), p. 263.

61. Barnes, *Wilson's Photogrpahic Magazine* (1891), p. 686.

62. "Women as Photographers," *Anthony's Photographic Bulletin* 22 (1891), p. 276.

63. Catherine Weed Barnes, "Photography from a Woman's Standpoint," *Anthony's Photographic Bulletin* 20 (1890) pp. 41-42.

64. See "Women as Photographers," *Anthony's Photographic Bulletin* p. 276 and Catherine Weed Barnes, "Women as Photographers," *Photographic Mosaics* (1891), p. 121.

65. Letter from Snowdon Ward to Frances Benjamin Johnston, December 29, 1893. Other letters (see Catherine Weed Ward to Frances Benjamin Johnston, April 25, 1901), affirm this.

66. Barnes, *Wilson's Photographic Magazine* (1891), p. 688.

67. Barnes, *Photographic Mosaics*, (1891) p. 118.

68. Barnes, *Wilson's Photographic Magazine*, 1 (1891), pp. 686-687.

69. Barnes, *Photographic Mosaics*, (1891), p. 119.

70. Sheila Rothman, *Woman's Proper Place* (New York: Basic Books, 1978), p. 63.

Chapter 4

1. Anthea Callen, *Women Artists of the Arts and Crafts Movement*, 1870-1914, (New York: Pantheon Books, 1979), p. 9.

2. See, for example, Germaine Greer, *The Obstacle Race* (New York: Farrar Straus Giroux, 1979) and Linda Nochlin, "Why Have There Been No Great Women Artists?", Thomas Hess and Elizabeth Baker, eds.) *Art and Sexual Politics* (New York: Collier Books, 1973).

3. Nancy Cott, Carroll Smith-Rosenberg, Blanche Weisen Cook agree that women's networks flourished throughout American history. Cott, *The Bonds of Womanhood* (New Haven: Yale University Press, 1977) examines the bonding pattern among women in the eighteenth and nineteenth centuries and notes the evolvement of a group consciousness of sisterhood that provided the impulse for nineteenth century feminism. Smith-Rosenberg, "The Female World of Love and Ritual," eds., Nancy Cott and Elizabeth Pleck *A Heritage of Her Own* (New York: Simon and Schuster, 1979), pp. 311-342, views nineteenth century friendship and rituals at all stages of the female life cycle and notes how this activity changed and enlarged historical perspectives on Victorian sexuality while Cook in "Female Support Networks and Political Activism: Lillian Wald, Crystal Eastman, Emma Goldman," *A Heritage of Her Own*, pp. 412-444, has insightfully noted the strength political activists derived from female associations. Similarly. Mary Ryan. "The Power of Women's Networks: A Case Study of Female Moral Reform in Antebellum America," *Feminist Studies* 5 (Spring, 1979), pp. 68-85, analyzes women's networks in the Female Moral Reform Society.

4. Rozsika Parker and Griselda Pollock, *Old Mistresses: Women, Art and Ideology* (New York: Pantheon Books, 1984).

5. Karen J. Blair, *The Clubwoman as Feminist* (new York, London: Holmes and Meier Publishers, Inc., 1980).

6. Letter from George Eastman to Frances Benjamin Johnston, February 3, 1891, Frances Benjamin Johnston Collection, Manuscript Division, Library of Congress.

7. *Brooklyn Eagle* (June 21, 1897), n.p. Clipping in Frances Benjamin Johnston Collection, Manuscript Division, Library of Congress.

8. *The Photographic Times* (July 3, 1891), Clipping in Frances Benjamin Johnston Collection, Manuscript Division, Library of Congress.

9. "Women About Town," *The Washington Post* (January 5, 1893), n.p. Clipping from Frances Benjamin Johnston Collection, Manuscript Division, Library of Congress.

10. Pete Daniel and Raymond Smock, *A Talent for Detail* (New York: Harmony Books, 1974), p. 87.

11. Letter from Boys Military Clubs, San Francisco California to Frances Benjamin Johnston, March 3, 1904, Frances Benjamin Johnston Collection, Manuscript Division, Library of Congress.

12. "Work of District Women," *The Washington Post* (April 2, 1893), n.p. Clipping in Frances Benjamin Johnston Collection, Manuscript Division, Library of Congress.

13. Toby Quitslund, "Her Feminine Colleagues," *Women Artists in Washington Collections* (University of Maryland Art Gallery, 1979), p. 97.

14. Letter from Ellen Henrotin to Frances Benjamin Johnston, April 12, 1900, Frances Benjamin Johnston Collection, Library of Congress.

15. At least the photographs were not seen in the United States until a recent (1979) exhibition at The International Center of Photography in New York City.

16. Frances Benjamin Johnston, "The Foremost Women Photographers in America," *The Ladies Home Journal* 18 (November, 1901), p. 13.

17. ———, "What a Woman Can Do With a Camera," *The Ladies Home Journal* (September, 1897), pp. 6-7.

18. Letter from Miss D. H. Ormsbee to Frances Benjamin Johnston, October 18, 1897, Frances Benjamin Johnston Collection, Manuscript Division, Library of Congress.

19. Letter from Gertrude Käsebier to Frances Benjamin Johnston, June 6, 1901, Frances Benjamin Johnston Collection, Manuscript Division, Library of Congress.

20. This summer holiday shared by Johnston and Käsebier is described in letters from Johnston to her mother, August, 1905, Frances Benjamin Johnston Collection, Manuscript Division, Library of Congress.

21. Letter from Käsebier to Frances Benjamin Johnston, June 6, 1903, Frances Benjamin Johnston Collection, Manuscript Division, Library of Congress.

22. David Travis and Anne Kennedy, *Photography Rediscovered* (New York: Whitney Museum of Art, 1979), pp. 160, 165.

23. Letter from Eva Watson-Schütze to Frances Benjamin Johnston, December 27, 1899, Frances Benjamin Johnston Collection, Manuscript Division, Library of Congress.

24. Letter from Mary E. Allen to Frances Benjamin Johnston, n.d. March 20, 1897, Frances Benjamin Johnston Collection, Manuscript Division, Library of Congress.

25. Letter from Allen to Frances Benjamin Johnston, March 20, 1897, Frances Benjamin Johnston Collection, Manuscript Division, Library of Congress.

26. Quitslund, "Her Feminine Colleagues," p. 112.

27. Eileen Boris, *Women's Culture, Women's Crafts: The Sisterhood of Art in Late Victorian America* (Female Sphere Conference, New Harmony Indiana, October, 1981).

28. Ibid.

29. Letter from Allen to Frances Benjamin Johnston, June 30, 1898, Frances Benjamin Johnston Collection, Manuscript Division, Library of Congress.

30. Letter from Virginia Sharp to Frances Benjamin Johnston, June 13, 1900, Frances Benjamin Johnston Collection, Manuscript Division, Library of Congress.

31. Letter from Sharp to Frances Benjamin Johnston, June 16, 1900, Frances Benjamin Johnston Collection, Manuscript Division, Library of Congress.

32. "The Educational Value of the Camera," *The Craftsman* 9 (March, 1910), p. 76.

33. Letter from Mattie Edwards Hewitt to Frances Benjamin Johnston, November 21, 1901, Frances Benjamin Johnston Collection, Manuscript Division, Library of Congress.

34. Letter from Hewitt to Frances Benjamin Johnston, November 7, 1907, Frances Benjamin Johnston Collection, Manuscript Division, Library of Congress.

35. Letter from Hewitt to Frances Benjamin Johnston, November 21, 1901, Frances Benjamin Johnston Collection, Manuscript Division, Library of Congress.

36. Letter from Hewitt to Frances Benjamin Johnston, December 2, 1901, Frances Benjamin Johnston Collection, Manuscript Division, Library of Congress.

37. Ellen Lagemann, *A Generation of Women's Studies in Educational Biography* (Cambridge: Harvard University Press, 1979).

38. Letter from Emily Mews to Frances Benjamin Johnston, November 12, 1894, Frances Benjamin Johnston Collection, Manuscript Division, Library of Congress.

39. Letter from Frances Barbour to Frances Benjamin Johnston, August 5, 1896, Frances Benjamin Johnston, August 5, 1896, Frances Benjamin Johnston Collection, Manuscript Division, Library of Congress.

40. Letter from I.W. Blake to Frances Benjamin Johnston, October 31, 1901, Frances Benjamin Johnston Collection, Manuscript Division, Library of Congress.

41. Letter from Lottie M. Hamilton to Frances Benjamin Johnston, January 26, 1902, Frances Benjamin Johnston Collection, Manuscript Division, Library of Congress.

42. Elizabeth Flint Wade, "Amateur Photography Through Women's Eyes," *The Photo-America* 15 (June, 1894), p. 235.

43. Ibid.

44. Myra Albert Wiggins, "Amateur Photography Through Women's Eyes," *The Photo-American* 15 (March, 1894), p. 193.

45. Adelaide Skeel, ed. "Our Women Friends," *Photo-American*. Column ran from 1892 to 1897.

46. Skeel, "Our Women Friends," (November, 1892), p. 41.

47. Skeel, "Our Women Friends," (November, 1897), p. 23.

48. A.H. Godfrey, "Cycling Clubs and Their Spheres of Action," *Outing* 30 (April–September, 1897), p. 341.

49. Ibid.

50. "Progress of Photography," *Anthony's Photographic Bulletin* (1885), pp. 429–430.

51. Quoted in Weston Naef, *The Collection of Alfred Stieglitz* (New York: Viking Press, A Studio Book, The Museum of Modern Art, 1979), p. 117.

52. See, for example, letter from J.C. Abel to Frances Benjamin Johnston, January 23, 1900, Frances Benjamin Johnston Collection, Manuscript Division, Library of Congress.

53. Welling, *Photography in America: The Formative Years, 1839–1900* (New York: Thomas Y. Crowell Company, 1978), p. 297.

54. Quoted in Welling, p. 297.

55. Charles Caffin quoted in Naef, *Collection of Alfred Stieglitz*, p. 15.

56. See Naef, *Collection of Alfred Stieglitz*, p. 18 for details about this controversy.

57. Herbert J. Seligman, *Alfred Stieglitz Talking* (New Haven: Yale University Library, 1966), p. 65.

58. William Innes Homer, *Alfred Stieglitz and the American Avant-Garde* (Boston, New York: Graphic Society, 1970), p. 46.

59. Gertrude Käsebier quoted in Naef, *Collection of Alfred Stieglitz*, p. 83.

60. S.D. Warlant, "Amateurs Kill the Business," *Anthony's Photographic Bulletin* (1885), p. 205.

61. "Gossip," *The Photographic Art Journal* (January, 1851), p. 61.

62. Ibid.

63. Oliver Wendell Holmes quoted in Robert Taft, *Photography and the American Scene* (New York: The MacMillan Company, 1938), p. 213. Taft also provides details on other aspects of exchange clubs. Also see *American Journal of Photography*, 4 (1861-1862), p. 329 and *Anthony's Photographic Bulletin*, 19, pp. 356, 403.

64. "Photographic Societies," *The Photographer's Friend*, 3 (May, 1873), p. 80.

65. Taft, *Photography and America Scene*, p. 376.

66. "Associations and Conventions," *Photographic Journal of America* 19 (May, 1882), pp. 135-136.

67. "The Postal Photographic Club," *The Photographic Times and American Photographer* 26 (February 26, 1886), p. 119.

68. Clarisse B. Moore, "Women Experts in Photography," *Cosmopolitan* 14 (March, 1893), pp. 580-590.

69. Oscar Van Engelin, "Organizing and Conducting a Successful Camera Club," *Photo-Beacon* 12 (May, 1900), p. 27.

70. "An American Camera Club," *The Photographic Art Journal* 11 (December 2, 1889), p. 238.

71. Dallet Fuguet, "Maker and Critic," *Camera Notes* (October, 1900), p. 80.

72. Theodore Dreiser, "The Camera Club of New York," *A Pictorial Vision*, ed. Peter Bunnell (Salt Lake City: Peregrine Smith, 1980), p. 120.

73. Ibid.

74. "The Camera Club," *Camera Notes* (January, 1901), p. 231.

75. Dreiser, *A Pictorial Vision*, p. 120.

76. Alfred Stieglitz quoted in Dorothy Norman, *Alfred Stieglitz* (Millerton, New York: Aperture, 1960, 1973), p. 43.

77. Sadachiki Hartmann quoted in Naef, *Collection of Alfred Stieglitz*, p. 121.

78. William Murray, "Miss Zaida Ben-Yusf's Exhibition," *Camera Notes* (April, 1899), p. 171.

79. Ibid.

80. Joseph T. Keiley, "Mrs. Käsebier's Prints," *Camera Notes* (July, 1899), p. 34.

81. Arthur K. Dow, "Mrs. Gertrude Käsebier's Portrait Photographs," *Camera Notes* (July, 1899), pp. 22-23.

82. "Two New American Links" *Camera Notes* (July, 1899), p. 75.

83. "Two New American Links" *Camera Notes* (June, 1901), p. 186.

84. "The Portfolio of American Pictorial Photography," *Camera Notes* (July, 1900), p. 23.

85. Child Bayley, "The English Exhibitions and the American Invasion," *Camera Notes* (July, 1900), pp. 162-175.

86. "American Pictures at the London Salon," *Camera Notes* (July, 1901), p. 182.

87. See, for example, membership lists, *Camera Notes* (October, 1897).

88. "Miss E.V. Clarkson," *Camera Notes* (July, 1897), pp. 8-9.

89. Quoted in Toby Quitslund "Her Feminine Colleagues," p. 104.

90. Naef, *Collection of Alfred Stieglitz*, p. 52.

91. Ibid., p. 52 and William Murray, "The Farnsworth Exhibition," *Camera Notes* (January, 1898), pp. 82-83.

92. "Exhibition of Prints by Miss Isabel Churchill Taylor," *Camera Notes* (July, 1899), p. 42.

93. "Associations and Conventions," *Photographic Journal of America* 19 (1882), pp. 13-137.

94. "Amateur Photography for Women," *Anthony's Photographic Bulletin* (1885), p. 721.

95. "Our Views," *The Amateur Photographer* 2 (May 15, 1885), p. 105.

96. "Our Views," *The Amateur Photographer* 2 (July , 1885), p. 205.

97. "The Ladies Section of the Chicago Amateur Photographer's Club," *Photographic Times and American Photographer* 16 (January 29, 1886), p. 70.

98. "Notes and News," *The Photographic Times and Amateur Photography* 17 (February 24, 1888), p. 92.

99. See *The Ladies Home Journal* during the 1880s and 1890s for examples of this.

100. "The Ladies," *The Photographer* 4 (April 10, 1906), p. 376.

101. "Photographer's Association of America," *The Photographer* 3 (June 10, 1905), p. 118.

102. *Camera Club Journal*, 2 (October, 1896), p. 23.

103. "Photography in Philadelphia," *Photographic Times and Amateur Photographer* 14 (July 1884), pp. 385-386.

104. "The Philadelphia Exhibition," *The Photographic Times*, 16 (February 12, 1886), pp. 93-94.

105. Ibid.

106. "Among the Clubs," *Photo-Era* 2 (April, 1899), p. 290.

107. "Miss F.B. Johnston's Exhibit," *Photo-Era* 2 (April, 1899), p. 292.

108. Ibid.

109. "The Chicago Salon," *Photo-Beacon* 12 (June, 1900), p. 151.

110. Quitslund, *"Her Feminine Colleagues,"* p. 104.

111. *Camera Craft*, 12 (May, 1900-April, 1901). Throughout these issues, women's activity is consistently reported.

Chapter 5

1. Weston J. Naef, *The Collection of Alfred Stieglitz* (New York: Viking Press, A Studio Book, The Museum of Modern Art, 1978), p. 72.

2. Alfred Stieglitz, "Four Happenings," *Twice a Year* 8-9 (Spring, Summer, Fall, Winter, 1942), p. 117.

3. Paul Strand, *Sixty Years of Photography* (Aperture, 1976), p. 143.

4. Letter from Alfred Stieglitz to Anne Brigman, June 24, 1914, Alfred Stieglitz Archive, Beinecke Rare Book and Manuscript Library, Yale University.

5. Herbert Seligman, *Alfred Stieglitz Talking* (New Haven: Yale University Library, 1966), p. 275.

6. Ibid., p. 279.

7. Ibid.

8. Strand, *Sixty Years*, p. 20.

9. Seligman, *Alfred Stieglitz Talking*, p. 148.

10. Letter from Alfred Stieglitz to Anne Brigman, December 26, 1913, Beinecke Rare Book and Manuscript Collection, Yale University. Alfred Stieglitz Archive (ASA).

11. Naef, *Collection of Alfred Stieglitz* p. 200.

12. Germaine Greer, *The Obstacle Race* (New York: Farrar, Straus, Giroux, 1979).

13. Ibid., p. 67.

14. Ibid., p. 35.

15. See Chapter VI, this volume, for further discussion of this subject.

16. Letter from Alfred Stieglitz to Brigman, December 24, 1919, ASA.

17. William Innes Homer. *Alfred Stieglitz and the American Avant-Garde* (Boston: New York Graphic Society, 1977), pp. 10-11.

18. Dorothy Norman, *Alfred Stieglitz* (Millerton, New York: Aperture, 1960, 1973), p. 16.

19. Ibid.

20. Ibid., p. 14.

21. *Georgia O'Keeffe: A Portrait by Alfred Stieglitz* (New York: Metropolitan Museum of Art, 1978).

22. Letter from Alfred Stieglitz to Frances Benjamin Johnston, June 8, 1900, Frances Benjamin Johnston Collection, Manuscript Division, Library of Congress.

23. Alfred Stieglitz, "An Apology," *Camera Work* 1 (January, 1903), p. 68.

24. Estelle Jussim, *Slave to Beauty* (Boston: David R. Godine, 1981), p. 289.

25. Letter from Mary Devens to Alfred Stieglitz, April 22, 1902, ASA.

26. Letter from Mary Devens to Alfred Stieglitz, December 26, 1902, ASA.

27. Letter from Rose Clark to Alfred Stieglitz, October, 1900, ASA.

28. Letter from Alice Boughton to Alfred Stieglitz, April 9, 1910, ASA.

29. Letter from Alfred Stieglitz to Elizabeth Beuhrmann, February 20, 1909, Manuscript Division, New York Public Library.

30. Letter from Paul Haviland to Elizabeth Beuhrmann, 1909, MD, NYPL.

31. Letter from Sarah Sears to Alfred Stieglitz, undated letters, ASA.

32. Letter from Alfred Stieglitz to Frances Benjamin Johnston, April 15, 1904, Frances Benjamin Johnston Collection, Library of Congress.

33. Harriet Livermore Rice, "Landon Rives and Her Work." *The Photographer* III (October 17, 1905), pp. 392-393.

34. William Innes Homer, *The Photographs of Gertrude Käsebier* (Delaware Art Museum, 1979), p. 26.

35. Jussim, *Slave to Beauty*, p. 137.

36. See Homer, *Alfred Stieglitz*, for further discussion.

37. Jussim, *Slave to Beauty*, p. 187.

38. Homer, *The Photographs of Gertrude Käsebier* p. 26.

39. Joseph Keiley, "The Philadelphia Salons," *Camera Notes* (1898), p. 118.

40. Quoted in Naef, *Collection of Alfred Stieglitz*, p. 100. The 1900 catalogue for Newark, Ohio Exhibition described Gertrude Käsebier as the "foremost professional photographer in the United States."

41. Letter from Gertrude Käsebier to Day, quoted in Jussim, *Slave to Beauty*, p. 174.

42. Letter from Alfred Stieglitz to Joseph Keiley, November 14, 1901, ASA.

43. Homer, *The Photographs of Gergrude Käsebier*, p. 26.

44. Letter from Alfred Stieglitz to Gertrude Käsebier, January 4, 1912, ASA.

45. Letter from Anne Brigman to Alfred Stieglitz, January 9, 1903, ASA.

46. Letter from Anne Brigman to Alfred Stieglitz, September 22, 1904, ASA.

47. Letter from Anne Brigman to Alfred Stieglitz, May 24, 1908, ASA.

48. Letter from Anne Brigman to Alfred Stieglitz, July 8, 1918, ASA.

49. Letter from Anne Brigman to Alfred Stieglitz, October 14, 1905, ASA.

50. Letter from Anne Brigman to Alfred Stieglitz, February 19, 1907, ASA. Arnold Genthe's autobiogrpahy, *As I Remember*, is dotted with the names of the rich and celebrated. Brigman's perception was probably not misplaced.

51. Milton Meltzer, *Dorothea Lange* (New York: Farrar, Straus, Giroux, 1978), p. 75.

52. Letter from Anne Brigman to Alfred Stieglitz, March 21, 1908, ASA.

53. Letter from Anne Brigman to Alfred Stieglitz, September 10, 1909, ASA.

54. Letter from Anne Brigman to Alfred Stieglitz, March 27, 1906, ASA.

55. Letter from Anne Brigman to Alfred Stieglitz, September 10, 1909, ASA.

56. Letter from Anne Brigman to Alfred Stieglitz, February 1, 1910, ASA.

57. Letter from Anne Brigman to Alfred Stieglitz, February 19, 1907, ASA.

58. Letter from Anne Brigman to Alfred Stieglitz, March 7, 1909, ASA.

59. Letter from Anne Brigman to Alfred Stieglitz, November 1, 1909, ASA.

60. Letter from Anne Brigman to Alfred Stieglitz, February 1910, ASA.

61. Letter from Anne Brigman to Alfred Stieglitz, March 2, 1911, ASA.

62. Letter from Anne Brigman to Alfred Stieglitz, July, 1910, ASA.

63. Letter from Anne Brigman to Alfred Stieglitz, March 21, 1911, ASA.

64. Therese Thau Heyman, *Anne Brigman* (The Oakland Museum , 1974), p. 6.

65. Letter from Anne Brigman to Alfred Stieglitz, March 2, 1911, ASA.

66. Letter from Anne Brigman to Alfred Stieglitz, November, 1910, ASA.

67. Letter from Anne Brigman to Alfred Stieglitz, November, 1911 (probable date), ASA.

68. Letter from Anne Brigman to Alfred Stieglitz, March, 1916, ASA.

69. Letter from Anne Brigman to Alfred Stieglitz, April 26, 1911, ASA.

70. Letter from Anne Brigman to Alfred Stieglitz, July 24, 1912, ASA.

71. Letter from Anne Brigman to Alfred Stieglitz, September 1, 1912, ASA.

72. Letter from Alfred Stieglitz to Anne Brigman, June 24, 1914, ASA.

73. Letter from Anne Brigman to Alfred Stieglitz, January 28, 1908, ASA.

74. Letter from Anne Brigman to Alfred Stieglitz, January 4, 1909, ASA.

75. Ibid.

76. Letter from Alfred Stieglitz to Anne Brigman, April 16, 1915, ASA.

77. Letter from Anne Brigman to Alfred Stieglitz, July 18, 1914, ASA.

78. See letters from Alfred Stieglitz to Anne Brigman circa 1919, ASA.

79. Letter from Anne Brigman to Alfred Stieglitz, May 24, 1908, ASA.

80. Letter from Anne Brigman to Alfred Stieglitz, March 3, 1907, ASA.

81. Letter from Alfred Stieglitz to Anne Brigman, June 24, 1914, ASA.

82. Letter from Alfred Stieglitz to Frank Crowinshield, October 6, 1915, ASA.

83. See Germaine Greer, *The Obstacle Race* for further discussion of this subject.

Chapter 6

1. The work of women who contributed to the photography exhibition organized by Frances Benjamin Johnston at the Paris Ex-

position in 1900 underscores this observation. The women's photography was overwhelmingly comprised of so-called "feminine" subjects. Only an occasional male portrait or a rare landscape could be found among the many representations of women, either with a child or alone. See the Frances Benjamin Johnston Collection. Prints and Photographs Division, Library of Congress.

2. *New York Times* (April 20, 1913), p. 12.

3. Ibid.

4. Mary Scott Boyd, "A Hint for Summer Work," *Anthony's Photographic Bulletin* 23 (1892), p. 335.

5. *The Professional and Amateur Photographer* 1902, p. 111.

6. Catherine Filene, ed., *Careers for Women* (Boston and New York: Houghton Mifflin Company, 1920), p. 63.

7. Marion Foster Washburne, "A New Profession for Women," *Godey's Magazine* 134 (February, 1897), p. 127.

8. Fannie Elton quoted in Toby Quitslund, "Her Feminine Colleagues," *Women Artists in Washington Collections* (College Park Maryland: University of Maryland Art Gallery, 1979), p. 118.

9. Ibid., p. 139.

10. Eva Watson-Schütze, "Portraits of Children," *The Photographer*, 1 (June 4, 1904), p. 93.

11. See, for example, the photographs of Beatrice Tonneson, Library of Congress, Prints and Photographs Division.

12. Marion Foster Washburne, "A New Profession for Women," *Godey's*, 1 (February, 1897), p. 127.

13. Quitslund, "Her Feminine Colleagues," p. 114.

14. Elizabeth Flint Wade, "Amateur Photography Through Women's Eyes," *The Photo-American* 5 (March, 1894).

15. Ann Sutherland Harris and Linda Nochlin, *Women Artists: 1550-1950* (Los Angeles County Museum of Art, Alfred A. Knopf: New York 1977), pp. 66-67.

16. Sidney Allen, "Pictorial Criticism: Constructive Not Destructive," *The Photographer* 5 (June 11, 1904), p. 105.

17. See Sheila M. Rothman, *Woman's Proper Place* (New York: Basic Books, 1978), Chapter 3, "The Ideology of Educated Motherhood," pp. 97-134.

18. Linda Gordon, *Woman's Body Woman's Right* (Penguin Books, 1977), pp. 135-158.

19. Lewis Erenberg, *Steppin' Out* (Westport, Connecticut: Greenwood Press, 1981), p. 7.

20. Charlotte Perkins Gilman quoted in Rothman, *Woman's Proper Place*, p. 197.

21. Giles Edgerton, "Photography as an Emotional Art," *The Craftsman* (April, 1907), p. 82.

22. Ibid.

23. "The Philadelphia Salon," *Camera Notes* (January, 1899), p. 129.

24. Edgerton, p. 80.

25. Ibid., pp. 91-92.

26. See Wanda Corn, *The Color Mood: American Tonalism, 1880-1910* (San Francisco: M.H. De Young Memorial Museum and California Palace of the Legion of Honor, 1978) for a fine analysis of the emotional nature of pictorialism.

27. Ann Novotny, *Alice's World* (Old Greenwich, Connecticut: The Chatham Press, 1976), p. 23.

28. John Haller and Robin Haller, *The Physician and Sexuality in Victorian America* (New York: The Norton Library, 1974), p. 175.

29. Ibid.

30. See Novotny, *Alice's World*, for representative photographs on this subject. Also see the Alice Austen Collection, The Staten Island Historical Society.

31. Haller, *Physician and Sexuality*, p. 175.

32. Maria Ward, *Bicycling for Ladies* (New York: Brenten's, 1896).

33. Haller, *Physician and Secuality*, pp. 182-183.

34. For these and following photographs see both Novotny, *Alice's World*, and the Alice Austen Collection, Staten Island Historical Society.

35. For reproductions of Johnston's work on these subjects see Pete Daniel and Raymond Smock, *A Talent for Detail* (New York: Harmony Books, 1974). Also see the Frances Benjamin Johnston Collection, Prints and Photographs Division, Library of Congress.

36. Jane Addams, *Twenty Years at Hull House* (New York and Scarborough, Ontario: New American Library, Signet Classic, 1910, 1960), p. 75.

37. Richard Hofstadter, *The Age of Reform* (New York: Vintage Books, 1955), p. 196.

38. Early in her career (1889), Johnston fulfilled assignments for weekly and monthly publications including *Demorests', Harper's Weekly,* and *Frank Leslie*. This work continued throughout the 1890s.

39. Barbara M. Wertheimer, *We Were There* (New York: Pantheon Books, 1977), pp. 89-90.

40. See *The Hampton Album* (New York: The Museum of Modern Art, 1966) for reproductions from this series. For original prints see the Frances Benjamin Johnston Collection, Prints and Photographs Division, The Library of Congress.

41. Anne Brigman, "Awareness," *Design* 38 (June, 1936), p. 17.

42. Ibid.

43. Susan Griffin, *Pornography and Silence* (New York: Harper and Row, 1981), p. 11.

44. See Ellen Moers, *Literary Women* (Garden City, New York: Doubleday Anchor Books, 1977). Moers, in Chapter 11, "Metaphors: A Postlude," discusses ocean water as used symbolically by women writers.

Bibliography

Primary Sources

Manuscript and Photograph Collections

Beinecke Rare Book and Manuscript Collection, Yale University, New Haven, Connecticut. Alfred Stieglitz Archive (ASA).

George Eastman House, International Museum of Photography Research Center, Rochester, New York.

Library of Congress Manuscript Division, Washington, D.C. (LC) Frances Benjamin Johnston Collection.

Library of Congress Prints and Photographs Division, Washington, D.C. Frances Benjamin Johnston Photograph Collection.

Museum of the City of New York, Photograph Division.

Nassau County Museum, East Meadow, New York. Mattie Edwards Hewitt Collection.

New York Public Library Manuscript Division, New York, New York (NYPL, MD) Elizabeth Beuhrmann Papers, Gertrude Käsebier Papers.

Arthur and Elizabeth Schlesinger Library, Radcliffe College, Cambridge, Massachusetts. Jessie Tarbox Beals Collection.

Staten Island Historical Association, Staten Island, New York. Alice Austen Photograph Collection.

Mina Turner, daughter-in-law of Gertrude Käsebier, unpublished personal notes.

Magazines and Newspapers

The Amateur Photographer, 1884-1885.
American Amateur Photographer, 1889.
American Journal of Photography, 1885-1896.
Anthony's Photographic Bulletin, 1885-1892.
Art Journal, 1872, 1898.
Burr McIntosh Monthly, 1903-1910.

Camera Club, New York Journal, 1896-1897.
Atlantic Monthly, 1880.
Brooklyn Eagle, 1891.
Camera Craft, 1900-1901.
Camera Notes, 1897-1903.
Camera Work, 1903-1917.
The Century, 1881.
Cosmopolitan, 1893.
The Craftsman, 1907-1913.
The Critic, 1897-1890.
Current Literature, 1903.
Demorest's Family Magazine, 1892.
Everybody's Magazine, 1899-1901.
Every Week, 1895.
Godey's Magazine, 1895.
The Illustrated American, 1892.
Journal of the Society of Amateur Photographers, 1896.
Kodakery, 1913-1923.
The Ladies Home Journal, 1884-1900.
Munsey's Magazine, 1894.
Outing, 1896.
The Outlook, 1897, 1900-1904.
The Philadelphia Photographer, 1883-1894.
Photo-American, 1892-1894.
Photo-Beacon.
Photo-Era, 1898-1899.
The Photogram, 1900-1908.
The Photographer, 1900-1905.
Photographic Journal of America, 1884-1920.
Photographic Mosaics, 1886-1901.
Photographic Times, 1880-1900.
Popular Science Monthly, 1904.
The Professional Photographer, 1900-1903.
The Washington Post, 1893.
Western Photographic News, 1874.
Wilson's Photographic Magazine, 1882-1891.

Articles

Allen, Sidney. "Pictorial Criticism: Constructive Not Destructive."
   The Photographer, 5 (June 11, 1905) 105.

"Amateur Photography—A Woman's View of the Art of Which Her Husband Is a Devotee." *Wilson's Photographic Magazine*, 28 (February 1, 1890) 69.

"Amateur Photography for Women." *Anthony's Photographic Bulletin*, 16 (1885) 721.

"Amateurs and Professionals." *Photo-Era* (October, 1898) 98.

"An American Camera Club." *The Photographic Art Journal*, 11 (December 2, 1889) 238.

"American Pictures at the London Salon." *Camera Notes*, 4 (July, 1901) 182.

"Among the Clubs." *Photo-Era*, ii (April, 1889) 290.

"An April Exhibit of California Studies by Anne Brigman." *The Bulletin of the Brooklyn Institute of Arts and Science*, 36 (1932) 295-300.

"An Artistic Photographer." *Current Literature*, 34 (January, 1903) 21.

"Associations and Conventions." *Photographic Journal of America*, 19 (May, 1882) 135-136.

Barnes, Catherine Weed. "Photography from a Woman's Standpoint." *Anthony's Photographic Bulletin*, 20 (1890) 41-42.

———. "Women as Photographers." *Anthony's Photographic Bulletin*, 22 (1891) 275-278.

———. "Women as Photographers." *Photographic Mosaics* (1891) 117-122.

———. "Women as Professional Photographers." *Wilson's Photographic Magazine* (1891) 687-688.

Bayley, Child. "The English Exhibitions and the American Invasion." *Camera Notes*, 3 (July, 1900) 162-175.

Bisland, Margaret. "A Home Photographic Studio." *The Amateur Photographer*, 7 (October, 1890) 384-385.

Bisland, Mary C. "Current Topics of Interest to Women." *The Illustrated American* (December 31, 1895) 15.

Boughton, Alice. "Photography, a Medium of Expression." *The Scrip*, 1 (1905) 75-80.

Boughton, Alice. "Pictures of the Stage." *The Scrip*, 1 (1906) 205-208.

Boyd, Mary Scott. "A Hint for Summer Work." *Anthony's Photographic Bulletin*, 23 (1892) 335.

Caffin, Charles. "Mrs. Kasebier's Work—An Appreciation." *Camera Work*, 1 (January, 1903) 17-19.

"The Camera Club." *Camera Notes*, 4 (January, 1901) 231.

"The Camera Girl." *The Photo-American*, 11 (October, 1900) 320.

"The Camera Has Opened a New Profession for Women." *New York Times* (April 20, 1912) 12.

Cameron, Julia Margaret. "Annals of My Glass House." *Photography in Print*, ed. Vicki Goldberg. New York: Simon and Schuster, 1981, p. 180.

"The Chicago Salon." *Photo-Beacon*, 12 (June, 1900) 151.

Crane, Frank W. "American Women Photographers." *Munsey's Magazine*, 11 (1894) n.p.

Crane, Julia. "That Horrid Photography." *Photographic Mosaics* (1891) p. 131.

Daniels, Marie-Antoinette. "Interiors." *Photo-Beacon*, 12 (August, 1900) 230-237.

"The Deadly Kodak Girl." *The Photographic Times*, xxi (October 16, 1891) 518.

Dow, Arthur K. "Mrs. Gertrude Käsebier's Portrait Photographs." *Camera Notes*, 2 (July, 1899) 22-23.

Dreiser, Theodore. "The Camera Club of New York," *A Pictorial Vision*, ed. Peter Bunnell. Salt Lake City: Peregrine Smith, 1980, 120-130.

"Early Days of Amateur Photography." *Anthony's Photographic Bulletin*, 120 (1889) 146-148.

Edgerton, Giles. "Is There a Sex Distinction in Art? The Attitude of the Critic Toward Women's Exhibits." *The Craftsman* , 14 (June, 1908) 239-251.

——. "The Lyric Quality in the Photo-Secession Art of George Seeley." *The Craftsman*, 14 (April-September, 1908) 303-305.

——. "Photography as an Emotional Art." *The Craftsman* 13 (April, 1907) 82-86.

"The Educational Value of the Camera." *The Craftsman*, 16 (March, 1910) p. 62.

Engelin, Oscar Van. "Organizing and Conducting a Successful Camera Club." *Photo-Beacon*, 12 (March, 1900) p. 40-44.

"Exhibition of Prints by Miss Isabel Churchill Taylor." *Camera Notes*, 2 (July, 1899) 42.

"Exhibitions." *The Amateur Photographer*, 2 (March 6, 1885) 347-348.

"A Fashionable Amusement." *The Amateur Photographer,* 1 (October 31, 1884) 60.

Fuguet, Dallet. "Maker and Critic." *Camera Notes* 3 (October, 1900) 80.

Glazier, Flora J. "A Postal Camera Club." *Photo-Beacon,* 12 (May, 1900) 91.

Godfrey, A. H. "Cycling Clubs and Their Spheres of Action." *Outing,* 25 (April-September, 1897) 341-351.

"Gossip." *The Photographic Art Journal* (January, 1851) 61.

Hartmann, Sadakichi. "A Purist." *The Photographic Times,* 31 (October, 1899) 449-451.

——. "A Walk Through the Exhibition of the Photographic Section of the American Institute," *Camera Notes,* 2 (January, 1899) 85-87.

Hersey, Heloise, E. "The Educated Woman of Tomorrow." *The Outlook* (August 1, 1903) 841.

Humphrey, Marmaduke. "Triumphs in Amateur Photography—V, Mrs. N. Gray Bartlett," *Godey's Magazine,* 136 (April, 1898) 368-378.

"Items of Interest-Empress as Expert Photographer." *Photo-American,* 17 (September, 1907) 77.

Johnston, Frances Benjamin. "Gertrude Käsebier, Professional Photographer." *Camera Work,* 1 (January, 1903) 20.

——. "The Foremost Women Photographers in America." *The Ladies Home Journal,* 18 (November, 1901).

——. "What A Woman Can Do With a Camera." *The Ladies Home Journal* (September, 1897) 6-7.

Käsebier, Gertrude. "An Art Village." *The Monthly Illustrator,* 4 (April, 1895) 9-17.

——. "Peasant Life in Normandy." *The Monthly Illustrator,* 3 (March, 1895) 269-275.

——. "Studies in Photography." *The Photographic Times,* 30 (June, 1898) 269-272.

——. "To Whom It May Concern." *Camera Notes,* 3 (January, 1900) 121-122.

Keiley, Joseph T. "Eva Watson-Schütze." *Camera Work,* 9 (January 1905) 23-26.

——. "Mrs. Käsebier's Prints." *Camera Notes,* 3 (July, 1899) 34.

——. "The Philadelphia Salon." *Camera Notes*, 1 (January, 1898) 118.

——. "The Philadelphia Salon." *Camera Notes*, 3 (January, 1899).

Kupper, L. V. "Photographer's Associations." *Photographic Mosaics* (1899) 200-202.

"The Ladies." *The Photographer*, 4 (April 10, 1906) 376.

"The Ladies Section of the Chicago Amateur Photographer's Club." *Photographic Times and American Photographer*, 17 (January 29, 1886) 70.

"A Lady Amateur." *Photographic Times*, 12 (1897) 117-118.

"The Los Angeles Camera Club." *Professional and Amateur Photographer*, 7 (May, 1920) 168.

Manson, George J. "Work for Women in Photography." *The Philadelphia Photographer*, 20 (February, 1883) 36-37.

McPhail, Mary. "Anne Brigman." *San Francisco Examiner* (November 23, 1924) n.p.

"Miss E. V. Clarkson." *Camera Notes*, 1 (July, 1897) 8-9.

"Miss F. B. Johnston's Exhibit." *Photo-Era*, ii (April, 1899) 292.

Moore, Clarisse Bloomfield. "Woman Experts in Photography." *Cosmopolitan*, 14 (March, 1893) 580-590.

Murray, William. "The Farnsworth Exhibition." *Camera Notes*, 1 (January, 1898) 82-83.

——. "Miss Zaida Ben-Yusuf's Exhibition." *Camera Notes*, 2 (April, 1899) 171.

"New Club Competition." *Camera Notes*, 2 (July, 1899) 41.

Newcombe, Edward W. "Chat Here and There." *The Photo-American*, 12 (June, 1900) 189-190.

Northrup, Amanda Carolyn. "The Successful Woman in America." *Popular Science Monthly*, 46 (1904) 239-244.

"Now Then Try It." *Photographic Mosaics* (1897) 313.

"The New York Exhibition of Photographs." *Photo-American*, 10 (January, 1898) 84.

"Notes and News." *The Photographic Times and Amateur Photographer*, 17 (February 24, 1888) 92.

"Our Views." *The Amateur Photographer*, 2 (July, 1885) 205.

"A Page for Women." *American Journal of Photography*, 17 (April, 1896) 190.

Parsons, J. H. "Women as Photographers." ed. M. C. Rayne. *What Can A Woman Do?* Detroit, Cincinnati, St. Louis: F. B. Dickerson and Company, 1884, 120-127.

Patten, Mary. "The Photographer." ed., Catherine Filene. *Careers for Women*, Boston and New York: Houghton Mifflin Company, 1920, 70-75.

"The Philadelphia Exhibition." *The Photographic Times*, 16 (February 12, 1886) 93-94.

"Philadelphia Salon of 1900." *Camera Notes*, 7 (January, 1910).

"Photographer's Association of America." *The Photographer*, 3 (June 20, 1905), 118.

"Photographic Societies." *The Photographer's Friend*, 3 (May, 1873) 80.

"Photographs of Mist and Twilight." *The Craftsman*, 14 (April-September, 1908) 62.

"Photography for the Girls." *Photographic Times and Amateur Photographer*, 17 (August 24, 1888) 404-405.

"Photography in Philadelphia." *Photographic Times and Amateur Photographer*, 14 (July, 1884) 385-386.

"The Portfolio of American Pictorial Photography." *Camera Notes*, 3 (July, 1900) 23.

"The Postal Photographic Club." *The Photographic Times and American Photographer*, 16 (February 26, 1886) 119.

Pragnell, Kate. "Photography." International Congress of Women, *Transactions*, (1899) 202-204.

"Progress of Photography." *Anthony's Photographic Bulletin*, 17 (1885) 429-430.

"Prominent Photographers of the Year." *The Professional Photographer*, 2 (February, 1899) 48.

Scott, Walter Dill. "The Psychology of Advertising." *Atlantic Monthly*, 93 (January, 1904) 29-36.

Skeel, Adelaide, ed. "Our Women Friends." *Photo-American*. Regular column from 1892-1897.

Snelling, A. Lee. "More Art and More Women Wanted in Our Art." *Photographic Mosaics* (1895) 120.

Somers, F. M. "The Ladies—And How to Deal With Them." *Photographic Mosaics* (1895) 260.

Spencer, Ema. "The White School." *Camera Craft*, 3 (July 1901) 95-103.

Spooner, Pitcher J. "Only a Photographer." *Photographic Mosaics* (1899) 54.

Stieglitz, Alfred. "An Apology." *Camera Work*, (January, 1903) 18.

———. "Four Happenings." *Twice A Year*, 8-9 (Spring, Summer, Fall, Winter, 1941) 117.

"Story of a Woman's Help." *The Photographic Art Journal*, 8 (June 1, 1888) 85-86.

"Studio Stories." *The Photographer*, 10 (November 21, 1905) 53.

"Studio Stories." *The Photogram*, 4 (February 20, 1906) 266-267.

"They Photograph the Smart Set." *Vanity Fair*, n.v. (December, 1912-1913) 18-19.

Thompson, Ray and Sue Thompson. "First Lady of the Lens." *The Woman*, 15 (December, 1945) 59-62.

"Travelling Daguerreotype Wagon." *The Photographic Art Journal*, 8 (March, 1852) 194.

"Two New American Links." *Camera Notes*, 3 (July, 1899).

Wade, Elizabeth Flint. "Amateur Photography Through Women's Eyes." *Photo-American*, 5 (June, 1984) 235-239.

Warlant, S. D. "Amateurs Kill the Business." *Anthony's Photographic Bulletin* (1885) 205.

Washburne, Marion Foster. "A New Profession for Women." *Godey's Magazine*, 134 (February, 1897) 123-128.

Waterbury, A.D., Mrs. "A Menu Hint for Housewives." *Photo-American*, 3 (April, 1897) 76.

Watson-Schütze, Eva. "Portraits of Children." *The Photographer*, 1 (June 4, 1904) 93.

Wells, Kate Gannett. "Women in Organizations." *Atlantic Monthly*, 17 (September, 1880) 360-367.

Wheeler, Candace. "Education for Women." *The Outlook* (January 2, 1897) 81-85.

Wiggins, Myra Albert. "Amateur Photography Through Women's Eyes." *Photo-American* v (March, 1894).

"Women and Business." *The Century*, 23 (1881-1882), 954.

"Women and Their Work." *The Outlook* (October 1, 1904) 256-258.

"Women as Photographers." *Anthony's Photographic Bulletin*, 22 (1891) 276.

"Women as Professional Photographers." *Wilson's Photographic Magazine*, 28 (November 21, 1891) 686.

"Women's Work in Photography." *The Photographic Times and Amateur Photographer*, 17 (March 18, 1887) 299.

"A Woman Worth Knowing." *The Photographic Times*, 21 (May 29, 1891) 262.

Wooley, Edward Mott. "The Best Paid Occupations for Women." *Every Week*, 15 (August 9, 1895) 15.

"Work of District Women." *The Washington Post*, (April 2, 1893) n.p.

"World's Photography Focusses." *The Philadelphia Photographer*, 17 (September, 1907) 47.

Yellott, Louis P. "Some Experiences of a Martyr." *Photo-American*, 9 (July, 1890) 259.

Books

Abbott, Edith. *Women in Industry*, London, New York: D. Appleton and Company, 1913.

Addams, Jane. *Twenty Years at Hull House*. New York: Signet Classic, 1910, 1960.

Beaux, Cecilia. *Background With Figures*. Boston and New York: s.d., 1930.

Blackwell, Elizabeth. *Pioneer Work on Opening the Medical Profession to Women*. New York: Source Book Press, 1970 (Reprint from 1895).

The Blue Book for Amateur Photographers. Beach Bluff, Massachusetts, 1894 and 1895.

Boughton, Alice. *Photographing the Famous*. New York: The Avondale Press, 1928.

Brigman, Anne. *Songs of a Pagan*. Caldwell, Idaho: The Caxton Printers, 1949.

Caffin, Charles. *Photography as a Fine Art*. Hastings-on-Hudson, New York: Morgan and Morgan, 1901, 1971.

Clement, Clara Erskine. *Women in the Fine Arts*. Boston and New York: Houghton Mifflin and Company, 1904.

Dorr, Rheta Childe. *What Eight Million Women Want*. Boston: Small, Maynard and Company, 1910.

Filene, Catherine, ed. *Careers for Women*. Boston and New York: Houghton Mifflin Company, 1920.

Genthe, Arnold. *As I Remember*. New York: Reynal and Hitchcock, 1936.

Gilman, Charlotte Perkins. *The Living of Charlotte Perkins Gilman*. New York: Harper Colophon Books, 1885, 1963.

Holme, Charles, ed. *Art in Photography*. Paris, New York: The Studio, 1905, 1979.

Hughes, Alice. *My Father and I*. London: Thornton Butterworth, Ltd., 1923.

Leonard, John William, ed. *Woman's Who's Who of America*. New York: The American Commonwealth Company, 1914.

Meyer, Annie Nathan, ed. *Woman's Work in America*. New York: Henry Holt and Company, 1891.

Rayne, Mrs. M.L. *What Can a Woman Do?* Detroit, Chicago, Cincinnati, St. Louis: F. B. Dickerson and Company, 1884.

Root, M.A. *The Camera and the Pencil*, New York: D. Appleton and Company, 1864.

Starrett, Helen Ekin. *After College What?* New York: Thomas Y. Crowell, 1896.

Strand, Paul. *Sixty Years of Photographs*. Millerton, New York: Aperture, 1976.

Ward, Maria. *Bicycling for Ladies*. New York: Brenton's, 1896.

Secondary Sources

Articles

"Alice Austen's America." *Holiday*, (September, 1952) 66-71.

"Alice Boughton, Photographer." *New York Times*, (June 23, (1943) 21.

Antler, Joyce. "After College, What?": New Graduates and the Family Claim." *American Quarterly*, 32 (Fall, 1980) 409-434.

———. "Feminism as Life-Process: The Life and Career of Lucy Sprague Mitchell." *Feminist Studies*, 1 (spring, 1981) 134-157.

Boris, Eileen. "Women's Culture, Women's Crafts: The Sisterhood of Art in Late Victorian America." Female Sphere Conference, New Harmony, Indiana (October, 1981).

Bunnell, Peter. "Gertrude Käsebier." *Arts in Virginia*, 16 (Fall, 1975) 2-15, 40.

Conway, Jill. "Women Reformers and American Culture, 1870-1930," eds. Jean Friedman and William Slade, *Our American Sisters*. Boston: Allyn and Baum, 1976, 301-312.

Cook, Blanche Weisen. "Female Support Networks and Political Activism: Lillian Ward, Crystal Eastman, Emma Goldman." eds. Nancy Cott and Elizabeth Pleck. *A Heritage of Her Own*. New York: Simon and Schuster (1979), 412-444.

Doherty, Amy S. "Photography's Forgotten Women." *A.B. Bookman's Weekly* (November 4, 1985) 3312-3372.

———. "Women in Focus: Early American Photographers." *Picturescope*, 31 (Summer, 1983) 50-56.

"E. Alice Austen, Photographed Earlier Gracious Days of Staten Island." *New York Times* (April 9, 1976) 35.

Heilbrun, Carolyn. "Hers." *New York Times* (March 5, 1981) 33.

Herman, Sondra. "Loving Courtship or the Marriage Market? The Ideal and Its Critics, 1871-1911." *Our American Sisters*, 233-251.

"Loveland Summer: The Forgotten Photographs of Nancy Ford Cones," *American Heritage*, 32 (August/September, 1981), 75-81.

Michaels, Barbara. "Rediscovering Gertrude Käsebier." *Image*, 19 (June, 1976) 20-31.

"The Newly Discovered Picture World of Alice Austen." *Life* (September 24, 1951), 137-144.

"Old Friends Honor Miss Alice Austen." *New York Times* (October 8, 1951) 62-65.

O'Neill, William. "Divorce in the Progressive Era." ed. Michael Gordon. *The American Family in Social-Historical Perspectives*. New York: St. Martin's Press (1973) 251-266.

Palmieri, Patricia A. "Patterns of Achievement of Single Academic Women at Wellesley College, 1880-1920." *Frontiers*, 1 (Spring, 1980) 63-67.

Peterson, A. E. "Frances Benjamin Johnston: Crusader With a Camera." *Historic Preservation*, 32 (January, 1980) 17-20.

Quitslund, Toby. "Her Feminine Colleagues—Photographs and Letters Collected by Francis Benjamin Johnston in 1900." ed. Josephine Withers. *Women Artists in Washington Collections*. University of Maryland Art Gallery and Women's Caucus for Art (1979) 97-143.

Ryan, Mary P. "The Power of Women's Networks: A Case Study of Female Moral Reform in Antebellum America." *Feminist Studies*, 5 (Spring, 1979) 68-85.

Taylor, William and Christopher Lasch. "Two 'Kindred Spirits': Sorority and Family in New England, 1839-1846." *New England Quarterly*, 36 (1963) 23-41.

Tighe, Mary Ann. "Gertrude Käsebier Lost and Found." *Art in America*, 25 (March ,1977) 94-98.

Tomes, Nancy and Joan Jacobs Brumberg. "Women in the Professions: A Research Agenda for American Historians." *Reviews in American History*, (June, 1982) 275-296.

Books and Catalogues

Ackerman, Carl W. *George Eastman*. Boston and New York: Houghton Mifflin Company, 1930.

Antler, Joyce. *The Educated Woman and Professionalization: The Struggle for a New Feminine Identity, 1890-1920*. Ph.D. Diss., State University of New York at Stony Brook, 1977.

Alland, Alexander, Sr. *Jessie Tarbox Beals: First Woman News Photographer*. New York: Camera/Graphic Press, Ltd., 1978.

Atwan, Robert, Donald McQuade and John W. Wright. *Edsels, Luckies, and Frigidaires*. New York: Dell, 1979.

Auer, Michel. *The Illustrated History of the Camera From 1839 to the Present*. Boston: New York Graphic Society, 1975.

Badger, R. Reid. *The Great American Fair: The World's Columbian Exposition and American Culture*. Chicago: Nelson Hall, 1979.

Barr, Alfred, Henry McBride and Andrew C. Ritchie. *Three American Romantic Painters*. New York: Museum of Modern Art, 19679.

Beaton, Cecil and Gail Buckland. *The Magic Image: The Genius of Photography from 1839 to the Present Day*. Boston: Little Brown and Company, 1975.

Bernard, Jessie. *Academic Women*. New York: Meridian, 1966.

Blair, Karen J. *The Clubwoman as Feminist*. New York: London: Holmes and Meier Publishers, 1980.

Bledstein, Burton J. *The Culture of Professionalism: The Middle Class and the Development of Higher Education in America*. New York: W. W. Norton and Company, 1976.

Block, Jean F. *Eva Watson-Schütze: Chicago Photo-Secessionist*. University of Chicago Library, 1985.

Boorstin, Daniel. *The Americans: The Democratic Experience*. New York: Random House, 1973.

Brandon, Ruth. *A Capitalist Romance: Singer and the Sewing Machine*. Philadelphia and New York: J.B. Lippincott, 1977.

Bunnell, Peter C. *A Photographic Vision: Pictorial Photography, 1889-1923*. Salt Lake City: Peregrine Smith, 1980.

Callen, Anthea. *Women Artists of the Arts and Crafts Movement, 1870-1914*. New York: Pantheon Books, 1979.

Coke, Van Deren, ed. *One Hundred Years of Photographic History*. Albuquerque: University of New Mexico Press, 1975.

Corn, Wanda. *The Color of Mood: American Tonalism: 1880-1910*. San Francisco: M.H. De Young Memorial Museum and California Palace of the Legion of Honor, 1978.

Daniel, Pete and Raymond Smock. *A Talent for Detail*. New York: Harmony Books, 1974.

Dijkstra, Bram. *The Hieroglyphics of a New Speech: Cubism, Stieglitz, and the Early Poetry of William Carlos Williams*. New Jersey: Princeton University Press, 1969.

Doty, Robert. *Photo-Secession: Stieglitz and the Fine Art Movement in Photography*. New York: Dover Publications, 1960, 1978.

Ehrenberg, Lewis A. *Steppin' Out*. Westport, London: Greenwood Press, 1981.

Faderman, Lillian. *Surpassing the Love of Men*. New York: William Morrow and Company, 1981.

Filene, Peter Gabriel. *Him, Her, Self: Sex Roles in Modern America*. New York, London: Harcourt, Brace, Jovanovich, 1975.

Finch, Edith. *Cary Thomas of Bryn Mawr*. New York: Harper, 1947.

Fischer, Claude S. *Networks and Places*. New York: The Free Press, 1977.

Frank, Waldo, et al. *America and Alfred Stieglitz*. New York: The Literary Guild, 1934.

Frankfort, Roberta. *Collegiate Women: Domesticity and Career in Turn of the Century America*. New York: New York University Press, 1977.

Freund, Gisele. *Photography and Society*. Boston: David R. Godine, 1980.

Gassan, Arnold. *A Chronology of Photography*. Athens, Ohio: Handbook Company, 1972.

Gernsheim, Helmut. *Creative Photography*. New York: Bonanza Books, 1962.

———. *Julia Margaret Cameron*. Millerton, New York: Aperture, Inc., 1975.

Glenn, Constance W. and Leland Rice, eds. *Frances Benjamin Johnston: Women of Class and Distinction*. Long Beach: California State University. The Art Museum and Gallery, 1979.

Gordon, Linda. *Woman's Body, Woman's Right*. New York: Penguin Books, 1977.

Greenough, Sarah and Juan Hamilton. *Alfred Stieglitz*. Washington: National Gallery of Art, 1982.

Green, Harvey. *The Light of the Home*. New York: Pantheon Books, 1983.

Greer, Germaine. *The Obstacle Race*. New York: Farrar, Straus, Giroux, 1979.

Griffin, Susan. *Pornography and Silence*. New York: Harper and Row, 1981.

Hale, Nancy. *Mary Cassatt*. Garden City, New York: Doubleday, 1975.

Haller, John S. and Robin M. Haller. *The Physician and Sexuality in Victorian America*. New York: W.W. Norton and Company, 1974.

The Hampton Album. ed., Lincoln Kirstein, New York: The Museum of Modern Art, 1966.

Hess, Thomas and Elizabeth Baker, eds. *Art and Sexual Politics*. New York: Collier Books, 1973, 1975.

Heyman, Therese Thau. *Anne Brigman*. The Oakland Museum, 1974.

Higham, John and Paul K. Conkin, eds. *New Directions in American Intellectual History*. Baltimore, London: Johns Hopkins University Press, 1979.

Hofstadter, Richard. *The Age of Reform*. New York: Vintage Books, 1955.

Homer, William Innes. *Alfred Stieglitz and the American Avant-Garde*. Boston: New York Graphic Society, 1977.

———. *Alfred Stieglitz and the Photo-Secession*. Boston: Little Brown and Company, 1983.

———. *The Photographs of Gertrude Käsebier*. Delaware Art Museum, 1979.

Jenkins, Reese V. *Images and Enterprise: Technology and the American Photographic Industry (1839-1925)*. Baltimore and London: Johns Hopkins University Press, 1975.

Jensen, Oliver. *Revolt of American Women: A Pictorial History of the Century of Change*. New York: Harcourt, Brace, 1952.

Jussim, Estelle. *Slave to Beauty*. Boston: David R. Godine, 1981.

Kahman, Volker. *Art History of Photography*. New York: The Viking Press, 1974.

Lagemann, Ellen. *A Generation of Women: Studies in Educational Biography*. Cambridge: Harvard University Press, 1979.

Lancaster, Clay, ed. *New York Interiors at the Turn of the Century*. New York: Dovic Publications, 1976.

Lesy, Michael. *Bearing Witness*. New York: Pantheon Books, 1982.

Lowe, Sue Davidson. *Stieglitz*. New York: Farrar, Straus, Giroux, 1983.

Lucie-Smith, Edward. *The Invented Eye: Masterpieces of Photography, 1839-1914*. New York: Paddington Press, 1975.

MacDonald, Gus. *Camera: Victorian Eyewitness*. New York: The Viking Press, 1979.

MacKinley, Helen. *John Marin*. Boston: The Institute of Contemporary Art and Pelligrini Cudahy, 1948.

Malcolm, Janet. *Diana and Nikon*. Boston: David R. Godine, 1980.

Mann, Margery. *California Pictorialism*. San Francisco: San Francisco Museum of Art, 1977.

Martin, Paul. *Victorian Snapshots*. New York: Charles Scribner's Sons, 1939.

Meltzer, Milton. *Dorothea Lange*. New York: Farrar, Straus, Giroux, 1978.

———. And Bernard Cole. *The Eye of Conscience: Photographers and Social Change*. Chicago: Follett Publishing Company, 1974.

Moers, Ellen. *Literary Women*. Garden City, New York: Doubleday, Anchor Books, 1977.

Moutoussamy-Ashe, Jeanne. *Viewfinders: Black Women Photographers*, New York: Dodd, Mead and Co., 1986.

Munro, Eleanor. *Originals: American Women Artists*, New York: Simon and Schuster, 1979.

Naef, Weston J. *The Collection of Alfred Stieglitz: Fifty Pioneers of Modern Photography*. New York: Viking Press, A Studio Book, The Metropolitan Museum of Art, 1978.

———. *The Painterly Photograph, 1890-1914.* New York: The Metropolitan Museum of Art, 1973.

Newhall, Beaumont. *The History of Photography.* New York: The Museum of Modern Art, 1964, 1982.

Norman, Dorothy. *Alfred Stieglitz.* Millerton, New York: Aperture, 1960, 1973.

Novotny, Ann. *Alice's World.* Old Greenwich, Connecticut: The Chatham Press, 1976.

O'Keeffe, Georgia. *Georgia O'Keeffe: A Portrait by Alfred Stieglitz.* New York: Metropolitan Museum of Art, 1976.

Parker, Rozsika and Griselda Pollock. *Old Mistresses: Women, Art, and Ideology.* New York: Pantheon Books, 1981.

Portrait of an Era in Landscape Architecture: The Photographs of Mattie Edwards Hewitt. Bronx, New York: Wave Hill, 1983.

Presbrey, Frank. *The History and Development of Advertising.* New York: Greenwood Press, 1968.

Rose, Barbara. *American Art Since 1900.* New York: Holt, Rhinehart and Winston, 1967, 1975.

Rothman, Sheila. *Woman's Proper Place.* New York: Basic Books, 1978.

Rubinstein, Charlotte Streiffer. *American Women Artists.* New York: Avon Books, 1982.

Rudisill, Richard. *Mirror Image: The Influence of the Daguerreotype on American Culture.* Albuquerque: University of New Mexico Press, 1971.

Ryan, Mary. *Womanhood in America.* New York: Franklin Watts, 1979.

Seligman, Herbert J. *Alfred Stieglitz Talking.* New Haven: Yale University Press, 1966.

Showalter, Elaine, ed. *These Modern Women.* Old Westbury: The Feminist Press, 1978.

Singer, Charles. *A History of Technology, Vol. 5.* Oxford: Oxford University Press, 1958.

Soby, James Thrall and Dorothy Miller. *Romantic Painting in America.* New York: Museum of Modern Art, 1969.

Smuts, Robert W. *Women and Work in America.* New York: Columbia University Press, 1959.

Sontag, Susan. *On Photography.* New York: Dell Publishing Company, 1977.

Taft, Robert. *Photography and the American Scene.* New York: The MacMillan Company, 1938.

Thomas, Allan. *Time in a Frame: Photography and the Nineteenth Century Mind.* New York: Schoken Books, 1977.

Travis, Donald and Anne Kennedy. *Photography Rediscovered.* New York: Whitney Museum of Art, 1979.

Tucker, Anne, ed. *The Woman's Eye.* New York: Alfred A. Knopf, 1976.

Turner, E. S. *The Shocking History of Advertising!* New York: E. P. Dutton and Company, 1953.

Walsh, Mary Roth. *Doctors Wanted: No Woman Need Apply.* New Haven and London: Yale University Press, 1977.

Weibel, Kathryn. *Mirror, Mirror.* Garden City: Anchor Books, 1977.

Welling, William. *Photography in America: The Formative Years, 1839-1900.* New York: Thomas Y. Crowell Company, 1978.

Welter, Barbara. *Dimity Convictions: The American Woman in the Nineteenth Century.* Athens: Ohio University Press, 1976.

Wertheim, Arthur. *The New York Little Renaissance.* New York: New York University Press, 1976.

Wertheimer, Barbara. *We Were There.* New York: Pantheon Books, 1977.

Wilson, Dorothy Clark. *Lone Woman: The Story of Elizabeth Blackwell, The First Woman Doctor.* Boston: Little Brown, 1970.

Women of Photography: A Historical Survey. San Francisco: San Francisco Museum of Art, 1975.

Woody, Thomas. *A History of Women's Education in the United States, Vols. 1, 2.* New York and Lancaster, Pennsylvania: The Science Press, 1929.

Index